The Uniqueness of Jesus

FAITH MEETS FAITH

An Orbis Series in Interreligious Dialogue
Paul F. Knitter, General Editor
Editorial Advisors
John Berthrong
Julia Ching
Diana Eck
Karl-Josef Kuschel
Lamin Sanneh
George E. Tinker
Felix Wilfred

In the contemporary world, the many religions and spiritualities stand in need of greater communication and cooperation. More than ever before, they must speak to, learn from, and work with each other in order both to maintain their vital identities and to contribute to fashioning a better world.

FAITH MEETS FAITH seeks to promote interreligious dialogue by providing an open forum for exchanges among followers of different religious paths. While the Series wants to encourage creative and bold responses to questions arising from contemporary appreciations of religious plurality, it also recognizes the multiplicity of basic perspectives concerning the methods and content of interreligious dialogue.

Although rooted in a Christian theological perspective, the Series does not endorse any single school of thought or approach. By making available to both the scholarly community and the general public works that represent a variety of religious and methodological viewpoints, FAITH MEETS FAITH seeks to foster an encounter among followers of the religions of the world on matters of common concern.

FAITH MEETS FAITH SERIES

The Uniqueness of Jesus

A Dialogue with Paul F. Knitter

Edited by

Leonard Swidler and Paul Mojzes

ORBIS BOOKS

Maryknoll, New York 10545

The Catholic Foreign Mission Society of America (Maryknoll) recruits and trains people for overseas missionary service. Through Orbis Books, Maryknoll aims to foster the international dialogue that is essential to mission. The books published, however, reflect the opinions of their authors and are not meant to represent the official position of the Society.

Manufactured in the United States of America.

Manuscript editing and typesetting by Joan Marie Laflamme.

ORBIS/ISBN 1-57075-123-4

Contents

Contributors

Kajsa Ahlstrand received a B.D. in 1979 and a Dr. Theol. in 1993, both from the University of Uppsala; her dissertation was on "Fundamental Openness: An Enquiry into Raimundo Panikkar's Theological Vision and Its Philosophical Presuppositions." She has published articles on religious pluralism in Europe, missiological issues, feminism, and disability. Since 1994 Ahlstrand has been working in the areas of theology of religions, missiology, and ecumenical studies at The Church of Sweden Research Department; she is the secretary of *Societas Oecumenica*.

Michael Amaladoss, S.J., is from South India and is currently professor of systematic theology at Vidyajyoti College of Theology, Delhi, India. He is former president of the International Association of Mission Studies and a former consultant to the Pontifical Council for Interreligious Dialogue. Among other articles and books, he is the author of *Making All Things New: Dialogue, Pluralism and Evangelization in Asia* (1990) and *Walking Together: The Practice of Interreligious Dialogue* (1992).

S. Wesley Ariarajah, a Methodist minister from Sri Lanka, was responsible for the Hindu/Buddhist-Christian dialogue program of the World Council of Churches (WCC) for twelve years and was the director of the WCC Sub-Unit on Dialogue with People of Living Faiths. His publications include *The Bible and People of Other Faiths* (1985), *Hindus and Christians: A Century of Protestant Ecumenical Thought* (1991), and *Did I Betray the Gospel?—Letters of Paul and the Place of Women*. He is currently the deputy general secretary of the World Council of Churches.

Michael von Brück, who holds the Dr. Theol., is professor of religious studies at the University of Munich, Germany. He studied theology, indology, and comparative linguistics at Rostock University; and Indian philosophy and religion at Madras University. He also received four years of training in Yoga at a Yoga-Institute in Madras and studied Zen Buddhism in Japan. He taught at Gurukul Lutheran College, Madras, from 1980 to 1985 and was professor of comparative religion at Regensburg University in 1988. He is editor of the journal *Dialog der Religionen*. For twenty years he has been a partner in dialogue with the Dalai Lama. His books include *The Unity of Reality* (1991), *Weisheit der Leere: Sutra-Texte des indischen Mahayana-Buddhismus* (1987), *Buddhism and Christianity: History and Perspectives of the Encounter* (with Whalen Lai) (1997).

Denise Carmody is the Bernard J. Hanley Professor at Santa Clara University, where she also chairs the Religious Studies Department. She received her M.A. and Ph.D. from Boston College. Together and alone, the Carmodys have written over sixty books.

John Carmody was senior research fellow in religion at Santa Clara University. He received his B.A. and M.A. from Boston College, a licentiate in philosophy from Weston College, a bachelor of divinity from Woodstock College, and the Ph.D. from Stanford University. He died on September 23, 1995.

John B. Cobb, Jr., is emeritus professor of theology of the School of Theology at Claremont and the Claremont Graduate School. He continues to be one of the co-directors of the Center for Process Studies and to participate in the Society for Buddhist-Christian Studies. Among his books, those most relevant to this discussion are *Christ in a Pluralistic Age* (1975), *Beyond Dialogue* (1982), and *Doubting Thomas* (1995).

Harvey Cox, professor of divinity at Harvard University, received a B.A. from the University of Pennsylvania, a B.D. from Yale Divinity School and the Ph.D. from Harvard University. His many books include *The Secular City* (1965), *Religion in the Secular City* (1984), *Many Mansions: A Christian's Encounter with Other Faiths* (1988), and *Fire from Heaven: The Rise of Pentecostal Spirituality* (1994).

Kenneth Cragg was the Anglican Assistant Bishop of Jerusalem and the Bishop of Egypt in Cairo and is now retired in England. He received his B.A., M.A. and D.Phil. from Jesus College, Oxford University. He has taught at Union Theological Seminary in New York, the University of London, the University of Ibadan, Nigeria, and the University of Sussex. His many books include *The Event of the Qur'an* (1971), *The Mind of the Qur'an* (1973), and *The Arab Christian* (1991).

Anthony Fernando has a doctorate in theology from the Gregorian University of Rome, a diploma in religious education from the Institut Catholique of Paris, the Ph.D. in Buddhist studies from the University of Sri Lanka, and has also studied Buddhism at the Ecole des Hautes Etudes of Paris. For a number of years he taught Buddhism to Christians and Christianity to Buddhists. At present Fernando is chairperson of the department of classical and Christian cultures of the Kelaniya University of Sri Lanka. His books include *Buddhism Made Plain* (1985, with Leonard Swidler), and *Christianity Made Intelligible* (1990).

Monika K. Hellwig retired as Landegger Professor of Theology at Georgetown University in 1996 to become the executive director of the Association of Catholic Colleges and Universities. She has long been engaged in both intra-Christian and interfaith ecumenism, and has lectured on all continents and in many countries. Among her publications are *Jesus, the Compassion of God* (1983), *Understanding Catholicism* (1981), and *The Eucharist and the Hunger of the World* (1976; revised and expanded 1992).

John Hick, formerly professor of philosophy of religion at the Claremont Graduate School in California, is now fellow of the Institute for Advanced Research in the Humanities at the University of Birmingham, England. His many books include *God Has Many Names* (1982), *An Interpretation of Religion* (1990), and *A Christian Theology of Religions* (1995).

Paul F. Knitter, professor of theology at Xavier University, received a licentiate in theology from the Pontifical Gregorian University in Rome (1966) and the doctorate in theology from the University of Marburg (1972). He is the author of *No Other Name? A Critical Survey of Christian Attitudes toward World Religions* (1985) and numerous other publications dealing with religious pluralism and interreligious dialogue. He is general editor of Orbis Books's Faith Meets Faith series and over the past decade also has also been active in peace groups working with the churches of El Salvador.

Karl-Josef Kuschel received the doctorate and habilitation in Catholic theology from the University of Tübingen in 1977 and 1989. In 1995 he was appointed professor of the theology of culture and interreligious dialogue in the Catholic theology faculty of the University of Tübingen. His many books include *Born before All Time? The Dispute over Christ's Origin* (1992), *A Global Ethic: The Declaration of the Parliament of the World's Religions* (1994), and *Streit um Abraham: Was Juden, Christen und Muslime trennt—und was sie eint* (1994).

John Macquarrie, born in Scotland in 1919, taught theology at the University of Glasgow; Union Theological Seminary, New York; and Oxford University. His latest book is *Mediators between Human and Divine: From Moses to Muhammad* (1996).

John Mbiti was born in Kenya. Educated in Africa, America, and Europe, he received the doctorate in New Testament studies from the University of Cambridge, England, and honorary doctorates from Gordon College (USA) and the University of Lausanne (Switzerland). He has worked with the churches and universities in all three continents, teaching and publishing in the areas of biblical and African theology, missiology, ecumenics, and African religions. He is an Anglican priest and is at present teaching missiology and extra-European theology at the University of Bern, Switzerland.

José Míguez Bonino has been the dean of the graduate school at the Protestant Institute for Advanced Theological Studies in Buenos Aires, Argentina. He received a Lic. Theol. from the Facultad Evangelica de Teologia,

Buenos Aires; an M.A. from Emory University, Atlanta; and the Ph.D. from Union Theological Seminary, New York. He was an observer at Vatican II, a member of the World Council of Churches Presidium, and co-president of the Permanent Assembly for Human Rights in Argentina. His many books include *Doing Theology in a Revolutionary Situation* (1975) and *Toward a Christian Political Ethics* (1983).

Paul Mojzes is professor of religious studies and academic dean at Catholic Rosemont College, Rosemont, Pennsylvania. A native of Yugoslavia who after two years of study at Belgrade University Law School came to America in 1957, he earned a B.A. from Florida Southern College in 1959 and the Ph.D. in church history from Boston University. He is co-editor of the *Journal of Ecumenical Studies*, editor of *Religion in Eastern Europe*, and president of Christians Associated for Relationships with Western Europe. His most recent book is *Yugoslavian Inferno: Ethnoreligious Warfare in the Balkans* (1994).

Raimon Panikkar, a Catholic priest, holds doctorates in philosophy (Madrid), sciences (Madrid) and theology (Rome). In 1966 he was appointed professor at Harvard University and in the two following decades he divided his time between India and the United States. In 1972 he was appointed professor of comparative philosophy of religion at the University of California in Santa Barbara, retired in 1987, and now lives in Catalonia. He has published more than forty books and a thousand articles, ranging from philosophy of science, to metaphysics, comparative religion, and indology. His English books include *The Unknown Christ of Hinduism* (1964), *The Trinity and the Religious Experience of Man* (1975), *The Vedic Experience* (1977), *The Intra-religious Dialogue* (1978), *Blessed Simplicity* (1982), *The Silence of God: The Answer of the Buddha* (1989), *The Cosmotheandric Experience* (1993), and *Cultural Disarmament: A Way to Peace* (1995).

Clark H. Pinnock, professor of theology at McMaster Divinity College, Hamilton, Ontario, Canada, is the author of *A Wideness of God's Mercy: The Finality of Jesus Christ in a World of Religions* (1992), and *Flame of Love: A Theology of the Holy Spirit* (1996).

John Sanders is head of the religious studies program at Oak Hills Bible College, Bemidji, Minnesota, and has authored or edited *No Other Name* (1992), *The Openness of God* (1994), and *What about Those Who Have Never Heard?* (1995). He holds the doctorate from the University of South Africa.

Ingrid Shafer, professor of philosophy and religion and Mary Jo Ragan Professor of Interdisciplinary Studies at the University of Science and Arts of Oklahoma, where she has taught since 1968, is a native of Innsbruck, Austria. She began her graduate studies at Vienna and

Innsbruck. She holds master's degrees in literature and human relations, as well as the Ph.D. in philosophy from the University of Oklahoma. Among her books are *Eros and the Womanliness of God* (1986) and *Incarnate Imagination* (1988).

Leonard Swidler, professor of Catholic thought and interreligious dialogue at Temple University and editor of the *Journal of Ecumenical Studies,* has a licentiate in theology from the University of Tübingen and a doctorate in history-philosophy from the University of Wisconsin. He is the author/editor of over fifty books, including *After the Absolute: The Dialogical Future of Religious Reflection* (1990), and *The Meaning of Life* (1993). He is also the director of the Institute for Interreligious, Intercultural Dialogue.

Seiichi Yagi did graduate work in Western classics at Tokyo University and completed the Ph.D. in New Testament studies at the University of Goettingen. He has taught at Tokyo University, the International Christian University in Tokyo, and the Tokyo Institute of Technology, and at present is professor of philosophy at Toin University of Yokohama. He is a leading figure in Buddhist-Christian dialogue in Japan. His books, such as *Christ and Jesus, Contact Points Between Buddhism and Christianity, Paul/Shinran-Jesus/Zen,* and *Language and Religion—Language of Religion* (all in Japanese), have sold widely in Japan. He is also the author of *Bridge to Buddhist-Christian Dialogue* (1990), available in English.

Introduction

PAUL MOJZES

In a memorable conversation recorded in all three synoptic gospels, Jesus asked his disciples, "Tell me, who do people say I am?" "Some say that you are John the Baptist," they answered; "others say that you are Elijah, while others say that you are one of the prophets." "What about you?" he asked them. "Who do you say I am?" Peter answered, "You are the Messiah." Then Jesus ordered them, "Do not tell anyone about me" (Mk 8:27-30; parallels Mt 16:13-20 and Lk 9:18-21). Was this the first or one of the first questions about Jesus Christ's uniqueness? The extensive variations of this passage indicate that the question of Jesus' role and significance was already under considerable reflection in the apostolic church and that there was a difference of opinion as to whether Jesus was like some other figure that preceded him, whether he was in some manner unique, or both. Paradoxically the passage seems to be affirming both Jesus' similarity and uniqueness. Jesus' insistence that they not tell anyone of their conviction appears to indicate some latitude in his own mind as to what his followers and contemporaries may believe about him, probably so as not to coerce a uniform christology upon those whom he encountered directly.

Despite the chronological increase in distance from Jesus and the incremental accrual of knowledge about him and the context in which he lived, the question of his identity and role agitates minds and hearts. The questions Paul Knitter raises are anything but new. Practically all the authors in this volume allude to the perennial need for christological reinterpretation in new circumstances. The new circumstance for our age is the relatively new phenomenon of world-wide interreligious dialogue. The meaning of the uniqueness and universality of Jesus Christ's nature and his identity and salvific role has animated lively confrontations throughout history. Some of these controversies, indeed, resulted in schisms and expulsion of "heretics" from the church. Even today, some people feel not only threatened and alienated by certain christological formulations but are willing to break communion over these issues. Paul Knitter's theses, which are placed at the beginning of the book, show that such questions still engender vigorous debate. The reader will see that, while not all segments of Christian opinion are represented in this volume, there is a healthy range of support and disagreement voiced in the pages that follow.

The structure of this book is threefold. Paul Knitter was asked to summarize his views on the central christological issues as they bear upon our contemporary awareness of religious plurality. Then, nineteen individuals representing a variety of theological viewpoints were invited to respond to the theses advanced by Professor Knitter. The theses revolve around the *uniqueness* of Jesus, what that term means, how it bears on christology and Christian identity, and how the uniqueness of Christ accords with the widespread contemporary judgment that religious plurality is not going to go away, indeed that it may be divinely willed. In a final section Knitter responds to his interlocutors.

It is interesting, though not surprising, that many respondents question the appropriateness of the key word, *uniqueness*. They point out that it is not a biblical claim and not even a term much used in traditional creedal statements. Granted. Of course, no word is likely to receive complete consent, and so we need to address the question of what is meant by a claim of uniqueness. A writer to the editor of a religious newspaper in the course of complaining about some of the findings of the so-called Jesus Seminar, which has undertaken the controversial task of determining the degree of genuineness of the reported sayings of Jesus in the gospels, asked, "If we take out of the gospel the things that make Jesus unique, disturbing, and miraculous, have we not denied the very essence and power of Christianity?" This lay person understands that there are certain Christian claims about Jesus that lift him above any other being that walked on this earth, making claims for the manner in which he reflected the nature and purpose of God and mediated to humans the gift of extrication from destructiveness and evil. Lay people, more than theologians, are likely to agree that this is what is meant by *uniqueness*. In this book we go with the plain understanding of the word *unique* and offer it for scrutiny by theologians who are bound to enrich and perhaps confuse the reader's understanding.

The question of Jesus Christ's uniqueness was raised by Protestant liberals of the nineteenth century, as they investigated the Bible and church history in the context of the growing knowledge about antiquity. Adolf von Harnack, for example, questioned the formulations of the Hellenized early church, maintaining that the ontology later ascribed to Jesus departed significantly from claims made by Jesus himself and his disciples. John Cobb, in his essay in this volume, points out that Ernst Troeltsch and Rudolf Otto continued this line and were followed in this century by the Swedish bishop Nathan Soederblom, Ernest Hocking, H. Richard Niebuhr, and Donald Bailey. They all explored the meaning of Jesus Christ's uniqueness.

As New Testament scholarship progressed and passed in phases from affirming the Jesus of history, to efforts at "de-mythologization" in order to understand the Christ of faith, to the "new quest" for the historical Jesus, it became obvious that the New Testament itself contains a pluralism of christological affirmations, which cannot be neatly ordered and synchronized. As the search for a better understanding of the Hebrew Bible, intertestamental writings, and the first-century Palestinian context began, it became clear that Jesus was intimately linked to the traditions, lifestyles, and beliefs of his own Jewish people. Again and again the question of Jesus' uniqueness was raised in new contexts.

Theologians like Paul Tillich, Teilhard de Chardin, Dorothee Sölle, John A. T. Robinson, and Hans Küng have approached the question of the uniqueness of Jesus by affirming the notion but pointing out that one needs to ask in what sense Christ is unique. Thus Bishop John A. T. Robinson stated:

> That Christ is in some way unique has been a constant presupposition of the Christian preaching—and one that has never been more of an offense than in this relativistic and pluralistic age. Yet how he is unique has been expressed in remarkably divergent ways, considering the unanimity on the fact and its indispensability. The divergence would suggest a certain fuzziness about the central certainty, which demands to be looked at before it is merely shouted more loudly to a particularly deaf generation.[1]

The purpose of this book, accordingly, is to consider how Jesus is unique in relation to the Christian dialogue with other religions.

The question whether the uniqueness of Jesus Christ can be maintained—along with the affirmation that God's revelation can be found in other world religions—emerged first in the Jewish-Christian dialogue and then, considerably later, in dialogues among Jews, Christians, and Muslims. In Jewish-Christian dialogue it became obvious, especially after the discoveries of the Dead Sea Scrolls and other spectacular archeological finds that shed light on first-century Judaism and on primitive Christianity, that little of what Jesus did or said was without precedent in Judaism. Such insights produced the very helpful works of Harry Emerson Fosdick's *The Man from Nazareth*, Günther Bornkamm's *Jesus of Nazareth*, Hans Küng's *On Being a Christian*, Gerard Sloyan's *Jesus in Focus*, Bishop John Selby Spong's *This Hebrew Lord*, and a myriad of similar works helping the modern reader come to grips with this issue.

---

[1] "In What Sense Is Christ Unique?" *Christian Century* (November 25, 1970), pp. 1409-12.

So, if there have been many contemporary thinkers who have addressed the question of the uniqueness of Jesus, why are Paul Knitter's essay and the accompanying responses so pertinent? The answer lies in Paul Knitter's deliberate wrestling with christological, theological, and soteriological questions in the light of the contemporary dialogue among people of various faiths, a dialogue that is expanding to global proportions. Professor Knitter published *No Other Name?* in 1985 and, with John Hick as co-editor, published *The Myth of Christian Uniqueness?* in 1987.[2] These works were controversial. While many found his arguments convincing and helpful, others were convinced that such thinking damaged the missionary and evangelizing task of the Christian church. Cardinal Jozef Tomko, for instance, targeted Knitter's views for criticism in "Missionary Challenges to the Theology of Salvation," which became the central essay to which a variety of respondents, including Knitter himself, responded in an anthology entitled *Christian Mission and Interreligious Dialogue*.[3] The present volume carries this process forward by focusing even more sharply on how a Christian may or should insist on the uniqueness and significance of Christ in the encounter with the claims of other religions either about their founders or uniqueness in their tradition.

Two things are constantly changing in our attempts to assess the nature of the uniqueness of Jesus, the task of every christology. One is the constantly growing body of information about the object of christology, Jesus the Christ. The second is circumstances that force the followers of Christ to deal with issues that either have not been encountered before or that have not been met in the same way as they are now. This twofold dynamic demands that every generation, perhaps every believer, answer anew the question, "Who do you say that I am?"

Paul Knitter's theses are not a final statement of position with which all must agree. But they prompt us to formulate positions based on the contemporary experiences of Jesus Christ and our continuous engagements in dialogue with others in love and respect. That is what this book is all about.

---

[2] Both titles were published by Orbis Books, Maryknoll, New York.

[3] Paul Mojzes and Leonard Swidler, eds. (Lewiston, N.Y.: The Edwin Mellen Press, 1990).

PART I

Paul F. Knitter's Five Theses

Five Theses on the Uniqueness of Jesus

PAUL F. KNITTER

Judging from a swarm of recent publications, it is clear that the much-debated issue of the uniqueness of Christ in a world of religious plural-ism continues to dog the Christian community.[1] So-called exclusivists and inclusivists accuse so-called pluralists of relativism and a deflation of the Christian message, while pluralists respond with counter-accusa-tions of imperialism and ideological abuse of the gospel.[2] I hope that the following five theses can bring some clarity and direction to the discus-

---

[1] Gavin D'Costa, ed., *Christian Uniqueness Reconsidered: The Myth of a Plu-ralistic Theology of Religions* (Maryknoll, N.Y.: Orbis Books, 1990); David Krieger, *The New Universalism: Foundations for a Global Theology* (Maryknoll, N.Y.: Orbis Books, 1991); Paul J. Griffiths, *An Apology for Apologetics: A Study in the Logic of Interreligious Dialogue* (Maryknoll, N.Y.: Orbis Books, 1991); John Tully and Denise Lardner Carmody, *Christian Uniqueness and Catholic Spirituality* (New York: Paulist Press, 1990); Carl E. Braaten, *No Other Gospel! Christianity among the World Religions* (Minneapolis: Fortress Press, 1992); S. J. Samartha, *One Christ—Many Religions: Toward a Revised Christology* (Maryknoll, N.Y.: Orbis Books, 1991); Jacques Dupuis, *Jesus Christ and the Encounter of World Religions* (Maryknoll, N.Y.: Orbis Books, 1991); David Tracy, *Dialogue with the Other: The Inter-Religious Dialogue* (Grand Rapids: Eerdmans, 1990); Schubert Ogden, *Is There Only One True Religion or Are There Many?* (Dallas: Southern Methodist University Press, 1991); J. A. DiNoia, *The Diversity of Religions: A Christian Per-spective* (Washington, D.C.: The Catholic University of America Press, 1992).

[2] To make sure that our terms are clear and to help those who have not been initiated into the complexities of theological jargon, let me define my terms: *exclusivists* are those who hold that there is only one true, saving religion—the religion founded on Christ; *inclusivists*, on the contrary, affirm many true religions but insist that Christ and his community make up the final, fulfilling norm for those religions (either constitutively, by being the causative source of God's saving truth, or representatively, by being the clearest and fullest embodiment of God's truth and grace). Finally, *pluralists* announce at least the possibility (some would hold the probability, if not the actuality) of many true religions, each carrying on a different though valid role in the divine plan of salvation.

sion. As succinctly and lucidly as possible, they seek to show that while the Christian affirmation of the uniqueness of Christ can and must be reinterpreted (theses 1 and 2), it need not be abandoned (thesis 3); indeed, precisely by reinterpreting Jesus' uniqueness, Christians can reaffirm it with greater relevance for our contemporary world (thesis 4). In the end, then, such a reinterpretation of how Jesus is unique will flow from and lend greater depth and strength to Christians' devotion to and following of Jesus (thesis 5).

THESIS 1:

Given the nature and history of christology, previous understandings of the uniqueness of Jesus **can** *be reinterpreted.*

This first thesis is as fundamental as, I hope, it is evident. Throughout their history, Christian communities have moved around the hermeneutical circle of experience and interpretation (or, as George Lindbeck and other post-moderns[3] would put it, interpretation and experience) in an ongoing attempt to state who this Jesus must be in order to have so affected and transformed their lives. The circle is never ending, because contexts differ and history changes; thus, as is commonly recognized today, there have been *many* christologies throughout the history of the church, even in the New Testament period.[4]

To recognize the pluralism of christologies is to admit two essential features of the christological task: that there can be no one way of talking about this Jesus, and that our efforts to talk about him embody an undertaking that is never accomplished. In other words, there is no *one way* and there is no *final way* in the attempts of Christians to say who this Jesus was, how he affected their lives, and what role he plays in the history of God's self-communication with humanity. In grasping, describing, and proclaiming the *person* and the *work* of Jesus, Christians can be open to new ways of talking, new images, deeper insights, yes, even re-visions of how God has acted and is acting through him. Such an openness to ever new ways of talking about who Jesus was and what he

---

[3] George Lindbeck, *The Nature of Doctrine: Religion and Theology in a Postliberal Age* (Philadelphia: Westminster Press, 1984); William C. Placher, *Unapologetic Theology: A Christian Voice in a Pluralistic Conversation* (Louisville: Westminster/John Knox Press, 1989).

[4] Paula Fredrikson, *From Jesus to Christ: The Origin of New Testament Images of Jesus* (New Haven: Yale University Press, 1988); Jaroslav Pelikan, *Jesus through the Centuries: His Place in the History of Culture* (New Haven: Yale University Press, 1985).

did must also include new ways of talking about what it is that makes him unique.

But here many would voice a caveat: there are limits to such interpretations. Christology is not a free-for-all, an anything-goes venture. Of course. Much can and must be said about the criteria for the ongoing task of christology. Let me formulate what I think is *a*, if not *the*, criterion or guideline for determining whether a new understanding of Jesus is valid. Following and expanding upon an ancient theological ground rule of the early communities, I would say that the *lex credendi* (norms for belief) must resonate with and foster the *lex orandi* (norms for spirituality), but that such norms for spiritual or devotional life are dangerously inadequate if they are not linked with the *lex sequendi* (norms for discipleship). In other words, any new understanding of Jesus—his person, work, or uniqueness—must flow from and nurture a saving experience of and commitment to Jesus (devotion) and a resolute following of him in the world (discipleship). If it does not do this, it is heretical; if it does, it merits our serious attention if not acceptance.

Thesis 5 will attempt to outline how the pluralistic reinterpretation of Jesus' uniqueness suggested in theses 3 and 4 does meet these requirements of the norms for spirituality and discipleship.

In what follows I hope it will become clear that I (and most other so-called pluralist theologians) am not questioning *whether* Jesus is unique but only *how*.

THESIS 2:

Given the ethical imperative of dialogue, previous understandings of the uniqueness of Jesus **must** *be reinterpreted.*[5]

Today, more urgently than ever, Christians (and, of course, others) are experiencing the ethical imperative of dialogue, especially of interreligious dialogue.[6] This imperative is seeping into Christian consciousness from both *external* and *internal* sources.

---

[5] Let me add a personal note: After five months of sabbatical travel and study in India (July to December 1991), I am more convinced of this thesis than ever. As I heard from many Indian Christians, both Protestant and Roman Catholic, traditional exclusive or even inclusive understandings of how Jesus is unique do not enable Indian Christians to live peacefully and productively with their many Hindu, Muslim, Sikh, Jain, and Buddhist neighbors.

[6] See Leonard Swidler, John B. Cobb, Jr., Monika Hellwig, and Paul Knitter, *Death or Dialogue: From the Age of Monologue to the Age of Dialogue* (Philadelphia: Trinity Press International, 1990).

Externally, the demands for dialogue coming from outside the Christian circle have been lucidly and powerfully laid out in Hans Küng's recent book *Global Responsibility: In Search of a New World Ethic*.[7] If the nations and cultures of the world are really going to confront and resolve the crises threatening humanity today—ecological devastation, human suffering due to unjust structures, the threat of conflict with uncontrollable weapons—nations and ethnic groups are going to have to cooperate as never before; but to make such cooperation possible, the religions of the world will have to cooperate as never before. This means they will have to dialogue. Dialogue, then, is a moral obligation.

Internally, our present age's new way of experiencing the old fact of religious plurality has made it clear to many Christians that they cannot truly and effectively carry out the *last commission* of proclaiming the gospel to all nations unless they are truly and effectively carrying out the *first commission* of loving their neighbors among those nations. If we don't love them, we cannot witness to them. But it has become clearer to Christian consciousness today that we cannot love our neighbors unless we are ready to dialogue with them. That's what love means; it calls us to the mutuality of dialogue. Love means to respect, value, and listen to the others, to be ready to learn from them. Negatively, if we do not extend to the others the same care and respect that we would wish for ourselves, we are not really loving them. If we enter a relationship with the others presupposing that we have the fullness of God's truth and they only partial rays of that truth, we all too easily view them (as has often been the case throughout history) as less able than we to know the truth or to live moral lives or to know God; with such an attitude, it seems to me, we are not really loving them. Thus, the ingredients for authentic dialogue are the ingredients for authentic loving.

As the recent Vatican statement *Dialogue and Proclamation*[8] states, we cannot proclaim unless we dialogue. Today, many Christians are recognizing that they have made proclamation more important than dialogue; they have talked more than they have listened. They have made the last commission more important than the first.

Thus, dialogue is an ethical imperative. Anything that prevents the fulfillment of this moral obligation is suspect. Here I would contend, respectfully but straightforwardly, that not just the exclusivist but also the inclusivist understandings of the uniqueness of Jesus are impedi-

---

[7] New York: Crossroad, 1991.

[8] The text can be found in *New Directions in Mission and Evangelization 1: Basic Statements 1974-1991*, ed. James A. Scherer and Stephen B. Bevans (Maryknoll, N.Y.: Orbis Books, 1992), pp. 177-200.

ments to real dialogue.[9] My inclusivist friends insist that this is not true. But they never adequately (at least for me) explain why it is not true. If we understand dialogue as an open-ended conversation in which all partners have equal rights, then all have to *listen* as genuinely as they witness, and all have to be ready to follow the truth wherever it may lead. But just such a process of dialogue, it seems to me, is hamstrung from the start if one of the partners insists that he or she has the God-given full, final, and unsurpassable vision of truth. Dialogue requires convictions, surely; but when those convictions are held to be divinely sealed as the "last word" or the "total word," then the dialogue cannot take place, as they say, on a level playing field.

If Christians think that they are in possession of the "fullness" of revelation and the norm for all truth, then no matter how much they might call for a dialogue "among equals," they retain the position of advantage. It is from *their* vantage point that any conflict of truth claims must be decided. If Christians have the norm, then they are not really able to recognize any truth or value in other religions that is genuinely different from what they already have; whatever truth or good may be found in other traditions has to be "fulfilled" or included within the final Christian truth. Such an attitude seems to me to be opposed to the nature and requirements of dialogue.

THESIS 3:

The uniqueness of Jesus' salvific role can be reinterpreted in terms of **truly** *but not* **only.**

A growing number of Christians around the world (I found many in India) are suggesting that in order to remain faithful to the New Testament witness and to nurture a true following of Jesus today, it is not necessary to insist that Jesus is the *only* mediator of God's saving grace in history. More precisely, it is not necessary to proclaim God's revelation in Jesus as *full*, *definitive*, or *unsurpassable*. Let me briefly spell out why one can qualify these three adjectives and still remain faithful to traditional Christian beliefs and convictions:

In Jesus we do not possess a *full* revelation, as if he exhausted all the truth that God has to reveal. This statement is grounded, I believe, in both theological and biblical convictions. Theologically, Christians throughout their tradition would take it for granted that no finite me-

---

[9] With Schubert Ogden in his recent book *Is There Only One Religion or Are There Many?*, I would identify both the exclusivist and the inclusivist models for a theology of religions as representing a salvific monism (see pp. 27-32).

dium can exhaust the fullness of the Infinite. To identify the Infinite with anything finite, to contain and limit the Divine to any one human form or mediation—has biblically and traditionally been called idolatry.[10]

Nor do we boast a *definitive* Word of God in Jesus, as if there could be no other norms for divine truth outside of him. Again, to claim definitiveness about anything is to hold that nothing essentially new or different can be said about it. To announce that we have the definitive divine Truth is to imply that the Wisdom that surpasses all knowledge and the Love that is eternally creative have been deposited in a container to which nothing more can be added. Again, if that is what we mean when we say we have the definitive "deposit of faith," then our "deposit" would seem to fit the definition of an idol.

Therefore, God's saving word in Jesus cannot be extolled as *unsurpassable*, as if God could not reveal more of God's fullness in other ways at other times. To hold that God could provide a revelation that would so contain God's truth as not to allow anything more to be said seems to me to be in tension, if not direct contradiction, with the more basic Christian belief that God is an unsurpassable Mystery, one which can never totally be comprehended or contained in human thought or construct. Such a notion of an unsurpassable revelation would also seem to contradict, or rule out, the role of the Holy Spirit that Jesus, in John's gospel, affirmed: "I have many things to say to you, but you cannot bear them now. . . . When the Spirit of Truth comes, he will guide you into all the truth" (Jn 16:12-13). If we believe in the Holy Spirit, we must believe that there is always "more to come."

But we can't stop there. Discipleship and fidelity to the New Testament witness do require Christians to know and proclaim Jesus as truly God's saving presence in history. If Christians no longer need to insist on *only*, they must continue to proclaim *truly*. Christians must announce Jesus to all peoples as God's *universal*, *decisive*, and *indispensable* manifestation of saving truth and grace. Once again, let me try to clarify briefly what each of those adjectives contains.

God's word in Jesus is *universal* insofar as it is experienced to be meaningful not just for Christians but for peoples of all times. I think

---

[10] But if this is idolatry, would not the Christian belief in the incarnation of the Divine in the man Jesus be idolatrous? Not really, for incarnation means that Divinity has assumed the fullness of humanity, not that humanity has taken on the fullness of Divinity. As Edward Schillebeeckx has recently reminded us, to believe in the incarnation is to believe that God has taken on all the limitations of the human condition (*Church: The Human Story of God* [New York: Crossroad, 1990], pp. 164-68). Thus, if Christians want to affirm that the Divine has truly been "made flesh" in Jesus, they cannot at the same time hold that the Divine has absolutely or totally been made flesh in Jesus. Flesh cannot be made into a total container of the Divine.

this runs through the multiple traditions of the New Testament: the insistence that the good news is good not just for a particular group of Jewish faithful but for all persons, and that therefore the followers of Jesus have to go into the whole world, to all nations, to announce this good news (Mt 28:19). To water down the universality of Christian truth claims is to violate the biblical witness.[11] But it is also to violate the way truth is experienced. If something is true, especially if it is a truth that touches the core of how we see the world and live our lives, it cannot be true only for me. If it is true, it has to be true for others also.[12]

The revelation given in Jesus is also *decisive*. It shakes and challenges and calls one to change one's perspective and conduct. It makes a difference in one's life; this difference, often if not always, will "cut one off" (*decidere*) from other perspectives and ways of living. Therefore, to say that Jesus is decisive means that he is normative.[13] But such a decisive norm is not unsurpassable, for as Roger Haight clarifies, in relation to persons of other religious traditions, Jesus provides Christians with a negative rather than a positive norm. While Christians can imagine that God may have more to reveal to humankind than what has been made

---

[11] Here I have some problems with the way Hans Küng, in his eagerness to promote dialogue, seems to restrict the transforming power of Jesus' truth only to Christians. With his distinction between "outside" and "inside" perspectives on religions, he suggests that it is only within Christianity that Christians would proclaim Jesus as savior. Küng compares allegiance to Christ with allegiance to the constitution of one's own country; just as one would not claim that one's own national constitution is valid for others, one would not claim that one's religion is valid for others. This, it seems to me, contradicts the New Testament affirmation of the universal relevance of what God has done in Jesus Christ (see Küng, pp. 99-100).

[12] As any post-modernist would remind us, such a grasp of truth is always limited and conditioned. Granting this, I still feel that what I am grasping as true is not confined by those limitations; it has to be "translatable" to other limitations and conditionings. Like salt that has lost its savor, truth that is not universal is not worth much.

[13] So I would want to clarify and qualify—which means correct!—the terminology I used in *No Other Name?* when I struggled to formulate the characteristics of a theocentric christology. No longer would I want to advocate a "non-normative christology," for that seems to imply that the encounter with God through Jesus cannot really be decisive insofar as it cannot really give us norms with which to direct our lives and take our stands. (See *No Other Name? A Critical Survey of Christian Attitudes toward World Religions,* Maryknoll, N.Y.: Orbis Books, 1985, Chapter 9.) What I was opposing at that time was a christology that holds up Jesus as the absolute, final, full, unsurpassable norm for all times and all religions. So, today, while I want to clearly affirm that Jesus is normative and universally so, I still am questioning whether he is, or can be, the only such norm.

known in Jesus, they cannot imagine that such a revelation would contradict the central ingredients of the truth they have found in Jesus.[14] In
serving as a norm, therefore, Jesus' good news *defines* God but does not
confine God; it reveals what Christians feel is *essential* to a true knowledge of the Divine, but it does not provide *all* that makes up such knowledge.

Finally, Christians continue to proclaim the truth made known in Jesus
as *indispensable*. If I experience something to be true not just for me but
for others, and if this truth has enriched and transformed my life, I auto-
matically feel that it can and should do the same for others. In other
words, to know Jesus Christ is to feel that Buddhists and Hindus and
Muslims need to know him too; this means they need to recognize and
accept the truth he reveals, even though this does not necessarily mean
that they will become members of the Christian community. Thus, it
seems to me that inherent in the Christian experience of Jesus is the
conviction that those who have not known and in some way accepted the
message and power of the gospel are missing something in their knowledge and living of truth. Whatever truth about the Ultimate and the human condition there may be in other traditions, such truth can be enhanced and clarified through an encounter with the good news made
known in Jesus. In a qualified but still real sense, persons of other religious paths are "unfulfilled" without Christ.

This, then, would be the skeletal outline of a reinterpretation of Jesus'
uniqueness: he is not God's total, definitive, unsurpassable truth, but he
does bring a universal, decisive, indispensable message. Notice, I said
"a" rather than "the" in the last sentence, for if we no longer insist that
Jesus is God's only saving word, we are open to the *possibility*—our
Christian belief in universal revelation would suggest *probability*—that
there are other universal, decisive, indispensable manifestations of divine reality besides Jesus.[15] If we Christians are deeply convinced that

---

[14] Roger Haight, "Towards an Understanding of Christ in the Context of Other
World Religions," *East Asian Pastoral Review* 3-4 (1989), pp. 248-65. Here, however, as Haight himself points out, one must be extremely careful not to identify
too hastily what is genuinely different with what is contradictory. Many of the
differences between Christianity and Buddhism that often have been held up as
contradictions are turning out to be complementarities. An example might be the
differences between the Buddhist notion of the No-Self and the Christian ideal of
the new person in Christ. Thus, when Christians say that Jesus is a norm that can be
applied to all religions, they are also open to the possibility or probability that
other religions may present Christians with norms that prove to have power over
Christian self-understanding.

[15] In *Is There Only One True Religion or Are There Many?* Schubert Ogden's
main criticism of the pluralists is that they too hastily conclude to the *actuality* of
many true religions when they should affirm only the *possibility*. Ogden's admoni-

whatever truth there may be in other traditions can be transformed and fulfilled in the Word that has been given to us, we must be as deeply open to being transformed and fulfilled by the Word spoken and embodied for us in persons of other paths. This new interpretation of Jesus' uniqueness seeks to promote the transformation of both other religions *and* of Christianity. Just what this transformation will imply and how much it will affect other faiths and Christianity can be known only through dialogue.

THESIS 4:

The content of Jesus' uniqueness must be made clear in Christian life and witness. This content, however, will be understood and proclaimed differently in different contexts and periods of history. Today, the uniqueness of Jesus can be found in his insistence that salvation or the Reign of God must be realized in this world *through* human actions *of love and justice.*

During my recent sojourn in India, it became clear to me that while Christians must abandon an understanding of Jesus' uniqueness that excludes or absorbs other religions, they also have to clarify what makes Jesus unique and what can attract, empower, and challenge other religious ways. What makes the message of Jesus universally, decisively, indispensably meaningful in today's world?

By *unique* I mean, first of all, that which stands at the heart of Jesus' message, without which you would no longer have the authentic, complete gospel. While this ingredient may also be present in other religions, it would not be unique to them insofar as it does not occupy the same centrality or possess the same clarity and challenge that it has within the message of Jesus. So the uniqueness of Jesus contains Christianity's essential and distinctive contribution to the interreligious dialogue.

---

tions are appropriate and, I hope, well taken, for many pluralists much too facilely and a priori announce that because all other religions *are* true, Christians must acknowledge and dialogue with them. Still, I would ask Ogden whether he himself is faithful to his own Christian starting points when he admits only the possibility that there are other true religions besides Christianity. Given the God of pure, unbounded love whom Ogden finds in the heart of the Christian message, and given the anthropological necessity of this love having to take historical-cultural form in order to be real in the lives of men and women, should he not recognize that it is *probable* that God's love will be found in and through other religions, thus rendering them, at least to some extent, true? In order to affirm the actuality and efficacy of God's saving love for all people, Ogden needs to affirm the *probability* of many true religions. That means he enters the dialogue, like the pluralists, expecting to find God's truth revealed in other religious traditions.

In searching for that which makes Jesus and Christianity unique, I am not trying to come up with the essence of Christianity. Such an essence, clearly defined and set in stone, is impossible to find, if it exists at all. I think that the history of Christianity bears out that the heart of the gospel or the core of Christian revelation is a pluriform, adaptive, changing reality. As the formulation of this thesis states, what Christians find to be most important or meaningful or saving in the good news of the living Christ will be experienced and formulated differently according to different stages of history or different cultures. The living Christ is the same yesterday, today, and tomorrow, but his transforming power will work in and be perceived differently by the medieval European peasant than by the contemporary Salvadoran campesino. What makes Christianity unique is, paradoxically, ever the same but ever different.

So how might we in the late twentieth century formulate the way Christians in varying cultural contexts are experiencing that which is at the heart of the gospel, that which most directly and decisively addresses their need for salvation? I would agree with those theologians—especially Asian, Latin American, and feminist—who locate Jesus' unique and much needed message in his insistence that the reality of God cannot be truly experienced and known unless one is actively engaged in loving one's neighbors and working for their betterment. As Jon Sobrino puts it, in Jesus' message "one thing is perfectly clear: it is impossible to profess God without working for God's reign. . . . There is no *spiritual* life without actual, historical *life*. It is impossible to live with spirit unless the spirit *becomes flesh*."[16]

For Jesus and Christians, the two commandments—love of God and love of neighbor—are inseparable, two aspects of the same experiential

---

[16] *Spirituality of Liberation: Toward Political Holiness* (Maryknoll, N.Y.: Orbis Books, 1988), p. 4. See also Jon Sobrino, "Eastern Religions and Liberation," in *World Religions and Human Liberation*, ed. Dan Cohn-Sherbok (Maryknoll, N.Y.: Orbis Books, 1992), pp. 113-26; George M. Soares-Prabhu, "The Liberative Pedagogy of Jesus: Lessons for an Indian Theology of Liberation," in *Leave the Temple: Indian Paths to Human Liberation*, ed. Felix Wilfred (Maryknoll, N.Y.: Orbis Books, 1992), pp. 100-15; Samuel Rayan, "Outside the Gate, Sharing the Insult," in *Leave the Temple*, pp. 125-45; Elisabeth Schüssler Fiorenza, *In Memory of Her: A Feminist Reconstruction of Christian Origins* (New York: Crossroad, 1984); Rosemary Radford Ruether, *Sexism and God-Talk: Toward a Feminist Theology* (Boston: Beacon Press, 1983), pp. 116-38.

Marcus Borg culls contemporary gospel scholarship and concludes that we do not have a true picture of Jesus and his message unless we hold two elements in unison: Jesus was both a spirit-filled mystic or teacher of wisdom, and at the same time an earth-rooted prophet and leader of a revitalization movement "whose purpose was the transformation of the Jewish social world" (*Jesus a New Vision: Spirit, Culture, and the Life of Discipleship* [San Francisco: Harper & Row, 1987], p. 125).

reality. Therefore, for Christians today, however else God may be known in other traditions, God must also be realized as a Call and Empowerment to transform this world from one of division and injustice into one of love and mutuality. "The transformation of the world to a higher humanity, to justice and peace, is therefore an essential part of the 'catholicity' or universality of Christian faith."[17] Divine Reality is a historical reality; the Divine, as made known in Jesus, calls us to struggle for the betterment of human beings in this world; and, as we realize today, human betterment is intertwined with ecological betterment. As Edward Schillebeeckx formulates it, if Christianity at one time defined its uniqueness in the dictum *extra ecclesiam nulla salus* (outside the church no salvation), today it finds that uniqueness in the proclamation *extra mundum nulla salus* (outside the world no salvation); that is, unless we are realizing salvation or well-being in and for this world, we are not realizing the salvation announced by Jesus.[18] This is the *unique* ingredient in his saving message.

Other religious traditions may have their own unique ingredients, from which Christians can and must learn, and perhaps be transformed; for instance, Hinduism's insights into the non-duality between the Ultimate and the Finite, or Buddhism's insistence that a transformation of our mindfulness (through meditation) is essential for any kind of genuine transformation on other levels, or the insights of Native American spirituality into the sacredness of the earth, or Islam's conviction that what is true in the spiritual-interior realm must be translated into the social-political arena.[19] Christians can agree with and be challenged by such truth claims without in any way losing their focus on and commitment to a God who acts in history and calls all peoples to do the same.

In a sense, this proposed understanding of the uniqueness of Jesus can be exclusive, inclusive, or pluralistic: *exclusive* in that it will challenge any religious belief or practice (also within Christianity) that does not promote a this-worldly engagement of love and justice; *inclusive* in that it will clarify and fulfill the potential of other religions to promote what Christians call the Reign of God; *pluralistic* in that it will recognize and be itself fulfilled by new insights found in other traditions as to how we can enable humanity and the earth to have life and to have it more abundantly.

---

[17] Schillebeeckx, p. 171.

[18] Ibid., pp. 5-9.

[19] In her marvelous study *States of Grace: The Recovery of Meaning in the Postmodern Age*, Charlene Spretnak outlines the unique but complementary contributions of different religious traditions to the well-being of the earth and human family (San Francisco: Harper, 1991).

THESIS 5:

The orthodoxy of this pluralistic reinterpretation of the uniqueness of Jesus must be grounded primarily in the ability of such a reinterpretation to nurture a holistic Christian spirituality, that is, a devotion to and a following of Jesus. The proposed understanding of Jesus as God's truly but not only saving word does meet this criterion.

As stated in thesis 1, the test of the orthodoxy of any new doctrinal declaration or theological viewpoint is not the way it logically dovetails with past normative statements, but rather the way it enables Christians to recognize, celebrate, and enact the power of God-in-Jesus in their lives. Devotion and discipleship, or spirituality and action, must both nurture and be nurtured by any theological position that claims to be orthodox.

As I speak for myself, I hope I can speak for other so-called pluralist Christians when I state that this pluralistic christology, which views Jesus as truly but not solely God's universal saving Word has arisen out of, and continues to sustain, an always faulty but determined devotion to Jesus and an effort to follow him. Speaking as a pluralist theologian, I also speak as a Christian who is nourished at the eucharistic table and who feels empowered to live the life of the risen Christ.

How does this work? How does a pluralist christology nourish such a devotion to Jesus the Christ? It does so insofar as pluralists continue to affirm, because they continue to experience, that God has truly spoken a saving Word in Jesus; as explained above, *truly* means decisively, universally, indispensably. Such adverbs arise not only out of a reading of the New Testament but also and especially out of one's own experience of Jesus as the place in which one encounters God, the place in which one's life is transformed and set in a new direction. For pluralist Christians, too, the story of Jesus becomes their story—a story by which they now know that their lives are grounded in a God of love, who calls and empowers them to love. In breaking bread and reading the scriptures, pluralist Christians can feel the Spirit of Christ alive in their communities and individual lives, a Spirit that "de-centers" them and enables them to feel that it is no longer they who live but Christ who lives in them (Gal 2:20). All this is what enables pluralists to say that God has truly acted in and as Jesus.[20]

---

[20] This means that as a pluralist Christian, I can with no difficulty whatsoever announce—indeed, I feel impelled to proclaim—that Jesus is truly the Son of God and universal Savior. The recognition and announcement of Jesus' divinity remains integral and essential to a pluralist christology. Out of my own experience I can endorse the explanations of what it means to call Jesus divine that have been proposed by Christian theologians such as Karl Rahner, Paul Tillich, Edward

But as was suggested above, the real test of fidelity to Jesus and his message is not whether one adheres to the proper titles for him or even whether one duly worships him; rather, one's fidelity and orthodoxy regarding who Jesus is have to be measured in one's ability and decision to follow him—to act as a disciple. And here too, as a pluralist Christian, even though I do not feel it possible or necessary to affirm that Jesus is the *only* Savior, I still experience him to be so *truly* a Savior that I feel impelled to cast my lot with him. What he reveals of God's Reign, his vision of a humanity united in love and justice as children of a God of love and justice, and the power of this vision as it lives on in the community after his death—all these call me to believe in this Reign and to act for it, even if it should require of me what it required of him. Contrary to what others have suggested, a pluralist Christian has sufficient clarity about and commitment to the gospel values of justice and love to resist those who trample on these values, whether Nazis or the Salvadoran oligarchy. One does not have to affirm Jesus as the only Truth in order to die for the Truth that he does reveal.

Insofar as pluralist Christians continue to experience and follow Jesus as God's Word, even though they question whether he is the only such Word, they can still be fully devoted to him. Indeed, what they find in him, the way he reveals God and God's Reign to them—leads them to expect that there *are* other ways and other words. I have found that my devotion to Jesus not only sustains, it also urges and clarifies my pluralistic christology and theology of religions. The God whom I know in Jesus and whose Reign I work for is a God of pure, unbounded love, a God who seeks to communicate with all persons and who wills to inspire all men and women to work for a world of love and justice. This is a God who cannot be confined, a God who, in speaking truly in Jesus, reveals that God cannot speak only in Jesus.

Therefore, according to John Cobb, as Christians come to know and follow Jesus, they realize he is the Way that is open to other Ways.[21] To know this Jesus and to be devoted to him is to be called to a relationship not only with him but also with others. In fact, I would say that the more deeply we enter into the Mystery of Christ, the more we will feel the

---

Schillebeeckx, Hans Küng, and Monika Hellwig: to feel and proclaim that Jesus is divine is to encounter him as God's sacrament—as the embodiment, the historical reality, the symbol, the story that makes God real and effective for me. To meet this Jesus is to meet the living reality of the Divine—this was the reason the early Christians proclaimed him as God's Son, and it remains the reason pluralist Christians continue to do so. Only someone who is utterly at one with God can so communicate God to me and be God for me. This, too, is contained in the pluralist affirmation of Jesus as truly divine.

[21] John B. Cobb, Jr., "The Meaning of Pluralism for Christian Self-Understanding," in *Religious Pluralism*, ed. Leroy S. Rouner (Notre Dame, Ind.: University of Notre Dame Press, 1984), pp. 174-75.

ability and need to embrace that Mystery wherever it may manifest itself. Secure in my commitment to Jesus the Christ, I am able to appreciate and even be startled by what God may be up to in other persons and other traditions. Indeed, I feel that if I am not open to the God of others, I am not truly open to the God made known to me in Jesus.

In the spirituality of a pluralist Christian, therefore, Jesus certainly remains unique. But as Gabriel Moran has recently suggested, his uniqueness is not a matter of superiority or arrogation of privilege; rather, it is a matter of distinctness, of specialness that will surely be different from but not necessarily better than others.[22] It is a distinctness that consists primarily and most importantly not in Jesus' ability to exclude or absorb others (although that can indeed happen) but rather in his ability to offer us a distinct, concrete, decisive way of knowing God and living God's life in this world. As William Burrows has put it, "The uniqueness of Christ and Christian life lies in a distinct structure of existence; the Christian manner of being a saint . . . is unique."[23]

In such an understanding of Jesus' uniqueness we are committed to Christ because of who he is and what we have found in him, not because we are certain that he is better than all others. A devotion to Christ based on distinctiveness has deeper roots, it seems to me, than one based on superiority or privileged place.

If there is any validity to these five theses, then a pluralist reinterpretation of the uniqueness of Jesus does turn out to be a reaffirmation of that uniqueness—a reaffirmation that can help Christians to be not only more open to followers of other ways but also more deeply committed to Jesus and his gospel.

---

[22] Gabriel Moran, *Uniqueness* (Maryknoll, N.Y.: Orbis Books, 1992).
[23] Personal letter to the author, February 11, 1993.

PART II

Responses
to Paul F. Knitter's Theses

What's So Special about Jesus?

KAJSA AHLSTRAND

INTRODUCTION

The pluralist position in the theology of religions has the advantage that it respects the integrity of the religious traditions of the world. Its new interpretations of the Christian doctrines of incarnation, redemption, christology, ecclesiology, sacramentology, and trinitarian theology, however, are more often than not embarrassingly shallow. The problem is whether it is possible to combine classic Christian theology in all its richness with a positive view of the many religious traditions of the world. Must the christological formulations of the Creed—"one Lord, Jesus Christ, the only Son of God, eternally begotten of the Father, God from God, Light from Light, true God from true God, begotten not made, of one being with the Father"—be reduced to "Jesus is an inspiring example in our struggle for justice, peace, and the preservation of the earth" if we want to maintain good relations with those who do not belong to the Christian tradition? I don't think so. I am convinced that self-respect is a prerequisite for respect of the other.

It might very well be that some of the christological assumptions of the Christian tradition are incompatible with fundamental assumptions of other religions, but I cannot see that as a good enough reason to abandon the Christian conviction. I do not demand of the others that they abandon their convictions just because they are contrary to my beliefs. The reinterpretation of christology, then, is not primarily induced by a desire to please believers outside the Christian community, but rather by an insight that the traditional christological formulations do not convey sufficient insight into the person and work of Jesus, whom the Christians call Christ, for people from different contexts and different religions to recognize God's liberating and life-giving Word and presence in this Jesus today.

QUESTIONS OF METHODOLOGY

Depending on the goal, the methodologies, the ways by which we arrive at the goals, must be of different kinds. Paul Knitter focuses on the present situation: "Any new understanding of Jesus—his person, work, or uniqueness—must flow from and nurture a saving experience of and commitment to Jesus (devotion) and a resolute following of him in the world (discipleship)." Although I concur that these are necessary, I would add some other criteria in order to avoid the danger of our christological formulations being subjected to the tyranny of current politically correct opinions.

Any new understanding of Jesus Christ must take the Christian scriptures seriously, make use of the best previous understandings of Jesus Christ, and see what kind of questions the classic christological formulations tried to answer. A new understanding of Jesus must have links with earlier interpretations of the person and work of Jesus. If there are no such links we are talking not about new interpretations but new religions.

It is also vital that our own thinking, knowledge, and experiences inform the present christological reflection. Although our own reflection is necessary, it should be challenged constantly by the other critical instances, so that it does not become lofty speculation or sheer wishful thinking.

Finally, the theologians of liberation have taught us that any theological reflection is incomplete without the experiences of the poor, not only poor Christians, but the poor from any or no religious tradition. The poor are primarily those who lack food, shelter, education, and political influence, but they are also the marginalized in any society. It is not quite true that christology has been a matter only for fair-skinned, educated, heterosexual men, but the dark, the unlearned, gays and lesbians, and heterosexual women certainly have not been given equal time and space in telling their stories of Jesus.

RESPECT FOR THE OTHER

An absolute prerequisite in interreligious dialogue is respect for the other. In the question of an inclusivist/pluralist christology we (the people who try to formulate such a christology) encounter several others.

The first other is Jesus, a Jewish peasant who lived in the eastern Mediterranean at the beginning of the Common Era. Something is definitely wrong if we see this Jesus as one of us, Western, Christian academics of the late twentieth century. Jesus is a scandal to Christians as well as to believers from different traditions and nonbelievers. Jesus does not compete with the Buddha or Krishna or Muhammad, not because he said essentially the same thing as they did, but because he said and did other things. He was a Jew, a landless, executed one.

Second, the other is also the Christian who has left everything and followed Jesus. Not a few Christians in India, Pakistan, Burma, and many other parts of the world have had to make a choice between commitment to Jesus and commitment to their families and friends. When Christians in secure positions make statements about the compatibility between commitment to Jesus and commitment to other religious traditions, respect for the other, in this case the other Christian, demands that we listen to those who have found loyalty to Jesus.

Third, the other is the person who does not belong to the Christian tradition. A good thing about exclusivism is that it takes the otherness of the other seriously; it respects the integrity of the other religion. Even though one might not agree with the other, one should not try to smooth out the differences between the two traditions in order to make the other seem more like oneself. Pluralism, on the other hand, may also respect the other as different from oneself, but it constantly runs the risk of smoothing out the contradictions. If, for example, I value liberation in all its aspects highly and regard it as the center of my (Christian) religion, or indeed any religion, it may be difficult for me to respect quietist attitudes in other religions or even my own, and I may tend to disregard such views as aberrations from "true" religion.

It is not self-evident that the non-Christian has the same goals as the Christian. Is it certain that everyone wants to be saved? Does salvation mean the same thing in the different traditions? The question can be even more pointed: what kind of salvation did Jesus promise? Before it is universalized, it should be understood in its immediate Jewish Mediterranean context. The Buddha came to show the way to enlightenment. That is not necessarily the same thing as salvation in Jesus' tradition.

JESUS IS SPECIAL TO US

Christians throughout the ages agree: There is something special about Jesus; "special" is more, not less, than "unique." Uniqueness and significance are not synonymous concepts. It is possible for something to be unique without being significant, and it is possible for something to be significant without being unique. The prime concern of christology is to vindicate the significance of Jesus, not the uniqueness of Jesus.

When coming home after work, always by bike and always with her hair in disarray, my mother used to get a quick glance of herself in the mirror and contentedly announce: "I may not be beautiful, but I am definitely rare." Not only is she rare, but she is indeed unique. Yet it is not the uniqueness that makes her special to me. To be special to someone is more important than to be unique. Even a snowflake is unique, but is it special to anyone?

The claim that Jesus is unique is not necessarily a significant theological statement. It could mean that he had his own particular DNA-combination. When traditional christology has claimed the uniqueness of Jesus, it is not this self-evident uniqueness the theologians have tried to formulate. When we ask for the uniqueness of Jesus, we state less than the Christian traditions have believed him to be.

The great risk is that the quest for uniqueness will lead to reductionist answers: only what Jesus does not have in common with others is significant. On the other hand, the question "what's so special about Jesus?" generates replies which lie at the center of the living Christian tradition. "Who is Jesus?" can only get a meaningful answer from someone to whom Jesus is special. Those to whom Jesus is special can be found both within and outside the boundaries of the church. Thus, to call Jesus special instead of unique will give us richer, more personal, more committed answers. While attempts to define the uniqueness of Jesus tend to be either arrogant or trivial, the personal question "what's so special?" elicits answers that arise from faith.

Jesus is special to many Muslims, Hindus, Buddhists, followers of traditional religions, and Atheists. The church, however, has an obligation to preserve and transmit the stories and experiences of how and why Jesus is special. When we state that there is something special about Jesus, we also contribute to the religions of the world by making accessible to others what we have found during the centuries—not because followers of other religions could not have found it, but because it has been the preoccupation of the Christians to find out what's so special about Jesus, without denying the possibility that others may add to that.

JESUS AS GOD'S TENTATIVE, PARTICULAR, AND REJECTABLE WORD

My own christological reflection, informed by Christian kenotic christology as well as by insights from Saivism, Buddhism and Western Atheism, is to see Jesus as God's tentative, particular, and rejectable Word. I do believe that Jesus is God's universal, decisive, and indispensable manifestation of saving truth and grace, but that he is so in a perspective of human brokenness. Because the oppressed of today are the oppressors of tomorrow, because the atrocities we see around us are committed by human beings like ourselves, there can be no "us" and "them" when it comes to the ability to inflict pain and suffering. In Jesus, divine reality, the ineffable mystery, became one of us.

Much has been said about Jesus as Omega—in this century from J. N. Farquhar's Christ as the crown or fulfillment of Hinduism to Knitter's description of him as God's decisive, universal, and indispensable Word. But he is Alpha as well as Omega. He is the beginning, "the most newly born among us," as Paul Claudel put it. God is not only infinitely greater than our thoughts, God is also smaller, to use a halting metaphor. In Jesus, God became vulnerable, particular, and rejectable. In fact, say the evangelists and apostles, God was wounded and rejected in Jesus. If this was possible then, it is still possible. We can reject Jesus.

The God I am looking for is the desecrated God, the one who identifies not only with the unjustly oppressed but with the most despicable creature: the oppressor. This was what Jesus did when he caused scandal by socializing with tax-collectors. And this Jesus, testify his followers through the centuries, was somehow God.

The incarnation means that God has become vulnerable and rejectable. It is not self-evident that everybody wants to accept a convicted and executed Jewish criminal as God's true Word. How do we handle the fact that although many Hindus and Buddhists love and respect Jesus, there are also those who say that he is indeed a very bad example: he ate meat and drank wine and allowed himself to be killed. The possibility to reject him must be safe-guarded in any christology.

Jesus can be rejected, but at the same time it is vital to remember that the letters J-E-S-U-S must not be confounded with the person and work of Jesus.

> And many followed him, and he healed them all, and ordered them not to make him known. This was to fulfill what was spoken by the prophet Isaiah: "Behold, my servant whom I have chosen, my beloved with whom my soul is well pleased. I will put my Spirit upon him, and he shall proclaim justice to the gentiles. He will not wrangle or cry aloud, nor will anyone hear his voice in the streets: he will not break a bruised reed or quench a smoldering wick, till he brings justice to victory; and in his name will the gentiles hope" (Mt 12:18-21).

One way of reading this text is to say that if hope is not conveyed, the people have not heard the name of Jesus. The combination of letters J-E-S-U-S is at times an obstacle for people to encounter Mary's son. When the person of Jesus is rejected, are hope and justice rejected? There is an unbreakable relation among justice, hope, liberation, and Jesus, Mary's son. So much so that Christians can say that it is impossible to encounter Jesus without encountering justice and hope, and also that it is impossible to encounter justice and hope without encountering Jesus, because he embodies hope and justice.

This may lead to a kind of inclusivism, but it is necessary to distinguish between what Paul Hacker has called "subordinating inclusivism," which means that other traditions are seen as less perfect forms of my own tradition, and what could be labeled "egalitarian inclusivism," which means that I may interpret other traditions through categories and images in my own tradition but also accept having my own tradition interpreted in the same way by believers from traditions other than my own. While I reject subordinating inclusivism, I accept egalitarian inclusivism insofar as it does not threaten the integrity of the other tradition.

When Christians say "Jesus," we think of hope, justice, and liberation. These are not abstract terms. They are embodied in the person of Jesus, and they can be realized in the world, albeit imperfectly, by human effort. When we look to Jesus, when we live in his communion (*koinonia*) and follow him in service, our perspective and direction must be toward hope, justice, and liberation; if they are not, it is not Jesus with whom we are in communion.

PLURALIST ESCHATOLOGY?

Even if there are many true revelations of God, are there also many "lives that kill death," many resurrected Lords who shall come again to judge the living and the dead? Is it only Jesus Christ or are there many "Returners"? Mythological as the eschatological language is, it is when it comes to eschatology that pluralist christology is challenged. If Christian eschatology is reduced to an action program for the betterment of the world, a christology that sees Jesus as example and inspirer is all right, but if a *lokuttara* dimension is allowed for, it becomes more difficult to maintain a pluralist christology. The inclusivists will say that the Buddha Maitreya, the Messiah, and Kalkin will remember what it was to be a landless Jew in the Eastern Mediterranean region. What will the pluralists say? Is pluralism provisional or ultimate? If it is ultimate, is there also a plurality of ultimate goals? Does that not imply a plurality of gods? A consistent pluralist christology questions monotheism.

A Simple Solution

MICHAEL AMALADOSS, S.J.

OVERSIMPLIFICATION

In his "Five Theses" Paul F. Knitter has offered a simple solution to a very complex problem. But the solution finally turns out to be no solution at all, because he has oversimplified the problem itself. Besides, this attempt makes us wonder whether the way of posing the problem itself has to be questioned.

Every human person is unique. There is no one else like that person. People differ by their natural gifts; the circumstances of their upbringing; the experiences and persons who have influenced them; the context of their life and work; and, finally, by their own creative initiative, reflection, and action. This is particularly so if a person happens to have leadership qualities and is at the origin of a group or movement. Such a person is not merely unique but leaves behind a unique tradition. The identity of some persons may be characterized by special spiritual experiences that have an impact on their followers. They add to the uniqueness of the persons concerned. Such persons command the loyalty and devotion of their followers.

To say that Jesus was unique in this way—namely, that one experienced the presence of God in him and that he left behind him a particular spiritual tradition which focused on the option for the poor and the oppressed and on struggling with them for their liberation and development concretely here and now in history—is true. Jesus has also commanded the passionate loyalty of many followers through history, who did not hesitate to sacrifice even their lives. Jesus is unique indeed. But so are the Buddha and Mahatma Gandhi and a host of others. The third thesis of Professor Knitter is key, and one could read it meaningfully, replacing the name of Jesus with that of any other great spiritual leader.

But people who speak of the uniqueness of Jesus Christ in the context of religious pluralism do not refer to this kind of uniqueness. So I wonder whether Knitter has not simplified the problem so much that it is no longer a problem. He says many beautiful things about Jesus but does not particularly address the problem that he set out to solve.

UNIQUENESS AND UNIVERSALITY

Talk about the uniqueness of Jesus Christ is linked to the affirmation of the universality of redemption through the paschal mystery of his death and resurrection. Christians believe that Jesus Christ died for all, though they may explain in various ways the significance of the act of redemption. If Jesus is reduced simply to one way that mediates the saving presence of God to some people, then he is not the redeemer that Christians are talking about. St. Paul contrasts the first and the second Adam: "For if, by the transgression of one person, death came to reign through that one, how much more will those who receive the abundance of grace and of the gift of justification come to reign in life through the one person Jesus Christ" (Rom 5:17). There may be different theologies of redemption, but all Christians normally agree on the saving significance of the paschal mystery for all peoples. I do not see how one can set about solving the problem of the uniqueness of Jesus without even adverting to this central affirmation.

Knitter seems to reduce the role of Jesus to mediating God's presence, communicating God-experience, or revealing the truth about God. Maybe he thinks that this is all that redemption means or demands. But then he must explain and defend that theory and not take it for granted and go on to propose a solution based on it.

HISTORY AND MYSTERY

Knitter also fights shy of mystery. In sacramental theology one used to discuss an abstract question like "If one had to baptize someone in danger of death and had to recall the basic mysteries of faith, on what should one focus?" The answer used to be basic mysteries like the Trinity, the incarnation, and the redemption.

I do not know whether one can talk about Jesus in a Christian context without talking about the mysteries of the incarnation and the Trinity. Like the mystery of the redemption, these are relevant to any discussion of the uniqueness and the universality of Jesus. If God is the Trinity, however this is understood, and if the Second Person of the Blessed Trinity became a human person, however this process is explained, then that person is not just unique as any other human person or spiritual leader is unique.

To talk about the uniqueness of Jesus and not even mention these mysteries seems an oversimplification of the issues of the discussion. How can one talk about any religion while carefully avoiding any reference to its basic creed?

I have the impression that Knitter carefully avoids the dimension of mystery. In thesis 5 his focus on the historical—earthly—dimension of liberation is welcome, provided one does not limit one's perspectives to that. Similarly, except in thesis 5, where he is talking in the context of Christian discipleship, Knitter talks about Jesus, referring I suppose to the historical person, while carefully avoiding any mention of Christ. I wonder whether this is an attempt to keep the dimension of mystery out of the discussion. But this again is an option that he has to explain to any Christian believer and not take for granted.

PHENOMENOLOGY AND FAITH

The problem with the approach of Knitter and many others who talk about the experience of religious pluralism in the categories of exclusivism, inclusivism, and pluralism is that sometimes they do not rise beyond the horizontal and phenomenological level of the historians of religions. Religions and/or their founders are reduced to their common denominators: "ways of salvation," or "mediations of divine presence," or "revelations of truth about the Ultimate," and so on. One does not take seriously the basic creedal affirmations of any of the religions. Then, of course, one gets caught in the numbers game of the one and the many. I wonder whether the question of uniqueness can be raised meaningfully and solved at the phenomenological level, without moving to the level of faith.

Maybe the language of uniqueness itself has to be abandoned. Such language arises out of a comparative perspective. One compares oneself with others and sees oneself as better or superior or having more truth, and so on. Given the operation of the hermeneutical circle in the process of interpretation, one finds in one's own tradition the criterion to evaluate and grade the others. As a matter of fact, the language of uniqueness, if it is consistent, should deny the possibility even of comparison.

I wonder whether, in the context of a growing realization among Christians of the positive role of other religions in the plan of God's self-communication to peoples, we should rediscover interreligious dialogue as an encounter of free persons who discover each other also as believers and who explore their basic differences in an ongoing process of living and working together, committed to building a common human community of fellowship, freedom, and justice, rather than engaging in comparative games on the abstract, intellectual level. Our identity depends on what we are positively and not upon what we are not, nor upon how we are different from the others.

Interreligious dialogue is a new experience for us Christians. In the light of this experience we will have to revise our vision of God's plan for the world and our theology of history—and, against this background, our theologies of revelation and redemption—as we dialogue with the other believers. We need not abandon or ignore the basic mysteries in which our faith is rooted, though they are always open to new experiences and understandings.

Dialogue requires respect for the others as human persons and believers who have encountered God and serious conversation with them with regard to the differences, which may be enriching but also sometimes divisive. It does not require an overall theoretical framework of comparisons and contrasts, attempting to solve all problems of difference, a priori and in the abstract, at a merely phenomenological level of the one and the many.

The Need for a New Debate

S. WESLEY ARIARAJAH

DIFFICULTIES WITH THE FIVE THESES

Modern science and technology have produced highly complex forms of entertainment since the time I was a little boy. My children grew up in the era of television, computer games, and high-tech amusement parks. And yet year after year I convinced them that we need to see the Circus Knie, a yearly circus in Geneva. As the girls became older, it gradually dawned on them that it was not all for their benefit. They realized that it was their dad who would not outgrow the habit of still regarding the circus as an outstanding form of entertainment. There is no more pretense. Now the family goes to the circus "because Appa (Dad) likes it." I too have admitted that my fascination with the circus as a whole must have come from the time I first saw a juggler who could keep five or six balls in the air. It was an act that I could never perform, and it was good to see someone who could.

Paul Knitter in his Five Theses has also decided to juggle with several balls, none of which he wants to drop:

1. The urgency of dialogue, which comes from external and internal pressures.
2. The need to respect and, where possible, affirm the religious experience of the other.
3. The Christian claim, rooted in scripture and tradition, that Jesus is unique.
4. Christian conviction that in Christ there is salvation, a message that needs to be shared.
5. The recognition that God can and does act in saving ways other than the one we know.

I say this with appreciation and respect for what Knitter has attempted. I am aware that the Five Theses come out of years of theological struggle and an attempt to break a stalemate in the discussions between the inclusivists and pluralists. As I have confessed, I have a healthy respect and admiration for juggling. All theological endeavor is an attempt to keep in motion and in interrelationship what we know in part of a mys-

29

tery yet to be revealed in its fullness. My question is a different one: Are these the balls that we should juggle with?

Useful as it was to classify positions within the theology of religions, it appears to me that the threefold paradigm of exclusivism, inclusivism, and pluralism has since increasingly become one of the stumbling blocks to progress in the discussions on how Christians should understand and relate to religious plurality. For one thing, people have begun to box in persons and theological explorations as belonging to one or another of the three positions. The debate on the theology of religions needs to be much more nuanced than these positions would allow. More discouraging, none of the three positions really seems to satisfy even the persons who claim to or are said to advocate it.

The exclusivists find it difficult, when pushed to the corner, to come up with an adequate basis for dialogue, except as a more respectable tool for mission. The inclusivists face the insinuation of being "spiritual colonialists" insofar as they define the other in terms of their own faith perspectives. The pluralists are accused of "throwing out the baby with the bath water."

Knitter is attempting in his Five Theses to show that the baby can still be there in the pluralist position. This he does by attempting to retain and reinterpret within a pluralist position some of the key concepts that are regarded as crucial to an interpretation of the meaning of the Jesus event from the perspective of the other positions, namely, the *uniqueness* of Jesus and the conviction that God's revelation in him is *full, definitive*, and *unsurpassable*.

He accepts that the uniqueness of Jesus is rooted in the Bible and Christian tradition and attempts to reinterpret that uniqueness in terms of *truly* instead of *only*. Then he substitutes the words *universal, decisive,* and *indispensable* for *full, definitive*, and *unsurpassable*. He then attempts to give an interpretation of these words that respects the sensitivity of the peoples of other faith traditions. But if the purpose of the exercise is to meet the charge of perceived relativism entailed in the pluralist perspective, Knitter is not persuasive, especially when he draws attention to the fact that he has used "a" and not "the" in respect of these claims.

If his purpose is not primarily to speak to the critics of the pluralist position but to explore a relevant christology for a pluralistic world, then one needs to ask whether any purpose can be served by revisiting words that have been so problematic in interpreting the meaning and mission of Jesus to people of other traditions. This is why I have posed the question whether these indeed are the balls one should juggle with today.

It appears, as he develops his theses, that his interest in retaining and giving new meaning to these words also stems from his concern to preserve the legitimacy of Christian witness to people of other faiths. He postulates, in his third thesis, three positions that seek to justify the importance of Christian witness, of course within the context and spirit of dialogue. They arise, however, from his primary assertion that Jesus is "universal, decisive, and indispensable."

> If something is true, especially if it is a truth that touches the core of how we see the world and live our lives, it cannot be true only for me. If it is true, it has to be true for others. . . .
>
> If I experience something to be true not just for me but for others, and if this truth has enriched and transformed my life, I automatically feel that it can and should do the same for others. . . . Whatever truth about the Ultimate and the human condition there may be in other traditions, such truth can be enhanced and clarified through an encounter with the good news made known in Jesus. In a qualified but still in a real sense, persons of other religious paths are "unfulfilled" without Christ.

Knitter's insistence that what is true for him *has to be true for others* and what has transformed his life *should transform others* smacks of being only the top side of the exclusivist position, softened up for the purposes of dialogue. For behind these assertions lies an understanding of truth, revelation, and God's relationship to humankind that the pluralist position has seriously questioned. This understanding naturally leads him to the conclusion that other religious paths "in a qualified but still real sense . . . are 'unfulfilled' without Christ." This is the conviction that prompts those who want to remain inclusivist.

Of more importance is to ask how the position he takes in this thesis relates to his argument in the second thesis that to claim to have the final norm is to "retain the position of advantage" in a dialogue "among equals." At the end of the same thesis he has also assailed inclusivists by saying:

> [A position that holds that] whatever truth or good may be found in other traditions has to be "fulfilled" or included within the final Christian truth . . . seems . . . to be opposed to the nature and requirements of dialogue.

Is Knitter, the reluctant pluralist, presenting a sugar-coated inclusivism, or is he, like the other Paul in the New Testament, wanting to be "all things to all people"? The Five Theses do succeed in minimizing what people find objectionable in the exclusivist position, primarily by reinterpreting, substituting, and giving new meaning to words, but they appear to me to fall short of giving a new and adequate basis for a Christian understanding and relationship to people of other faiths, one which truly respects the otherness of the others. Knitter seems to drag his feet on the confidence we have as people of dialogue—that God can and does indeed deal with people in ways other than what we claim to be true on the basis of our own experience.

Knitter, however, goes further to make his own specific contribution to the discussion by insisting that the uniqueness of Jesus is made clear in the life and witness of his followers. He also recognizes that the content of that uniqueness will be understood and proclaimed differently in different contexts and periods of history. In our own time he sees the uniqueness of Jesus expressed in his insistence that salvation or the reign of God must be realized in this world through human actions of love and justice. One is left with the feeling that the word *uniqueness* is qualified so much that the word itself loses its uniqueness.

DO WE REALLY NEED THESE WORDS?

What is difficult for me with Knitter's theses is his basic assumption that an interpretation of Jesus must contain such concepts as unique, decisive, indispensable, and so on. I am convinced that these words, however carefully interpreted, have no place in our Christian witness. They come from the period when the significance of Jesus was interpreted in the context of the church's polemical relations with the Jewish people and were further reinforced when Christianity became associated with imperial power and colonial expansion. They were, of course, also used in the language of faith and love to indicate the depth and profundity of the experience of Christ, even as people of other religious traditions speak of their own faith experience. But they are understood today to reflect a power relation that existed between Christianity and other religions. In any case, this is how they have been perceived by people of other faith traditions. These words appear to me to be unredeemable and, in any case, do not help us in an interpretation of Jesus in the context of an open relationship with others.

The hope for an interpretation of Jesus appropriate for our witness today lies in our ability to come up with a new framework that both sets out what we believe God to have done in Jesus and remains genuinely open to being surprised by God's freedom to act within the life and experience of other people and outside the history that has shaped our own faith.

Does this mean that we go in the opposite direction and openly deny that there is any uniqueness in Jesus or that God might have done something decisive, indispensable, universal, and so forth, in the Jesus event? There is no need to do this, because it is possible to come to an understanding of who Jesus is in which these issues and words become pointless and irrelevant. It is interesting that most of the interpretations of the

life and ministry of Jesus in third-world contexts pay little or no attention to the issue of uniqueness. The *minjung* theologians of Korea, for
example, when thrown into jails and tortured for taking sides with the
dispossessed, awoke to the fact that Jesus identified himself with the
brokenness of the people and met the fate that befell them. They recognized that to follow him is to participate in their misery (*han*) and to be
willing to pay the price for so doing. Such an understanding of Jesus
may be challengingly relevant to all peoples and all times, and to enter
that discipleship might be life-transforming to anyone. But the very spirit
that undergirds this interpretation rules out the possibility of using such
words as *decisive*, *indispensable*, and so on. The uniqueness issue was
not consciously dropped; it had become irrelevant and meaningless both
to their understanding of who Jesus was and to their witness to him.

It appears to me that Knitter's Five Theses suffer from the limited
scope he set for himself; namely, to give an interpretation of the uniqueness of Jesus in the world. This is too narrow a scope for the task that
confronts us. An adequate interpretation of Jesus for our time, in my
experience of dealing with the issue, cannot be arrived at without beginning with a much wider framework that takes the earth and all its people
into account. And it certainly cannot be achieved by beginning with
christology. Such a framework, to be truly biblical has to begin with
God and end with God, within which we need to place the significance
of Jesus and his challenge to discipleship.

TOWARD A WIDER FRAMEWORK

A wider framework needs to take account of several aspects, including the following:

1. God is the creator, preserver, and provider of all that is; nothing is
   outside God's love and care.
2. In our experience we know that the world is not what God intends
   it to be. God's love, compassion, and justice, however, are at work
   to bring wholeness to the whole creation.
3. Religious traditions witness to how people in all ages and places
   have attempted to know, understand, and relate to God, or to grasp
   the meaning of life, sometimes without using God language.
4. In our experience we also know that all human attempts to relate
   to God and live a life that God intends have been ambiguous; all
   religious life participates in this ambiguity. But all of them also
   give undeniable witness to people's life with God and to God's
   life with people.
5. Christians have, in and through the life, death, and resurrection of
   Jesus, come to a knowledge and understanding of who God is,

how God deals with us, and what God requires of us. To be a Christian is to be caught up in this profound reality and to accept the discipleship to which this knowledge calls us.

6. This discipleship is exercised in the world in the way we relate to God, ourselves, and others. In so doing, we believe that we participate in God's rule, which will in its own time bring fullness of life to all creation.

7. As Christians live with others they witness to the one who called them to this discipleship. Even as they give an "account of the hope that is in them," they are open to listening and learning about the ways God has been active in the world and in the lives of other people.

8. As people who have come into the discipleship of God's Reign we participate wherever we discern the Spirit of God to be active to bring wholeness. We are also open to inviting all who stand for the values of the Kingdom to work with us, despite religious labels, in seeking to fulfill God's will for the world.

The above considerations are not alternate theses, nor do they provide the framework that resolves the issue of Christian faith among the plurality of religions. All such lists invariably raise more questions than they answer. But the attempt has one main purpose; namely, to show that it is possible to deal with the specificity and distinctiveness of the Christian experience and relate it to other faith traditions without having to use the concepts of uniqueness, decisiveness, and so on, which only cloud our witness to God's rule and to the One who calls us to its discipleship.

In other words, as someone who personally knows Knitter's intention and has worked with him in some of the struggles to arrive at clarity on this issue, I retain my admiration for his theological struggle and the Five Theses he has produced to further the discussion. But I do think that he needs a different paradigm to juggle with. The uniqueness debate and the conversation between the inclusivists and pluralists seem to go round in circles. We need a new debate.

My daughters come with me to the circus every year. It is to the credit of Circus Knie that, despite being a circus, where new possibilities are somewhat difficult to come up with, it manages to do something radically new every year!

Identifying Constructively Our Interreligious Moment

MICHAEL von BRÜCK

Paul Knitter rightly points out that the question is not *that* Jesus is unique but *how* he is so (thesis 1). Any answer, of course, is not a revealed fact but already an interpretation, which we cannot avoid. Thesis 4 gives a rather formal criterion: "It" is the saving good news that changes all the time, and "loving one's neighbors and working for their betterment." But this is a common human appeal we find in many traditions. One would have to be more precise to make a real liberating contribution. This *how*, I would like to suggest, seems to be the transformation of the world based in an *extra nos*.

CHRISTIAN ROOTS

Christian faith is rooted in the unconditional love of God, which God has revealed in Jesus Christ in a unique way. This love extends to the whole cosmos (Jn 3:16). Cosmos means the whole world in space and time, and perhaps even more. Christ is the embodiment of the true light that enlightens all humankind (Jn 1:9), even if the human situation is marked by an experience of the absence of God insofar as this light is not being fully recognized (Jn 1:11). In Christ, however, the atonement of the world is certain (Rom 5:11; 11:15), even if knowledge of this fact is always broken, incomplete, and may be questioned. The specific Christian contribution in a world of religious plurality is not so much a distinct way of life, as Paul Knitter suggests at the end of thesis 5, for genuine life of unbounded love and justice is happening also outside the Christian tradition. Rather, it is to witness to this unconditionality of the love of God.

Unconditionality implies that the love of God cannot be limited spatially or temporally, nor can it depend on the condition of knowing this fact. Faith as trust in God's unconditional love, therefore, is a pure gift of the loving God. In Christian theology God is conceived in trinitarian dynamics so that God's actions *ad extra* are indivisible (*opera trinitatis ad extra indivisa sunt*). Consequently, the very act of reconciliation is present also in creation and in the free presence of the Spirit everywhere, at all times, not only implicitly but also explicitly. What follows is that human beings in all their languages, religions, circumstances of life, and attitudes of consciousness are being reached by God's reconciling presence. The presence of this reconciliation is universal, and non-Christians *ante* or *post Christum natum* cannot be excluded from it.

These seem to be possible cornerstones for the foundation of a Christian theology of religions. However, I fully agree with Paul Knitter when he points out (thesis 5) that it is not the dovetailing with past normative statements, but how "it enables Christians to recognize, celebrate, and enact the power of God-in-Jesus in their lives," that makes a theology truly Christian. Christians are to accept all human beings as having equal dignity precisely in their religious distinction; that is, they can love them precisely in their otherness. This is how Christians may witness to their trust in the unconditional and prior love of the one God, who wants to be close to all creatures without exception.

However, in the dualistic processes of decision-making in history, humans need orientation and values. Theologically speaking this means that we require criteria for where and in which ways God's actions can be distinguished from human projections and wishes. For Christians the criterion is Jesus Christ; for others it is a witness of the self-revelation of God in other languages. The knowledge of this criterion is always under dispute, both within the history of Christianity and among religions. Therefore, a never-ending discourse to recognize the truth must be carried on, one which is based on trust, love and mutual respect.

This is not to say that all religions actually express the same insight. Of course the principle of the Golden Rule exists in many religions. The unity of love of God and love of the neighbor (or their equivalents) is known not only in Christianity. We might express the unity of religions in a shift from ego-centeredness toward reality-centeredness (John Hick). A hermeneutic community of scholars can patiently figure out a common ethics of the world's religions that looks very much like a human rights declaration. I do not argue that all this would be futile, just the opposite—such general statements and documents can be a court of appeal for those people on the basis of religions who are being oppressed even in the name of religion by their own hierarchies!

But a common denominator of religions in ethics is not sufficient. Ethics requires a foundation, and this implies—at least in the field of religious unconditionality—the whole understanding of self, world, and salvation of a religion. Here the economic, ecological, political, and psychological aspects of communication between social groups and people are becoming constitutive for the process of understanding. Any search for a common denominator or world ethics therefore has to be careful not just to prolong the status quo, which might be worth prolonging from an European, American, or Japanese perspective, but certainly not from a Latin American, African, or South Asian perspective. Interreligious understanding does not take place in a space free of power structures! The trustworthiness of the interreligious search in the struggle for peace, justice, and integrity of creation depends on the willingness of all partners to share power.

Therefore, interreligious communication and community are dependent upon the following:

1. Just socioeconomic relations between the rich and the poor;
2. Mutual renunciation of establishing one's own identity at the cost of the other;
3. The insight that other human beings are equal before God, that they are also a possible source for knowledge of truth and salvation and so other religions cannot be made objects of mission that might be institutionally legitimized in order to strengthen one's own religious social group;
4. A radical change of behavior that has to be practiced and experienced first in the basic groups where human beings organize themselves across the traditional borderlines of religions and, in fact, discover antagonistic social structures in every religion.

These four points are an expression of the fact that God is not at our disposal and that we are to keep distance to a certain extent from our ego. This distance liberates and establishes a composure that not only accepts our own relativity but accepts it gratefully. In the Qur'an it is said in a similar way: God created human beings in their differences so that they may learn to love each other in their otherness. Love works on the basis of difference and celebrates unity. But, I could also say, it lives on the basis of unity and celebrates difference.

DIALOGUE AND MISSION

How about the whole problem of mission? Christianity is a missionary religion, but so too are Buddhism, Islam, and others. Are we to discard mission? Are we to give up any search and struggle for truth that imply also arguments and conversion of ourselves and perhaps others? This is a thorny subject, but it is the touchstone for any theology of religions. Are there several truths or only one, and how can this question be decided if we are always talking on the basis of different claims of truth?

Religions with universal claims and respective experiences of life have shaped and influenced other cultures and religions during the last three millennia or so. Each religion of this type has not only the right but maybe the duty to express itself and witness its basic event and experience to other people. The Christian understanding of mission and its respective history has two aspects:

1. Mission is the legitimate expression of the witness of Christian faith in the world as an offer of salvation for all human beings.

2. The history and the notion of mission are aspects of a bloody power struggle and very much connected to the colonial history of Europe and North America. Therefore, the whole concept of mission today is unbearable, because too much historical guilt and aberration is connected with it.

Mission today actually covers and hinders precisely what is to be done in a dialogical way: to give witness to the original experience of the Christian community, a witness of the unconditional love of God expressed in the person of Jesus Christ. Should we not recognize this fact and give up our hidden or open interests of power and identity, which are so connected with the Christian understanding of truth, salvation, and mission?

The universal claim of unconditional love of God in Christ has to be expressed in a totally different language in order to say theologically and in a hermeneutically reflected way precisely what it said to the early Christians—but now under the conditions of interreligious communication. Otherwise we run the risk of a total mix-up of notions and understandings. That is why the concept of the church's "dialogue in mission" or "mission in dialogue" (as expressed also in recent Vatican statements) is not only weak but confused and therefore a source of suspicion for our partners. We have to say clearly that we do not regard our truth claims as superior, although we still feel that we need to be embedded in our truth claims even if they are relative. Any theology of religions has to be very precise at this point.

Even Paul Knitter does not say clearly (thesis 3) whether he wants to give up converting people of other religions—though perhaps not to a classical form of Christianity and perhaps not in the name of a classical theological understanding of salvation, but maybe in the name of a liberated liberation theology. What does he mean by asserting that the truth made known in Jesus is "indispensable," though Hindus, Buddhists, and Muslims do not "necessarily" have to become members of the Christian community? They do not need to join at all, if this truth is really an event in but also beyond form (of language and institution). Again, this is a case of contradicting claims of identity. Religions are not essentially just private judgments of faith but sociopolitical systems. On the other hand, if we do not want to preserve the status quo, we need conversion or *metanoesis*—individually and collectively. What does this mean in dialogue? Who is the subject of this process?

To argue against the position I am trying to suggest here on the basis of Matthew 28:19-20 would not provide a basis for a helpful Christian theology of religions, first, because other ideas in the Greek Bible are also being reinterpreted since they are time-bound (for instance, the expectation of the end of the world during the lifetime of the apostles, Luke 21:32), and second, because the world of the early Christians and also of Matthew was so small and knowledge of the cosmos at that time was limited to the Mediterranean area. They had no idea of cultures beyond those horizons. This is totally different today. That the Christian message is a message for every human being is as true today as it was at that time, but this does not mean to export the forms of thinking and language and other institutions that made up the theology or church of the last two thousand years. They are not universal for the rest of the world—and not even universal for today's theology in Europe and America.

Knowledge is particular, limited and inseparable from a specific tradition in language. Inasmuch as today's field of interpretation is interreligious, so our conditions for the possibility (*Möglichkeitsbedingungen*) of knowing the truth are changing as well. In terms of Christian theology, precisely insofar as in Christianity only Christ himself is experienced as truth, this truth cannot be identified with truth claims that are historically conditioned in space and time. Otherwise conditioned circumstances would be given an unconditional validity, which would be idolatry. There is, however, no interreligious Esperanto, because any Esperanto would have to be explained again in specific languages. Religions are not one, and we cannot create a world religion or even a world ethics, and we should not even strive for it, because this would be a spiritual impoverishment, an abstraction of the concrete myths, histories, experiences of life, and claims of different human beings and cultures.

However, languages can be learned. Religions can be learned, too. How far one can go into another religion depends on many factors, such as one's personal biography and hermeneutical awareness. In any case, it is a process of experiences of learning; it is not easy, for it requires effort and changes the person. Such efforts are being made by those who live with people of other languages or other religions. When such persons return to their own homes, they are no longer the same. Patterns of thinking, values, judgments, and their own religious perception have changed. They see that there are different possibilities and interpretations of life. This is an enrichment insofar as the specifics and the uniqueness of one's own language and religion become conscious. In relation to the other we change ourselves.

This is precisely the history of all religions that have developed in encounter with others. One only has to recall the history of Christianity, which started in Judaism; developed in Hellenistic environments; came under the influence of Platonism, Neo-Platonism, and so forth; changed in the Middle Ages under the influence of Islam; and once again changed as the Renaissance made possible a new contact with Greek Antiquity, which created the Scholastic system. For the last one hundred years Christianity has changed in its contact with other cultures and other religions. The whole process could be described also for Buddhism, Islam, Judaism, and other religions.

NEW EXPLOITATION?

Here a very important objection needs to be raised. Until recently Europe and America exploited other cultures in terms of their material as well as human resources. Is interreligious dialogue a means to exploit non-European and non-American cultures in a spiritual way insofar as their religious traditions are being made "available" to us? This is a tremendous danger indeed and can be avoided only when we, as partners in dialogue, are ready to move so that partners in other religions are not objects of our mission or even subjects of our enrichment, but real partners. The notion of partnership—which we know from psychology—can be applied here: In partnership both partners change inasmuch as both walk a common path. They learn from each other, take from each other, but also give to each other—not only psychologically and materially but also spiritually. Therefore I would like to speak of a "partnership in identity."

LANGUAGE AND SPIRITUAL PRACTICE IN DIALOGUE

Verbal dialogue is important, but it touches only one level of interreligious communication. Spiritual practice that intensifies motivations and forms or changes consciousness leads into deeper aspects of the human being and therefore also of understanding. Christians today practice Zen, Yoga, Sufi paths, and other spiritual techniques. This is certainly a great chance for deepening the Christian experience. My own experience is that God does not speak to us only in books and through the great teachers of our tradition but also through other religions and their teachers. Practicing the spiritual paths of other religions enables one to gain a new look into one's own tradition. What happens at these times of interreligious encounter is precisely that Christian mysticism is newly discovered, and this is certainly one of the best fruits of the encounter over the last few decades. This, however, is not sufficient. It is important to walk together in spiritual experience in order to shape life accordingly, so that the different traditions may draw from the sources of all religions to make life on earth more just, more peaceful, and more sustainable in the future.

PLURALISM, IDENTITY, AND FUNDAMENTALISM

In interreligious encounter pluralism and identity are sometimes experienced as contradictions. Pluralism is the equality of different claims; identity is the search for continuity in the midst of our constructed borderlines, so that identity turns often into the denigration of the other or the stranger. But at the same time all religions are syntheses of originally different traditions.

All modern world religions have their roots in different cultures or several origins. In Christianity, for example, what we know as Catholic, Protestant, or Orthodox Christianity, that is, the confessional plurality, has had many roots and influences. Religions would become sclerotic or rigid if their identity were fixed, if they would not move and integrate new aspects. I see this matter as analogous to the biological process, as a simultaneous distinction and assimilation. A spiritual movement, culture, or religion can assimilate what corresponds with it, what somehow does not throw this movement off from its own center or its own axis. This can, from time to time, imply dramatic changes in basic attitudes in terms of a rediscovery of the original impetus or experience of a given religion. A religious tradition, however, must distinguish what does not correspond with it. And here, dialogue as an expression of love is more than "to respect, value, and listen to the others, to be ready to learn from them" (thesis 2); it is also to argue, to contradict, even to fight. For instance, in the Christian faith basic human inequality, injustice, and human sacrifice (there are certainly modern equivalent forms of the destruction of human beings) must be excluded because they would contradict categorically the experience of the presence of God in all creatures, the *imago Dei*, and the love of the neighbor.

Each tradition forms a unique identity and still can integrate others. This is precisely what happens today in the whole world. Religions are in a fundamental crisis facing secularism and the economized culture into which the world seems to be developing. This is similar in India, Japan, Europe, and America. All religions, therefore, face the question of what their unique and important contribution to humankind is. They are called not just to legitimize or strengthen their religious institutions but to offer selfless service to human beings on the basis of their original impulses.

What is called *fundamentalism* (a very ambiguous and semantically unclear term) today is the denial of a reflection on and relativizing of one's own knowledge in view of other claims, as well as a refusal of this assimilation or integration just spoken about. However, different forms of fundamentalism, which are always politically motivated and supported, have to be distinguished. Yet these forms of denial and refusal of a living change probably have two basic roots.

One root is an individual point: fear. It is the fear of losing something because faith in the reconciling God is not strong enough. Clinging to traditional forms or rigid institutions or certain dogmatic formulations is an attitude of weakness. To speak with Paul: Those whom nothing can separate from the love of God (Rom 8:38ff.) do not need delimitation and demarcation due to a fear of losing identity.

The other root is a social point: The search for power. The ardent desire for safety and security we just have described can be and is being politically exploited. Different parties or groups use the search for identity in order to legitimize their interest in power, that is to say, they organize and proclaim fixed identities.

The notion of identity, however, has to be clearly understood. We live simultaneously in different identities, for example, in regional and national identities. Confessional and wider religious identities always intermingle. A confessional identity that might be important and demarcating within the context of a specific religion loses ground and importance in the horizon of encounter with other religions (this is one of the interesting experiences in interreligious dialogue not only for Christians but also for Buddhists and others). Further, the differentiation into different religions loses in importance in view of the secular atheistic context in the present world (this is one of Nishitani's and Abe's motivations for dialogue).

Identities also change according to the system to which they are related. They are, however, not exchangeable but place the subject in a specific horizon, in a pyramid of identities as it were, since we today find ourselves in a situation of global responsibility in view of the crisis of the one humankind on spaceship earth, or, speaking in the religious idiom, we recognize that we all are children and creatures of one God. Such a statement relativizes traditional religious identities through which different cultures had been held apart.

The emergent understanding and practice of the one humanity have no parallel in the previous history of humankind, even if certain institutions are struggling against these developments because of their interest in power. This is another root of the tendency of delimitation (which often is called fundamentalism without being really fundamental). What we are looking for is the lived and experienced identity that all human beings share on the basis of their humanness, that (theistically speaking) all human beings are creatures of one God. Or, if we want to avoid the notion of God in order to make Buddhists feel comfortable, that we all are responsible to the one inexpressible Mystery of life.

My argument is that in the present partnership of religions on all levels of human expression and formation a common identity emerges that has not yet been there in our respective traditions and therefore has no model we could draw on. Therefore, I would be more cautious than Paul Knitter in reinterpreting classical models (thesis 3). That Jesus reveals truly God's saving presence can be established only if this "truly" implies that this revelation is also sufficient (*satis est*); if so, all other claims have to be interpreted again in the horizon of this sufficiency, and this is basically an inclusivistic model of understanding, which I think is unavoidable and justified if it does not swallow up the space for the otherness of the other.

Paul Knitter, too, cannot avoid an inclusivistic structure. For if Jesus defines (not confines) God as a decisive and normative claim, this is challenged by counter-claims that are to be validated. Any such validation on a normative basis (Christ, in our case) calls for a certain type of inclusivism, particularly if the other tradition is being recognized as "resonating" with what Jesus is and says.

In any case, my point does not mean that respective religious identities would disappear or should disappear—quite the contrary. According to all present experiences Christians, for example, discover in their encounter and partnership with Buddhists, Hindus, Jews, Muslims, tribals, and so forth, their specific identity in a new way—but without the constraint to celebrate one's superiority complex, which always implies aggressive claims of truth and mission.

This is very important, for today we witness movements of delimitation that legitimize themselves again on the basis of nation, race, and religion and lead to terrible excesses of violence (of about fifty contemporary wars more than 50 percent are connected to religious sentiments). Religions here play a very unhealthy role, because they point toward an absolute and unconditionally valued horizon of reality that ideologically is misused for the legitimation of power—a limited, relative, partial identity claims unlimited validity and identity. This is an idolatrous deification of the relative. Christian churches and their dogmatic language games have been and still are guilty in this respect. This is related to the idolatry in mission, a mission that has replaced the unconditional presence of God and God's coming toward human beings (*missio Dei*) with human and institutional self-consciousness.

In God, or the Absolute Reality, the differences of religions are already reconciled. For us it is important to argue mutually what we have recognized as true and to live in a witnessing way what we have faith in as our final support. The first aspect is the critical correction, the second the existential deepening that all religions today require urgently.

Do Knitter's Theses Take Christ's Divinity Seriously?

DENISE AND JOHN CARMODY

THESIS 1

It seems obvious that previous understandings of the uniqueness of Jesus can be reinterpreted—no cause for quarrel. As Knitter notes, the history of christology is replete with new understandings of Jesus, fresh developments of earlier views. The historical nature of human culture, including Christian theology, means that at least a minimal pluralism (a variety of understandings and appreciations) is inevitable. So does the historical and limited nature of all the human knowers, both individuals and groups, from which Christian cultures derive. If pluralism in christology means affirming that there can be no single way of talking about Jesus, nor any way that is final in the sense of answering all questions, then pluralism is a shoo-in, a position as obvious as the manifestly historical character of the whole theological enterprise.

Further, it seems completely legitimate to suggest that over time Christians are bound to generate numerous ways of understanding the uniqueness of Jesus. Conceptions of what makes Jesus *sui generis* are sure to develop and vary, as people study the question in different temporal, geographical, political, and other circumstances.

Finally, the three laws that Knitter offers when sketching a criterion for determining the validity of a new understanding of Jesus are probably as good as any other trio. Creedal belief, worship, and (practical) discipleship are three basic modes in which Christians manifest their grasp of Jesus, what he means to them. Each mode admits of considerable flexibility, when faith is properly relaxed and confident. When dealing with any of the three, a healthy Christian will be slow to accuse other Christians of deviancy, rather assuming good understanding and good will until forced to conclude otherwise.

The overall criterion for healthy Christian faith that we ourselves favor is simpler than what Knitter proposes, vaguer, more existential, and closer to Jesus' own: the fruits that a given disciple generates. People whom love of Christ, allegiance to Christ, make ardent at prayer and

44

resolute at work for social justice are orthodox in the most important sense. This does not mean that their doctrinal language will be impeccable, any more than it means that they could not pray better or do more for the welfare of their neighbors. It does mean that, to the limited degree that human beings can or should or must make judgments about the orthodoxy of others, such Christians seem to be led by the Spirit of Christ and so to be healthy.

THESIS 2

It is fine to say that dialogue is an ethical imperative today, because saying this focuses well a widespread, well-grounded conviction. Unless human beings speak to one another regularly, ongoingly, with both honesty and mutual respect, we are not likely to increase the quanta of justice and peace in our world or decrease the quanta of injustice and conflict. Moreover, the dialogues most crucial today both flow from people's deepest ethical and religious convictions and bear on those convictions. When we talk adequately about how to make the world more just and peaceful, we are bound to deal with what diverse people believe about God, human nature and destiny, human dignity, both the realities and the ideals that ought to govern relations among disparate human beings.

So, if the question of the uniqueness of Jesus bears on (religious) dialogues such as these, and if prior Christian approaches to this question now seem either problematic or insufficiently developed, then the time is ripe for reconsidering, reinterpreting, the uniqueness of Jesus. Indeed, there is some moral imperative to do so. Christian theologians need not feel this moral pressure as something foreign to their craft or calling. From New Testament times, "faith seeking understanding" has entailed responding to the questions and needs of a given era, church, or socioeconomic group.

There is no blackmail, then, in saying that the dialogical signs of today's times require Christian theologians to think again about the uniqueness of Jesus, and those who propose getting on with this task need not resort to moral earnestness. On the whole, dialogue is attractive because of the goods that it holds out, and mature Christians tend to find reflection on Jesus, their beloved, cause for delight. We prefer the reading of thesis 2 that joins these two positive motives simply, downplaying any rhetoric of obligation.

THESIS 3

The uniqueness of Jesus' salvific role *cannot* be adequately reinterpreted in terms of adverbs: *truly* but not *only*. Without considerable nuance and distinction, so simple a reinterpretation does violence to traditional Christian faith—unnecessary violence, we believe.

Jesus truly saves human beings (or, God saves human beings in and through Jesus)—with that we have no quarrel. Other figures can and do mediate God's saving grace in history—with that we also have no quarrel. But whether there is any mediation of the salvation that Christians find in Jesus apart from Jesus is a further question. If one holds, with the traditional Christian creeds, that in Jesus the eternal Word of God took flesh, in such wise Jesus was the incarnation of "God from God, light from light," then one will probably think that no salvation occurs apart from Jesus—outside the single, comprehensive, ontological order centered in the Incarnate Word. Then the soteriological functions of other saviors—figures such as Buddha and Muhammad, who mediate the historical processes of healing and sanctification manifest in their people—occur in an ontological Christian order of salvation. We see no alternative, unless one is going to scrap either traditional Christian faith in the full divinity of Jesus the Christ or traditional Christian monotheism.

Concerning whether the revelation of God in Jesus is full, definitive, or unsurpassable, the answer depends on how one manages the twofoldness of traditional christology. Inasmuch as one stresses or looks to the fully real humanity of Jesus, one can qualify or even deny fullness, definitiveness, or unsurpassableness, pointing to the historical limitations that fully real humanity entails. Inasmuch as one stresses fully real divinity, an incarnation warranting the Orthodox phrase "Christ our God" and worship that is *latria*, one ought to retain a sense that the revelation God gives in Jesus the Christ is full, definitive, and unsurpassable. In our opinion, it eviscerates a proper Christian faith to say that in any historical personage other than Jesus the fullness of the godhead dwelt corporeally. We find that Knitter does justice to the humanity of Jesus but not to his divinity.

It is well to say that the manifestation of God's saving grace in Jesus is universal, decisive, and indispensable. However, it is not sufficient, in our opinion, if one is to keep faith with the doctrine, worship, or social praxis handed down the Christian line. Down that line, Jesus the Christ, true God and truly human, is a scandalous singularity. Christians believe that something unique happened in him—an incarnation qualitatively different from what has happened anywhere else. In our opinion, retaining this belief is essential to an undiluted Christian discipleship.

However, in our opinion this belief also does not limit salvation to Christians, does not mean that other historical figures cannot mediate salvation, does not deny that such historical figures have expressed some truths, some aspects of the one God, better than Jesus and his followers. Buddhists, Muslims, and adherents of any other traditions can be better human beings than Christians, holier, richer in the signs that suggest salvation. Christians can and should sit at the feet of such people in docility and veneration.

Moreover, Christians do not have to ask people flourishing through other faiths to give up their convictions and convert their ways to Christian ones. On the other hand, neither ought Christians to deny that they find Jesus and the Christian way more adequate, overall, than any other paths of salvation, and so imagine conversion to Christianity as gain for the adherent to any other pathway. Finally, Christians should defend the complete right of the adherents to other pathways to practice their faith without hindrance or pressure to convert to Christianity. Indeed, Christians should exercise their imaginations so that they see, along with how Christ might enrich the lives of non-Christians, how the lives of non-Christians fill out, enrich, the limited picture of God and salvation that Christianity provides on its own.

THESIS 4

It is useful to stress the this-worldly character of the salvation that Jesus mediates. At some conceptual point such a this-worldliness may well be uniquely clear in function of uniquely Christian claims about the enfleshment of God's Word, the profoundly historical character of the revelation and passover available in Jesus. For this reason, thesis four has considerable merit.

However, it is dubious that such a stress, alone, does justice to the full Christian message. Nowadays this-worldliness may be the emphasis to place, as Christian spirituality strives to give liberation theologies their due and overcome inadequacies in past proclamations of the gospel. But in some simple yet lovely way, we believe, any adequate proclamation of the gospel is also going to be other-worldly—mystical, intent on honoring the ontological as well as the moral transcendence of God. The same high christology that in Johannine fashion makes time and the flesh of Jesus sacramental also breaks faith out of time, speaks passionately and longingly of eternity and everlasting life. Is Paul Knitter willing to speak this way, as well as merely politically?

Some liberation theologies give the transcendence of God and the strict divinity of Jesus their traditional due, but other liberation theologies do not. When a theology so deconstructs traditional Christian sacramentality that nothing stands over and against language, history, and culture, counterbalancing their claims and opposing their imperialism, it has, in our opinion, lost its soul. Both Christian mysticism and leading voices from the spiritualities of other religious traditions insist that God is God's only ultimate norm or exegesis.

Christians can and should say that God wants mercy rather than sacrifice, countenances no love of divinity set at odds with love of humanity. But an undiluted Christian commitment to the realities symbolized by the paschal mysteries, especially the resurrection, ascension, and movement of the Spirit taking the faithful into eternal life, refuses to understand history or death in ways that let them limit God or imprison the human spirit. The truth of the prophet Amos ought not to take away the truth of the mystic John of the Cross.

THESIS 5

Thesis 5 is attractive for making existential Christian living the criterion to which we ought to bend our christological reflections. Whether Knitter's proposed understanding of Jesus as truly but not solely God's saving Word meets this criterion cannot be determined in the abstract, on conceptual grounds. If a given Christian used such an understanding of Jesus to develop a holy life, signal for both love of God and love of neighbor, that understanding would be vindicated. If given Christians used other criteria to develop such a signal faith, those other criteria would be vindicated. Rejecting the notion that Jesus is solely God's saving Word seems to us to carry a positive potential for removing both Christian claims to superiority and Christian senses of uniqueness that have hampered the development of a holistic Christian spirituality, a full Christian holiness, in the past. Insofar as it in fact brought this benefit, Knitter's understanding would be desirable.

On the other hand, insofar as downplaying the soleness of Jesus' incarnation of God's Word in fact lessened Christians' love of God and neighbor, such a downplaying would be lamentable. Christians who thought that Jesus was only a good man, an upright moral teacher, might well do less at worship and less for the poor than those who thought that Jesus had unique words of eternal life, because he was uniquely God's eternal Son. When one is discussing existential, lived faith, much depends on the actions, the worship and the politics, to which given conceptions lead. Holistic spirituality runs ahead of the doctrines, the understandings, that people think they are enacting. That is the point to the liberationists' insistence on the priority of praxis, as well as to Michael Polanyi's wonderfully rich notion of "tacit" knowledge.

CONCLUSION

The Christian faith that we treasure is delicately balanced. It holds to Jesus as to its unique treasure, but not so as to deprecate any other goodness or wisdom. Its spirit is that of Philippians 4:8f.: "Whatever is true, whatever is honorable, whatever is pleasing, whatever is commendable, if there is any excellence and if there is anything worthy of praise . . . "

Yet, its spirit is also Johannine: All (of these excellent) things were made through him, and without him was made nothing that was made (Jn 1:3).

There are many excellent insights and motives attaching to Paul Knitter's theses about the uniqueness of Christ. Their deficiency, in our opinion, is their (unnecessary) forfeit of the full divinity of Christ, without which Christian salvation becomes only a shell of its traditional self, not the faith of Hebrews' great cloud of witnesses.

Toward Transformation

JOHN B. COBB, JR.

On past occasions, despite my appreciation for Knitter's basic concern to open Christians to the wisdom of other religious traditions, I have felt it necessary to dissociate myself from some of his formulations. I rejoice that with regard to these theses I have no such need. If it were a matter of signing or not signing this statement as a manifesto, I would sign. Hence, the following criticisms are to be read as indications of ways in which I would reformulate the theses in order better to express my own convictions. They are not serious objections. The pluralism Knitter here affirms, unlike the one to which he seemed to subscribe at times in the past, is one I also affirm. To distinguish my position from other, more common, forms of "pluralism," I prefer to call it *transformationism*. But I am grateful for this opportunity to express my solidarity with Knitter in the important project to which he has given himself so selflessly and so long.

Nevertheless, since there are formulations with which I am not quite satisfied, I will continue my long argument with Knitter on the details that still separate us. I will take up the theses in succession.

THESIS 1

I find the first thesis excellent. There is nothing in what is said with which I disagree. However, I am troubled by the impression it leaves, namely, that the kind of reinterpretation now needed is simply a task for the future. It *is* a task for the future. But we do not begin *de novo*. The need of which we are now keenly aware was already sensed a century ago. Ernst Troeltsch and Rudolf Otto paved the way. Nathan Søderblom not only advanced this preparation but also inspired a dialogical mission that continues to the present. More recently William Ernest Hocking, H. Richard Niebuhr, and Donald Baillie can be cited for their quite diverse contributions. In still more recent times many of us have been engaged in this project. Not only *can* christology be reinterpreted, much reinterpretation of the sort required has already occurred. The task is not completed. Indeed, the work of theology is never finished. But we should locate our current efforts in a long tradition rather than depict them as something quite new.

THESIS 2

I am less comfortable with thesis 2. One of the things I most like about Knitter's essay is that for the most part it is written explicitly from a Christian, and therefore Christocentric, perspective. But in the development of this thesis, Knitter adopts Küng's distinction between external and internal reasons for change. When I read these external reasons as a Christian, they seem to me quite fully internal. That is, it is as a Christian that I care deeply about the threats to human well-being. It is as a Christian that I feel the imperative that the great religious communities should cooperate for the well-being of all. I do not find moral obligations coming to Christians from without. Our moral obligations arise out of devotion to Christ.

My second concern is less emphatic. I have previously discussed with Knitter the issue of prerequisites for dialogue. My own judgment is that the only prerequisite is willingness to dialogue. I thought that Knitter did not seriously disagree. But in this section he seems to be saying that one should be a pluralist in order to engage in dialogue. I expect dialogue to lead many Christians into a more pluralist position. I would expect those who enter dialogue as inclusivists, for example, to find that as they listen to what their partners have to say, they will recognize that much of it is not simply a less adequate way of formulating Christian teaching. And I agree with Knitter that entering dialogue with inclusivist assumptions might make it harder to hear what the partner is saying.

But unless the inclusivists in question are unwilling to consider any idea that does not fit their scheme, I would certainly not discourage them from entering the dialogue in which they express willingness to participate! The problem would then not be the particular beliefs brought to dialogue but unwillingness to listen to the partner. Such unwillingness is the problem, not the particular starting point. But that unwillingness is in fact unwillingness to engage in dialogue at all. If one begins as an inclusivist, or even as an exclusivist, and then engages in genuine dialogue, one will learn. If one is able so to develop the inclusivist or exclusivist position so that it expresses real learning from the dialogue partner, this can be a distinctive and valuable contribution to the needed transformation of Christianity. The resultant forms of inclusivism and exclusivism will not be the same as those with which we are now familiar, for these arose apart from actual involvement in dialogue.

THESIS 3

The third thesis may be the most important. Its distinction between thinking of God's revelation in Jesus as "full, definitive, or unsurpassable" and as "universal, decisive, and indispensable" is a major contribution. We do not all hear exactly the same meanings in these terms, but Knitter's exposition makes the rejection of the first set and the affirmation of the second acceptable to me. I am in his debt.

Nevertheless, there is a subtle implication of many of the formulations that still troubles me. It sounds as though other traditions are to be affirmed only insofar as they also reveal God or mediate saving grace in history. In other words, what we are open to in other traditions seems to be defined in Christian terms. I doubt that this is truly what Knitter wants to say. But because so many pluralists do talk this way, one who wants to say something different must do so carefully and emphatically. It has been my constant protest against most pluralists that they are insufficiently pluralist, that they define the terms of the dialogue without taking into account what the dialogue partners want to say.

If I thought that this was really what Knitter is saying in this essay, I would not lend it my support. But I am confident that he wants to let the dialogue partners define what they have to contribute. He knows that Buddhists want to show us the way to enlightenment, not to point to a revelation of God or show how saving grace is mediated in history.

If we are looking for a formulation of what all the great religious communities or traditional Ways are offering, we must work hard to find more neutral language. For example, perhaps they all want to offer an account of what is most profoundly wrong with the human condition and to point out the way in which this can be alleviated or overcome. Even this may turn out to be an unsuitable formulation for some of these traditions. And certainly it is not useful when we approach the primal traditions, from which we also have much to learn. But it is better than supposing that they all want to offer revelations of God or mediate saving grace to history.

When we listen carefully to what each offers to all the others, it may turn out that mediating saving grace to history is, after all, a distinctively Christian contribution. If so, we should not hesitate to say so. If, on the other hand, Jews say that they also offer such mediation, then this alternative way of mediating saving grace is to be acknowledged. What is shared by whom and what is unique are to be learned through dialogue. Dialogue may bring out the uniqueness of Jesus Christ more radically than Knitter seems to think.

Nevertheless, for Christians to recognize that there *may* be other revelations, or that what other communities describe in quite different ways may be appropriated as revelations by Christians, is an excellent point.

It is because I understand this as Knitter's concern that I continue to support the statement as a whole. As long as Christian categories are not allowed to filter what we can learn from others, they can be useful as a starting point for opening ourselves. The problem is that they may function not only as a starting point but also as a limit.

THESIS 4

In thesis 4 Knitter recognizes that the content of Jesus' uniqueness as understood and proclaimed changes from time to time. Commendably, Knitter introduces a pluralism into Christianity itself. But this pluralism disappears in his formulation of the content of this uniqueness for today. I find myself sympathetic with what he affirms for today, but I am troubled by its exclusivism. There is always the danger that in the process of recognizing the wisdom and value in other great Ways, we may deny the wisdom and value in other forms of our own Way. We need continuing dialogue among Christians as well as dialogue with representatives of other religious traditions.

Knitter's formulation of Jesus' uniqueness focuses on his message. There are other understandings of that message which have scholarly support. There are also those who understand the uniqueness of Jesus Christ through the kerygma or through the later development of tradition. We have much to learn from one another. I would argue on Knitter's side, in such intra-Christian dialogue, in support of an emphasis on Jesus' own message, but I am troubled by his effort to define the content of Jesus' uniqueness for all Christians today in terms of just one living Christian tradition.

A second problem with Knitter's account of Jesus' uniqueness is that it appears to deny that other Jewish teachers taught and teach "that salvation . . . must be realized *in this world* through *human actions* of love and justice." Before announcing that this is unique to Jesus, we need to ask our Jewish dialogue partners whether they agree. We would also have to consult our Muslim dialogue partners. Knitter writes of "Islam's conviction that what is true in the spiritual-interior realm must be translated into the social-political arena." Is this so different?

THESIS 5

As I read the fifth thesis I find little of this effort to define the truth for others. It is a beautiful confessional statement showing how deeply a pluralist can be devoted to Jesus Christ, how, indeed, the pluralism flows from that devotion. With this statement I have no quarrel at all.

Indeed, my deepest concern is that we Christians find in our faith in Christ the reason for opening ourselves to others. These others include both other Christians and also those who are not Christian. Among the latter we have become especially aware that we have much to learn from those who can share with us the living wisdom of other great ancient Ways.

Against those who teach that faith in Christ should restrict our openness to our neighbors, I am prepared to argue passionately. The "Christ" who closes us to the neighbor is, in my view, an idol. I would also say that the "Christ" who closes us to criticism of our beliefs and practices, including our christological beliefs, is also an idol. To serve Christ is to be ever open to such criticism. Of course, one is responsible to decide, in light of Christ, what is valid and what is invalid in that criticism.

If any theory of how Christianity relates to other religious traditions closes us either to the neighbor or to criticism of our cherished views, then, in my view, it is faithless to Christ. This can happen to pluralists as well as to exclusivists and inclusivists. For example, if pluralists hold fast to the view that Jesus is one savior among others or one revealer among others, that may blind them to what the dialogue partner has to say and to valid criticism of their own theories just as fully as insistence that Jesus is the only Way may blind exclusivists. This need not happen to any of them. If it does not happen, then openness to the neighbor and to criticism will bring about change, repeatedly. Change that comes about in this way I call transformation. For me, faith in Christ and openness to the transformation of my thinking and my life are inseparable. That is why I call myself a transformationist. Knitter's formulation of pluralism in these theses moves so far in this direction that I feel no need to distance myself from him.

It is another question whether commitment and devotion formed in other great Ways provide similar reasons for openness to the neighbor and to criticism. This question is not for Christians to answer one way or another in advance of dialogue. If others are willing to dialogue, one of the questions we can ask them is why they are willing. Perhaps we will learn from them reasons for dialogue that can enrich and transform our own. Perhaps not. We cannot know, and we do not need to know, in advance of dialogue. Dialogue does not presuppose common motives on the part of the dialogue partners. But whatever the purpose of the partner, one purpose of the Christian will be to witness to Jesus Christ in hopes that through that witness the partner also may be transformed.

Jesus and Pentecostals

HARVEY COX

One of the strengths of Paul Knitter's recent thought on christology is his attempt to hold together both the challenge of religious pluralism and the characteristically Christian perception of God's preferential option for the poor and the outcast as it is clearly highlighted in the gospel accounts and has been recovered more recently by the various liberation theologies. I commend him for holding these two dimensions in dynamic tension, but I believe there are three additional dimensions of contemporary Christian spirituality that need to be woven together as well. These are:

1. The growing recognition, garnered from documentary, archeological and other sources, that the christologies found in our present New Testament canon represent only a few of the many strands to be discovered in what was in fact the richly complex tapestry of multifarious christologies that thrived in the first centuries of Christian history. Dominic Crossan makes especially excellent use of these materials in his recent work.

2. The expanding renaissance of the feminine component in the churches and the new hermeneutical vantage point that this awareness brings to bear on all questions of theology including christology. Elisabeth Schüssler Fiorenza shows how much difference this illuminating perspective brings to our grasp of the significance of Jesus.

3. The astonishing expansion of Pentecostalism, charismatic movements, and other forms of Christian spirituality that bring the importance of the Holy Spirit, and consequently of pneumatology, very forcibly back into the theological conversation. There are, I believe, critical theological implications in the fact that these movements are the fastest growing ones in the Christian world, especially among poor and dispossessed peoples.

In my own view, too much of the current discussion about the uniqueness of Jesus isolates the religious pluralism issue—as important as it is—as though it can be usefully considered apart from these other vectors that cut through it from various angles.

I want to comment briefly on the first two of these three additional dimensions, asking what they say to the question posed by Knitter's theses on the uniqueness of Jesus. I will devote a little more space to the third issue, that of the uniqueness of Jesus in relation to current pneumatological movements and theologies, which are the principal subject of my own current research and writing.

SOURCE MATERIALS

The discovery of buried scrolls near the Dead Sea and later at Nag Hammadi, the enormous refinement of archeological methods, and the application of the social scientific analysis of peasant societies to first-century Palestine have combined to produce a curious reversal of fortune. Although we are—by definition—the farthest generation away from Jesus temporally, we have more data about him than any previous generation since the first century. Admittedly the data has not all been sorted and evaluated, and I have little doubt that new material will appear. Still, we can no longer say with Albert Schweitzer, "He comes to us as one unknown." Today he comes to us as one about whom a lot more is known than even Schweitzer could have imagined, and all the evidence suggests that Jesus was even more a participant in the political, economic, and social—as well as the religious—history and culture of his time than anyone had known.

What we are learning is that there is an irreducible sure, hard core of historical facticity about Jesus that no responsible scholar can afford to overlook. This is true despite some modifications in certain recent, sometimes ahistorical, claims about a "cosmic Christ." I do not mean that the historical Jesus and the cosmic Christ cannot be reconciled. I mean that the tough particularity of the Palestinian peasant, rebel rabbi, and freewheeling healer who emerges from the shadows as the new quest for the historical Jesus continues is not, in my mind, as easily assimilable to other religious sensibilities as Schweitzer's "unknown One" appeared to be.

I think the introduction of this perspective into Knitter's discussion will cut in different directions. How can we discuss the "uniqueness" of Jesus without wrenching him out of a culture that was in part unique but which shared structural elements with other cultures? How much does the clearly political dimension of Jesus' mission in Roman-occupied Palestine suggest a commonality that is not narrowly religious? What does the obvious centrality of healing in his mission say about his uniqueness and/or commonality with modes of religious healing and spiritual healers in other faiths?

THE FEMINIST COMPONENT

Feminist hermeneutics brings a much needed corrective to uncritical male interpretations of the gospel texts, especially when those texts are read, as Elaine Pagels reads them, in the light of the extra-canonical treatments of Jesus in the Nag Hammadi texts and others. What we find is that even our earliest sources about who Jesus was come to us picked over and edited from a patriarchal point of view. Allusions to Jesus' sexuality and especially his relationship to Mary Magdalene seem to have been bowdlerized in the canonical texts. The feminine qualities of the God Jesus reveals appear to have been purged or muted.

The mind boggles at the interfaith implications of recovering a flesh-and-blood Jesus who might not have been the sexual ascetic we have been led to believe. The further question then arises of how our expurgated picture of Jesus has skewed our understanding of the God he reveals and whose love he brings into the world. Think of what all this might mean for relations with Vaishnavite Hinduism or Tantric Buddhism, where the erotic and the spiritual components of human life are held much more closely together. Jesus was obviously no Krishna sporting in the forest with a bevy of cow maidens. But we must ask what energies in the God Jesus reveals, and in ourselves, have been distorted by the biases of the process of canonization and textual transmissions, and what implications this has for the uniqueness of Jesus.

PENTECOSTAL CHRISTIANITY

For the past three years I have been studying Pentecostal Christianity, the fastest growing religious movement in the world. From its relatively obscure beginnings around 1900, it grew to 75 million adherents in 1970, and now encompasses an estimated 400 million people, one of every four Christians on the planet. Pentecostals are multiplying in virtually all countries, largely but not exclusively among poor and marginated people. The largest (Pentecostal) Full Gospel Church in the world is in Seoul, Korea. It has 800,000 members. But other congregations in Korea and Latin America are nearly as large. Two million people regularly turn out for the Easter service of the Zion Apostolic Church in South Africa. Yet the movement's growth seems to occur more often in small face-to-face congregations, often meeting in storefronts or living rooms. In the United States thousands of Latino immigrants leave the Catholic church every year to join Pentecostal congregations, most of them small ones. As I have worked on my book *Fire From Heaven* I have constantly asked myself why this astonishing growth is happening and what it means for our understanding of the uniqueness of Christianity and of the challenges of interfaith dialogue.

I believe Pentecostalism is growing so rapidly because it speaks to the spiritual emptiness of our time by reaching below the levels of creed and ceremony into the core of human religiousness, into what might be called "primal spirituality," that largely unprocessed nucleus of the human psyche in which the unending struggle for a sense of meaning and a feeling of belonging goes on. The early Pentecostals believed they were restoring the original faith of the first apostles. Scholars have sometimes glibly dismissed them as one more "restorationist" movement. My own conviction is that Pentecostals have touched so many people because they have indeed restored something. They have helped countless people to recover, on a very personal level, a direct experience of God, through the Holy Spirit. Although Pentecostals do not talk much about the *filioque* clause, they are engaged in a functional removal of that longstanding obstacle to Christian unity and interreligious fellowship.

I also believe that this massive eruption of primal spirituality, which I see as the presence of the Spirit of God in all peoples, is altering our understanding of Christianity's relationship to the wellsprings of other religious traditions. It is doing so, however, not at the conceptual but at the experiential level, by tapping into three dimensions of primal spirituality which I call "primal speech," "primal piety," and "primal hope."

The *first*, primal speech, pinpoints the spiritual import of what scholars of religion sometimes call "ecstatic utterance," what the earliest Pentecostals called "speaking in tongues," and what many now refer to as "praying in the Spirit." In an age of bombast, hype, and doublespeak, when ultra-specialized terminologies and contrived rhetoric seem to have emptied and pulverized language, the first Pentecostals learned to speak— and their successors still speak—with another voice, a language of the heart. They believe this capacity to transcend the hegemonic language system and to live in a multicultural community are gifts of the Holy Spirit. This is an operative theology in which Jesus plays an important role but not as exclusive as in the more christocentric theologies of the established churches.

A *second*, primal piety, touches on the resurgence in Pentecostalism of trance, vision, healing, dreams, dance, and other archetypal religious expressions. These primeval modes of praise and supplication comprise what the great French sociologist Emile Durkheim once called the "elementary forms" of religious life, by which he meant the foundational elements of human religiosity. The reemergence of this primal spirituality came—perhaps not surprisingly—at just the point in history when both the rationalistic assumptions of modernity and the strategies religions had used to oppose them (or to accommodate to them) were all coming unravelled.

Again, this is a Christian but not a christocentric theology. It is actually more authentically trinitarian. Through the Holy Spirit Christians experience these elements of primal spirituality that they share with many other religious traditions.

The *third*, primal hope, points to Pentecostalism's apocalyptic outlook—its insistence that a radically new world age is about to dawn. This is the kind of hope which transcends any particular content. It is what the German philosopher Ernst Bloch once called "Prinzip Hoffnung," the kernel of all utopianism, the principled refusal to believe that what we see is all there is or could be. It is also viewed as a gift of the Holy Spirit and is believed to be what the epistle to the Hebrews calls the "evidence of things not seen."

It is important to note that Hebrews is also the text that refers to Jesus as "the pioneer of our faith," a title that, to my regret, was not developed in subsequent christologies. Here Jesus becomes one who has gone before, to open the future. Thus the hope that is engendered does not fail because it is more an orientation to the future than a detailed scheme. It persists despite the failure of particular hopes to materialize. I believe this underdeveloped christology could be of enormous help in a world of many religions in which so many people desperately need a basis for hope.

For many thoughtful people, all three of these qualities of the Pentecostal phenomenon—glossolalia, dreams and trances, and apocalypticism—appear at best merely bizarre and at worst downright scary. But if we think of the three in the broader perspective of religious history, as the recovery of primal speech (ecstatic utterance), primal piety (mystical experience, trance and embodiment), and primal hope (the unshakable expectation of a better future), then their contemporary recovery becomes a little less baffling. Long before primal scream therapy, dream journals, liturgical dance, psycho-drama, and futurology made their appearances at elite conference centers and expensive weekend workshops, the early Pentecostals were spreading their own versions of all of them.

I believe the unanticipated reappearance of primal spirituality in our time, with its massive implications for what Roger Haight calls a "Spirit christology," has enormous significance for interfaith dialogue. It suggests an experiential rather than a doctrinal basis for our relations to people in other faith traditions (and I know this cuts against the grain of the currently fashionable cultural "linguistic" current of academic theology).

The lightning growth of Pentecostal and charismatic movements today transcends all merely social or psychological explanations. For Christians it must be seen as a work of the Holy Spirit which, among other things, will force us to redefine our regnant christologies. It also tells us a lot about who we human beings are as we approach the twenty-first century. In an age that has found exclusively secular explanations of life wanting, but is also wary of religious dogmas and ecclesial institutions, the unforeseen eruption of this spiritual lava reminds us that somewhere deep within us we all carry the image of the *Creator Spiritus*. Pentecostalism is not an aberration. It is a part of the larger and longer history of human religiousness. To try to understand the significance of the uniqueness of Jesus without giving it serious consideration is to miss what the Holy Spirit may be saying to the churches through what may seem a very unlikely instrument.

Beguiled by a Word?

KENNETH CRAGG

I

"In Ireland," wrote Dean Jonathan Swift, "no man visits where he cannot drink." That reads like a good instinct too for our interreligious hospitality. We can assume that there is always much to savor. Yet the vexing problems remain that have to do with the authority to believe; the what and why of conviction, symbol, and worship; and the competing warrants they present for inner assurance or for outward credential. These are well broached in Paul Knitter's Five Theses, though some may feel the Aquinas-style tabulation and process of case-making is in need of the poetic and the imaginative—those vital elements in religious meaning. Perhaps one can be over-analytic where mystery belongs. This is not, however, a plea for obfuscation.

However, my main contention in grateful response is one that has often come inevitably to mind in a long encounter with the three theisms in their contemporary stage. It is that *unique* is not the right, or the useful, term either to claim or to make central. *Unique*, anyway, is not a biblical word, nor is *only*, except in reference to the unity of God (e.g., Jn 17:3, Jude 25, etc.) or in incidental reference to "only son" or "only daughter" of suppliants in the gospels for Jesus' help. Otherwise "only" is used adverbially. The phrase which becomes creedal—and crucial to the whole issue—comes in John 1:14, 18; 3:16, 18; in Hebrews 11:17; 1 John 4:9. It is vital to read *monogenes* aright, for "one" and "only" are the profoundest of metaphors.

We are not in the realm of arithmetic, as when we note, for example, that John Ruskin (to his great privation) was "an only child." We are not in a series that was meant to go on but was arrested before it reached two. The "conceiving of the Holy Spirit" is not of that order. What we believe we have of "God in Christ" is not like "one of the works of Shakespeare." *Exclusive* and *inclusive* here are irrelevant language for the unity of the "originality" which is at once the well and the water, the mind and the meaning.

Unique is thus seen to be an inhibiting word to carry the appropriate sense of *only* in Christian discourse. *Only* there means "wholly," "entirely," "completely," consistent with the sphere, that is, the human, in which the divine is understood to be self-expressed. It is the antonym of *partially*, or *proximately*. It has to do with a *pleroma*, a wholeness, in the confidence that if God is revealing, then God is revealed. The "one" is predicate, as if we say "Beethoven is one—the man and the music." We do not denote either without the other. *Begotten* creedally is very much in this idiom and in no sense serial. Jesus is not "one with the Father" in the way in which the earth is one in the solar system. He is so in the sense of the third, and crucial, clause in John 1.1: "and God [*theos* not *ho theos*] was the Word." This is perhaps analogous to how one might exclaim after being at the theater: "And Shakespeare was the play." "Only begotten" is about the unity of God.

It is this necessary alignment of theology and christology—the one within the other because they co-inhere—that makes *unique* a prevaricating word to employ. For it suggests what cannot co-inhere but has to be isolated, immunized as an entity which can only obtain as self-explained and in necessary disjuncture from all else. No faith in the incarnate Word can intelligently, or intelligibly, be of that order. To be sure, we are still left with the question that, doubtless, beguiles us into using the word *unique*; namely, whether divine revelation in the human is not somehow multiple, here, there and anywhere, as something diverse and haphazard and inconsistently plural. But, given the unity of God, the question cannot arise. God's self-revelation will not pluralize that self. Faith in it, however, will be distinctive among other perceptions of the capacities of the Divine that may not share it. When the authors in *The Myth of Christian Uniqueness*[1] gave their contributions that title there was perhaps a larger irony than they knew.

II

So *distinctive* has to be the wiser word. What Christianity believes to be *definitive* concerning God will certainly discriminate between faiths, and it will decide believers. But it will not isolate these as if they held no intellectual or spiritual society with others or with the questions and answers of humans everywhere, whether in confidence or conjecture, perplexity or propagation. Mutualities, overlaps, concords within que-

---

[1] John Hick and Paul Knitter, eds., *The Myth of Christian Uniqueness* (Maryknoll, N.Y.: Orbis Books, 1987). *The Relevance of Christian Distinctiveness* would have been, in every way, a more incisive, effectual, not to say modest, entitlement for the useful issues the book explored, vitiated as they were by the disservice done to them by the book's title.

ries, are inseparable from all discourse around the human, all common mortality, and every shared wistfulness. None is ever unique in the context where its clues belong.

Seeing further why this must be so, there is first a caveat about *definitive* used above. We must always reserve infinitude from ever being in "the grasp of our reach," but unless we are playing games or indulging in futility, what will always transcend about transcendence will not cancel or decry what faith properly holds. Knowledge will be knowledge even though truly of that which passes knowledge. Assurance must always be reverent—which it can never be if it is also irrelevant. Faith is more than fideism and sometimes less pretentious than dogma. But it "holds and is held."

That caveat noted, we can go on to note how all that is distinctively Christian stands within a doctrine of creation which is not uniquely Christian. There are views of the world, Greek, Hindu, nihilist, or other, which posit a basic malevolence at the heart of things. For these, there is no "oneness" of God in the sense of a "sovereignty of good." The gods themselves are at odds, malign, chaotic, devious or deviant, mirroring human enmities or sporting with a pointless world. These notions Judaic, Christian, Islamic, and perhaps other theism roundly repudiates. They are thereby distinguished from views that doubt or deny their confidence. Having it in common, none of the three is unique. Though within this commonality distinctivenesses emerge, this single denominator remains vital, unitary, and precious. Moreover, its implications will continue to inform, and to that extent unify, the significant *differentia* that belong with it. There is an enormous togetherness in believing in divine purposiveness of good, in creaturehood under it, in the good earth and the sacramental clue to all things physical, in a trust in the God who entrusts humans. Where christology diverges from the Judaic and the Islamic understandings it still belongs within a universe of theism to which its need to diverge persistently relates and, so relating, it continues to belong with them. This means that we do not need to make Jesus somehow carry all that other faiths might want to ascribe to him, as if christology could accommodate whatever they or we might wish to have it mean. Christian christology has its own distinctive parameters, in history and ethics and the anthropic, which other faiths query or dispute. But the "distinctive," unlike the "unique," does not totally exclude or need contrivance to include, since it relates multilaterally.

III

Given the common divine context of creation, the common human dignity of creaturehood, fully cognized between us and shared, it follows intrinsically that there will be divine action vis-à-vis the human scene, some sense of divine sending, "enscripturing," enjoining, guiding, and other dimensions of a transcendent initiative that wills in its own terms to relate to the human realm as the crux of what intention in creation expresses. Do not Judaic concepts of divine "agency," in "word," "wisdom," "deputy-ship," underlie if not educate the first Christian christology?[2] A God out of relation, in perpetual privacy, in sublime indifference, would be altogether devoid of what "being God" means— though despair and doubt on the point have often burdened the deepest biblical theism—witness Job and the psalmist, and Jeremiah. Even so, such agonies were the surest clue that meaninglessness only demonstrates the meaning of what it threatens.

If the being of God must mean relationship reciprocal to the "being" in our being human, that common creation-theism may well diverge in the terms in which the reciprocal is understood, the reach it might have, the lengths to which it might go. For example, will it have an ethnic predilection? preparatorily? or forever? So the Judaic. Will it be content with guidance, law, direction, ordinances and final judgment? So the Islamic. Or might it incorporate dimensions of suffering, vulnerability, the tragic as the key to the redemptive?

Such issues finally turn on two counts; namely, what is most opposite to the human scene, and what is most properly worth, or—may we say— "expectable" of God. Answers have defined themselves variously in the several theisms and have fortified themselves in scriptures, prophets, covenants, and creeds, which, in part, "exclusify" themselves. That is our problem. Yet they also "inclusify" themselves within the common concern of God with humanity and of humanity with God. They are distinctive within a unity. What is at issue between them can surely be explored by gentle appeal to mind and spirit so that they no longer confront or diverge on the *ipse dixit* of sheer authority or assertion, but acknowledge a common liability for and to each other.

Those two criteria of God's worthiness and adequacy to the human predicament may be resolved in exclusive certitudes religiously institutionalized, but they are also plainly susceptible of enquiry out of inclusive experience. In an intriguing passage the Qur'an speaks of a necessary reproach against God had there been no prophethood sent. Christianity sees the dimensions of what is necessarily expectable of

---

[2] Though it is often alleged that the Christian sense of "the Son of the Father" or of "God descending to earth" derives from Greek or gnostic sources, corrupting a Hebraic original that knows nothing of them, it is truer to see christology within Hebraic themes of divine agency, of divine will and word in their interaction. A christology of action is entirely consistent with Hebraic paradigms in "word," "wisdom," and "*fiat*," and only needs a christology of "substance" to interpret itself in a Greek world and to ensure that divine willing is not seen as some demi-god but as inherent in the nature of the God who is One.

God in the Christ-event and the cross. Therein it is distinctive, but only with a tremendous relevance to all that in Judaism and Islam that sense of things does, and must, incorporate.

It aligns with a deeper diagnosis of humanity as not susceptible of rightness by dint of command, prohibition, exhortation and direction alone. For these take no account of a propensity in us to sin against the light. That perception of a perversity in selfhood per se brings Christian faith into a deep affinity with the Buddhist mind. The Buddha was not unique in perceiving that there is a snare in "desire" and therefore a crisis inherent in selfhood. The gospel is not unique in warning that there is that about ourselves which requires to be negated ("mortified" was Paul's word, see Romans 8:13 and Colossians 3:5). There is vital distinction, however, in that this Christian "negation" is not of a selfhood inherently illusory and incapable of unselfishness, but of an authentic selfhood—such as Buddhism denies—that has to be redeemed by grace *from* the toils of selfishness and *for* its true fulfilling. The Buddhist and the Christian share a common realism about our being as critical, but do so in sharp contrast about the answer it deserves. The self and "desire" are the crux for both, but only on incompatible reading of time, flux, and the egocentric situation we all alike experience.

It was, and is, precisely this realism which requires of Christianity a corresponding measure of what it must entail for faith in God; namely, a place for what old-fashioned theology called *theodicy*. If God is indeed "a faithful Creator" (1 Pt 4:19), there is more at stake about humanity than law and requital. Does it not seem like a test case for omnipotence, or even a challenge to the very feasibility of omnipotence? For "the sovereignty of love" seems at stake in our evident recalcitrance. We can, no doubt, ignore the issue, but only at the expense of the reality of sin as we know it and of the credibility of any divine reign. There would seem to be need for an answer worthy to be identified as divine and big enough for our human situation, lest God should be seen in default, as it were, of what being God must mean. If we may not say here "must mean" is not theism vacuous?

This necessity, put in biblical terms, is "messianic." Because they believe "God in Christ" and, therefore, "the Christ in God," Christians are distinctive in the predicates they then have about God. They are not unique, however, in respect to the situations which lead them to what those predicates confess. The situations remain relevant to all, though others may be oblivious or merely sanguine about their import. For some divine relatedness to us is implicit in all theism. Ours entails the love that cares and participates, an Emmanuel nail-printed. Transcendence is not finally betokened in advice, counsel, guidance, words, the exodus of one people, these alone, but further in grace, divine self-giving, the Word-made-flesh, in bread and wine, and the cross of a risen Christ. These "distinctives," however, converse hopefully with all the clues by which the faiths in their diversity aspire to interpret and encounter one singular mortality, one bonding experience as human.

There are aspects of Indian piety that share a vision of divine/human relationship as an exchange of love, of infinite compassion in the one and utter devotion in the other. Here two questions persist; that is, whether such inter-love between the personal Lord and the ardent soul is compatible with the Brahma Oneness that must evermore preclude it, and whether it matters if the condescension of the divine is purely fictitious, imaginary, mythical. On the one count the reader may refer, for example, to the strenuous effort of Raimundo Panikkar to reconcile *Brahma* and *Bhakti*. On the other count the question must be whether history matters. Is there a truth of fiction—about Krishna or whomever—which does not require that things really happened? Can history ever actually contain the eternal or the historian confine the theologian?

Christian faith has long been at odds with itself about the degree to which historicity is verifiable, discernible, or negotiable about Jesus and the Christ-event. There are those who see the kerygma, the affirmation per se, sufficing as challenge to an existential commitment in which alone the authentic can reside and to which it may adhere in neglect of what may have "happened" in "the days of his flesh." But if the story is "out of this world," can it avail it? There may well be a sense in which we Christians are "deceivers and yet true" (as, in measure, all believers must be). Yet that paradox can have two forms, the one in complacence, the other in integrity. The historical can never of itself guarantee the things of faith since, in truth, the things of faith are not susceptible of guarantee and would cease to be themselves if they were. Nevertheless, faith stands in and by evidentiality, and this, in part, means where and when and how. In this requirement the gospel will always be distinctive. "Crucified under Pontius Pilate" will be where it finds its warrant. But just as metaphor is constituted by tenor and vehicle, so the hinges of the Christ-event in birth, life, death, and risen-ness must be known, not as arbitrarily constituted in the sheer miraculous, where acknowledgment could only be credulous, but by conveying, as metaphor must always do, the tenor of one realm in the idiom of another. When Timon's servants in Shakespeare's *Timon of Athens* say "Leaked is our bark," we know what they mean. Hope-wreck is like shipwreck—they have been a loyal crew and are come to disaster. We need the literal but only, reading past it, for the sake of the significant. Is it not likewise in the gospel, with "conceived by the Holy Spirit," and "ascended into heaven?" There is divine conception, authorship, origin, behind all that happened. Everything so transacted belongs with the glory that is God's and is clued into divine sovereignty as its sure credential.

Is it not true that "history" belongs with "meaning" in the Christian gospel? As image goes into word, word into metaphor, metaphor into story, and story into history, so "God was in Christ reconciling the world."

The Christian metaphor of divine fulfillment and expression of divine Being is distinctive but its reliance on time, story, imagination and perception engages it with everything human.

These thoughts are far from exhausting the issues the Five Theses raise. To have questioned the point of departure means we have no need to "reinterpret," but only better to understand what always was. Greater devotion need not be in doubt since it need never have been lost or suspect. There remains one final point. It is that the Christian belief in a concrete, veritable, paradigmatic "manifest" in history of divine *kenosis* as the secret of divine glory is eminently imitable. Found in those terms nowhere else, it can generate and empower, outside its doctrinal house of faith and symbol, an emulation in action of how it sees and reads our humanity as a vocation into love. Insofar as it does so, its distinctiveness is anywhere reproduced. It differs only to belong.

An Asian's View of Jesus' Uniqueness

ANTHONY FERNANDO

I find Paul Knitter's Five Theses thought-provoking, and I value the educational aim with which they have been written. I am sure they will provoke a very healthy discussion among theologians and thinking Christians. However, since Knitter has apparently written them with a primarily Western Christian audience in mind, and because I am an Asian, I am confused about where I stand in my attitude or ideas on the uniqueness of Jesus. Said briefly, I am uncertain whether I am an "inclusivist," "exclusivist," or "pluralist," and I wonder whether the categories themselves are adequate.

I leave to the reader to discern into which camp I should be put, but let me as my initial response to Knitter's Five Theses show first how I profess my faith in this basic tenet of Christianity and, thereafter, show how scholars of world religions explain the notion of uniqueness. An explanation of that term can not be ignored, if the integrity of the Christian belief is to be safeguarded, and misconceptions and misuses of it are to be avoided. Nevertheless, since my attitude and language may sound strange to Western theological ears, let me begin by giving a word of introduction to myself.

I am, by birth and nationality, Sri Lankan. The majority of the people in my country are Buddhist, but I was born into a Christian family. I belong to the Roman Catholic tradition. By commitment, I consider myself a Christian missionary. But my missionary work is purely a matter of goodwill and conviction. I am not officially delegated for that work by any religious organization. I just want to see our people understand, value, and use for their betterment the sublime life-ideals that Jesus preached.

Academically, my main field of interest is the science of religion. But since this science has a number of forms, and I am concerned only with the spiritual or the life-transformational dimension of religion, I tend to consider myself more a religionist than a scientist or theologian. For me, the general scientific approach to religion looks secular, and the present theological approach far too confined to one religion. Because of my interest in religions, I have studied and taught Hinduism and Islam for a number of years.

By profession I am a teacher of Christianity. I head a university department that conducts a course on Christianity. But that course is very different from those conducted in theological faculties. Here Christianity is taught as one of the world's religions. Among the graduates and postgraduates following the course a number are not Christians. One permanent member of the staff is a Buddhist monk.

JESUS, THE WAY

In spite of my academic interest in all the religions, I have never for a moment felt inclined to give up my affiliation to Christianity, the religion I inherited from my parents. And because I consider myself Christian not only by birth but also by conviction, Jesus is for me unique. He has been a source of untold healing for me. His life and teachings have given me great strength and the courage to cope with my problems in life and to live that life in an increasingly liberated way. I therefore subscribe wholeheartedly and without reservation to what Jesus, according to St. John's gospel is supposed to have said of himself: "I am the way, the truth and the life. No one can come to the Father except through me" (Jn 14:6). But, of course, I take that verse in the context of the whole sermon of Jesus—that lengthy Last Supper sermon—of which it is only a part. In that sermon, he also said:

> A new commandment I give you: Love one another. . . . By this all men will know that you are my disciples. . . . If you obey my commands, you will remain in my love, just as I have obeyed my Father's commands and remain in his love. I have told you this so that my joy may be in you, and your joy may be complete. My command is this: Love each other as I have loved you. Greater love has no man than this that he lay down his life for his friends (Jn 13: 34-35; 15:10-13).

When we take both these assertions together, we see better what Jesus meant when he introduced himself as "the Way." By his example and his teaching, Jesus was an authentic expression of the only Way by which a human being can be human to the fullest degree ordained by nature. The main element of that Way is love to the extent of self-sacrifice.

That Way of selfless love is the eternal Way for human beings to achieve in its fullness the divine "joy" of being human. That is the Way after the birth of Christ. That had been the Way for innumerable centuries before the birth of Christ. That is the way for people who are born into a Christian family and for people who are not born into a Christian family. Christians know of that unique Way only because of their contact with Jesus. He is for them the best life-symbol of that unique universal way. And so by them Jesus has necessarily to be taken as unique. Thus when I profess that Jesus is unique, it is in the sense of the "supreme Way" that I take the word *Jesus*.

RELIGION: TWO MEANINGS, TWO FORMS

But that is not the only sense in which the word *Jesus* can be taken or that it has been taken. *Jesus* can be a cover for quite another reality, and "Jesus is unique" could have a sense that has nothing to do with Jesus as "the way, the truth, and the life." That, no doubt, sounds perplexing, but it is a fact. To understand that, however, we have to be well-acquainted with what the contemporary science of religion has to say about the reality called religion.

According to the science of religion, *religion* is not a word with one fixed meaning. Rather, it falls into the category of so-called equivocal words. Just as, for example, the word *file* could mean in one instance a container of papers, and in another, a sharpener of blades, so too the term *religion* can convey different meanings and, as a result, represent totally different realities. Of these, two are predominant. Christianity, or any religion for that matter, can be conceived of in either of these two forms.

In one sense, religion is what we are "born to"; in the other, it is what we are "re-born to." Jesus told Nicodemus: "I tell you the truth, no one can see the Kingdom of God unless he is born again" (Jn 3:3). Religion by birth and religion by conviction (and taking their primary functions into account, we will here designate the former as "religion as clan-solidarity" and the latter "religion as life-vision") are not only very different from each other, they are also poles apart from each other. It is only the second that is religion proper.

The first, or the religion that a person is born to, is religion as part of culture. Culture belongs to a clan (taken here in the nonderogatory sense of a group linked together by a sociologically common living pattern). Culture and clan are rooted in a locality. The religion of a locality is more often than not decided by the one who governs the locality. The Latin summed up that truth very pithily in the aphorism *Cujus regio ejus religio* (Whose reign, his religion).

Religion of this cultural form, though not to be mistaken for religion proper, still has a great value of its own. As a constituent element of culture, it fulfills an important sociological function vital for human existence. Like culture's other constitutive elements, such as the history of the clan, the geography of the clan, and the language of the clan, religion ensures the solidarity of the clan. It is all those elements taken together that make a person in America, American; a person in Japan, Japanese; and a person in Africa, African. For that reason, we have to admit that religion as clan-solidarity answers a basic human need.

Religion as life-vision answers quite another need of human beings. Its purpose is purely and simply to make a person grow into full mental adulthood. In Christianity of the life-vision form, it is this adultness that is referred to as being a child of God, as living in the Spirit, or as being submissive to the commandment to "love one another as I have loved you" (Jn 13:34).

Being more provincial than universal in its concerns, religion as clan-solidarity has characteristics all its own. Those characteristics and also what it considers as virtues are all culturally conditioned. People of a culture, for example, are under an almost insurmountable subconscious compulsion to extol the religion of their culture above those of other cultures. They have to talk of other religions and their adherents disparagingly, and that for no other reason than that these are outside their camp. People of a culture have to fight for their religion, its security, its enlargement. Bloodshed for such purposes is not only just but also meritorious. Wars become "holy wars." Taken exclusively in the clan-solidarity form, Hinduism, Buddhism, Christianity, and Islam are irreconcilable and even antagonistic to each other.

For people of a particular clan-solidarity religion, that religion is the greatest in the world. Thus Buddhism is the greatest religion for Sri Lankans and Tibetans; Christianity, for Europeans and others of a Western culture; Hinduism, for the Indians; and Islam, for Arabs. With regard to personalities, Gautama Buddha is for Buddhists the greatest human figure in the world; Muhammad is so for Muslims. It is not only Christians who say that their founder is unique.

But when voiced by people for whom religion is just part of their culture, such affirmations have a special connotation. In a subtle way such affirmations insinuate that their culture is the greatest and that as a people or clan, they are superior to others. Probably because, in fact, everybody is born to the religion of his or her parents, all human beings—if not all through their life, at least at one non-adult stage in their life—adopt such an attitude. And so, whether we like it or not, the fact of that subconscious compulsion, to which nobody is immune, has to be taken into account when we try to understand introspectively an assertion such as "Jesus is unique." In such a statement "Jesus" may not necessarily stand for "Jesus, the supreme Way"; "Jesus" can just as well be a substitute for "we of Western culture," and then "Jesus is unique" could mean simply, "We of the Western culture are unique"!

By saying this I am not belittling people who happen to be Western. Even though I am Asian, through being Christian I share that culture of the West; further, what I am saying here of Christians is equally true of other religions. Hinduism, Buddhism, and Islam, too, can stand for race, nation, or culture rather than for a way of life. What I wish to stress is that *Christianity* is an ambiguous word, because it can represent either of two totally distinct realities. In one sense, it is the kingdom of Christian culture or Christendom, an offshoot of the Holy Roman Empire. In the other sense, it is the religion created by the humble carpenter-preacher of Galilee. Adherents of that religion are recognizable only by the life of love and selflessness they lead ("They will know that you are my disciples, if you love one another" [Jn 13:35]). The Christianity of Constantine and the Christianity of Jesus are not always identical.

To avoid possible confusion and even misconception, we must also underline here that the two forms, though clearly distinct, are not necessarily separable. They represent two mentalities much more than two camps. These two mentalities operate within the same individual. To become adult is to grow out of one into the other. Christians must realize that birth or registration as Christian does not make them genuinely Christian. Christianness is a level of life that they have to acquire with effort and perseverance.

AS A MISSIONARY PROCLAMATION

The distinction made above between clan-solidarity religion and life-vision religion is new, a very recent topic among scholars of world religions. But without taking that perspective into account, the uniqueness of Jesus cannot be professed by a Christian in an authentic way. The uniqueness of Jesus, further, is not a belief that Christians have to affirm just among themselves; it is also what they have to proclaim to the rest of the world. In other words, it is only to the extent that this affirmation is correctly understood and subscribed to that missionary work itself becomes meaningful.

If missionary work has fallen into confusion today, it is because the distinction has not been made about the mentality with which it has to be conducted. Though more unconsciously than consciously, most Christians so far have engaged in missionary work with a clan-solidarity mentality. They have tried to diffuse and enlarge Christendom rather than the Reign of God of Jesus' expectation, which actually stands for the reign of right life-ideals in the hearts of people.

True missionary work liberates people from their inner misery and restlessness by awakening them to the life-ideals that make them mentally adult. The great weakness of contemporary humanity is the immaturity of the vast majority. The root cause for the frightful rifts and the growing tension in the modern world is exactly there. Given that background, missionary work is not something to be shunned. Mission is really needed. But it must be missionary work of the right form.

Missionaries motivated by a right life-vision mentality do not feel threatened by preachers of other religions, as long as what they preach is also life-vision religion. Christian missionaries would even join hands with them and collaborate with them. When taken as preachers of sublime life-ideals, the founders of other religions, such as the Buddha and Muhammad, are not opponents of Jesus. The healing ministry exercised by them in other cultures is implicitly affirmed when a missionary proclaims aloud that Jesus is unique.

All that goes to say how important it is for Christians in general, and theologians in particular, to take seriously the distinction made above about the two forms of Christianity and the two mentalities they engender. If that distinction is not taken into account, "Jesus is unique" becomes an ambiguous statement. But if it is interpreted in the light of religion proper, that is, Christianity as life-vision, it becomes not only an unassailable tenet of Christians but also an affirmation admired and respected by non-Christians.

Rethinking Uniqueness

MONIKA K. HELLWIG

RESPONSES TO THE FIVE THESES

My initial response to Paul Knitter's Five Theses is not exactly that I disagree, but rather that I would prefer to express myself differently and with different emphases. The foundation of my different emphasis is that I find that the designations "inclusivist" and "pluralist" insufficient. They do not do justice to the nuances and perspectives of the various writers who have attempted to explain the Christian claim of the uniqueness of Jesus as part of a wider ecumenism. I have a similar problem with responding to the Five Theses, as this limits what I can express to a frame of reference that I do not find conducive to dealing with the problem. However, I shall attempt here first to give a response to each thesis and then to proceed to my own suggestion. (I have made these points before in several publications, although it seems to me that Paul Knitter has misinterpreted them when referring to my position.)

To *thesis 1* I respond that certainly there has been considerable reinterpretation in christology through the centuries, and what has occurred in the past in the development of doctrine can occur again. However, the real question is in the area of what is being reinterpreted, by whom, for whom, and what distinctions are being made, for example: between texts of scripture, ancient and surviving texts of prayer, titles, and designations widely disseminated since ancient times, solemnly declared dogma, and theological positions held with more or less authority and clarity.

The field of christology and, in particular, statements which in various ways express the uniqueness claims cannot easily be reduced to straightforward propositions. At one level we are concerned with the believers' sense of the trustworthiness of the faith they have been taught. At another level we are concerned with guaranteed common ground for the expression of faith by Christians of many cultures who therefore look to classic formulations and hold them conservatively. At yet another level we are concerned with the nature and the many types and many uses of religious language, the problem of semantic shift, inevitable losses in translation, various degrees of sensitivity to symbolism, and varying degrees of tolerance of ambiguity. These are different challenges to be met in different ways, not in the abstract, but with careful attention to context.

It would seem that Knitter more or less acknowledges all this in the text following the formulations of thesis 1. But on his own proclaimed pluralist assumptions, it is not clear why it should then be necessary to arrive at a consensus statement in the abstract, noncontextually. It is not even clear why it should be necessary for theologians to take a stand in relation to the thesis noncontextually, nor is it clear what type of authority such statements would have so as to be judged as valid or invalid, to use Knitter's words. While I agree that the formulations of the faith must be expressed in harmony with the established language of public prayer and with the established criteria of discipleship, I think that the testing of any formulation is ecclesially contextual, beginning in a particular situation and gradually gaining or not gaining acceptance on a wider basis.

To *thesis 2* I respond again that it is clear that doctrine has always been shaped in the context of the praxis of discipleship and faith exercised in response to the experiences, challenges, and interpretive frames of reference available. In second-century, largely gentile churches with Greek cultural assumptions, the term *logos* had a great deal more intelligibility than the term *messiah* in giving expression to the uniqueness of Jesus. It should be noted, however, that this adaptation had Hebrew roots on which to build on in the notion of the *memra* of God. It should also be noted that a huge leap like this was not entertained again for the solid historical reason that these formulations soon acquired the authority of classic positions guaranteeing the unity of the community's faith.

This being said, however, it is not clear that "an ethical imperative of dialogue" requires any particular stance on the uniqueness of Jesus. Theologians and church officials of very varied theological positions are deeply, sincerely, and fruitfully engaged in dialogue with those of other faiths. I have been a participant and observer in conversations that included people of ultra-orthodox and uncritical persuasion in their own traditions who were respectfully curious about the tenets and practices of their dialogue partners from other traditions, eager to correct any misapprehensions they themselves might have had, and very pleased to learn how the others approached matters of common concern. There has been in such meetings a profound level of exchange on creedal, moral, social justice, and prayer or meditation traditions. It has not been my experience that such exchanges depended upon any particular interpretation of the uniqueness of Jesus.

To *thesis 3* I respond that I have no objection to Knitter's position, but I myself prefer an entirely different approach. I will explain my approach in the second half of this chapter.

To *thesis 4* I must divide my response in two because I think there are really two separate theses here. That the content of the uniqueness of

Jesus must be made clear in Christian life and witness is a thesis I heartily endorse. To quote a slogan from the 1960s, the medium is the message. The impact of Jesus in the world is made through his followers, and it is this impact which reflects what is specific about him. That the particulars of that impact in human society will depend not only on Jesus himself but also on changing cultures and circumstances is evident.

It is, however, with the final sentence of thesis 4 that I have some difficulty. I find it difficult to locate the uniqueness of Jesus in our times "in his insistence that salvation or the Reign of God must be realized *in this world* through *human actions* of love and justice." I find this difficult because most of our dialogue partners are not speaking of salvation or the Reign of God in any case; on the other hand, anyone who speaks on behalf of Christians must be aware that vast numbers of Christians doggedly resist any focus on this worldly salvation and see the role of the Christian believer as rather passive before a redeeming Christ. When Knitter refers to his Indian experience as the basis of his fourth thesis, I wonder whether he can maintain his uniqueness claim in this shape in the face of the social concerns and community building, uplifting, and transforming activities of the Sikh temples and agricultural project in the New Delhi area, to give but one example of such initiatives of religions foundations outside the Christian tradition. My sense is that the contrast is drawn too sharply for some traditions and is not relevant for others.

To *thesis 5* I respond with the agreement, mentioned before in relation to thesis 4, that orthodoxy must be grounded in the orthopraxis of discipleship. I also agree with the implicit assumption behind the Five Theses, namely, that the demands of discipleship can and do unfold in the course of time and in relation to changing contexts. I am inclined, however, to be less casual about the need for continuity with past normative statements, again for reasons already given—the need to maintain unity and communion among Christians of varying times and cultures, the link of trustworthiness with classic statements, and the need not to confuse the faithful into a state of discouragement and indifference from a sense of disorientation.

As to the distinction between "truly" and "solely," I am quite willing to accept Paul Knitter as an authentic Christian independently of the adverbs he uses, but I do not find the adverbs particularly helpful. I find too many variations in the uses of religious language. The creeds do speak of Jesus as *filius unicus Patris*, but scripture also speaks of our being made "children of God," patristic tradition has it that "he became what we are that we might become what he is," and the churches of the East speak unabashedly of divinization, while the tradition of the West has described the ordained priest as *alter Christus*, to mention only a few paradoxes in the use of the terms. What is obviously called for is some analysis of the language as rhetoric.

MY APPROACH

It is my understanding that the purpose of ecumenical dialogue is not to persuade the others of my beliefs but to be willing to discuss them, to make every effort to make them intelligible to those who want to try to understand, and reciprocally to take a genuine interest in the beliefs and practices of the others, to try to learn about them to correct prejudices and grow in empathetic understanding. When I say "empathetic" I mean the exercise of that characteristically human faculty that makes it possible to cross over into the experience of others by using our analogical imagination. Therefore I find it important not only to read about other faiths but to encounter their practitioners face to face, to listen to their voices and look at their gestures and facial expressions to notice what excites their enthusiasm and inspires their reverence. I do this to learn both about their religious experience and to learn something about mine from the encounter. I find it important to pray or meditate with people of other traditions so long as the prayer does not deny my own faith. I like to visit temples and shrines of other traditions to experience the atmosphere, the symbolism, and their approach to the sacred. I like to learn about their mystical and ascetical traditions, and about the devotional practices of popular piety. I have found all of this immensely enriching, and have acquired great admiration, respect, and friendship for certain members of other traditions whom I have met often and come to know well.

I have never found that others held back because I profess faith in Christ as universal savior. On the contrary, it is my impression that they would suspect me of not engaging seriously in dialogue if I were to deny it, because I would not be showing them my tradition as it really is in my community's own consciousness. I have never found that the others expected me to distance myself from the beliefs and sensitivities and piety of my own community in order to come into dialogue with them. If I were to do that, I should be useless as a dialogue partner, because I would no longer represent my tradition.

It is my experience that other dialogue partners take it for granted that Jesus is unique, because founders of traditions are necessarily so. But they also take it for granted that we who are followers of Jesus will have a unique explanation of the uniqueness of Jesus, because that is the kind of teaching that gives a religious tradition its shape and coherence. None of this has ever troubled my dialogue partners; that is the way they expected to meet me. Moreover, I have found that most of the other traditions are not so concerned about the notion of salvation as we are, and some have to make great efforts to make any sense of it at all. They may be more concerned with law, cosmic harmony, inner peace, oneness with nature, loyalty to community traditions, the art of meditation, the asceticism of the discovery and full use of the higher human faculties, communication with the spirit world, and so forth.

It seems to me that in the actual experience of the wider ecumenism the preoccupation with who may be saved and by whose agency or mediation is entirely an internal issue for the Christian partners. I have reflected on it, though it has cost me no sleepless nights or gray hairs. My own attitude is based in the first place on the understanding that human beings really know very little about ultimate questions and generally do not advance that knowledge by speculation but can live quite happily by faith, seeking only one kind of verification, namely, that their faith should make progressively more sense as they live by it. Operating by this principle, it becomes clearer to me every day that Jesus is offered to the world as universal savior, but that the vast majority of human beings will never see it that way, while most of the minority who acknowledge him as savior do not take this as a serious operating principle in the structuring of human society and its activities. Aware that my conviction is based not on publicly available conclusive evidence but on faith supported by private and internal evidence of praxis of discipleship, I am cheerfully prepared to live my life as a friendly wager against all contrary convictions and arguments—a wager that Jesus really does have the secret because he really is at the center. I am also prepared to live quite peacefully with the realization that I may never know the outcome of the wager.

Five Misgivings

JOHN HICK

Paul Knitter's purpose in presenting his Five Theses on the uniqueness of Jesus[1] is clearly to commend the Christian pluralist point of view within the church by stressing its elements of continuity with the past tradition. This is a valuable service, and if his theses succeed in gaining a greater Christian acceptance of religious pluralism the project will have been fully vindicated.

The misgivings that I shall register do not concern the Five Theses themselves. The five propositions seem to me, with the caveat that I shall enter below about thesis 4, to be excellent, but I shall take issue with Knitter's more detailed explanation of them. These seem to me at certain crucial points to be ambiguous, capable of being understood in both pluralist and inclusivist ways. He seems, in his desire to make the pluralist position as widely acceptable as possible, to be offering the illusory possibility of having it both ways.

My first misgiving concerns Knitter's account of pluralism. He defines it as announcing "at least the possibility (some would hold the probability, if not the actuality) of many true religions, each carrying on a different though valid role in the divine plan of salvation" (note 2). But both exclusivists and inclusivists could hold that it is possibly but not actually the case that there are other true religions as well as Christianity. St. Thomas argued with great cogency that there could in principle have been other divine incarnations. There could have been incarnations of the other Persons of the Trinity, for "what the Son can do, the Father can do, for otherwise the three persons would not be equal in

---

[1] Strictly speaking, *uniqueness* is not the right word. Jesus, and of course everyone else, is unique; that is to say, there was only one of him. But the word is commonly used in the present context to signal the claim that Jesus uniquely was God (that is, God the Son, Second Person of the Holy Trinity) incarnate, the only savior of the world from sin and perdition. The question is whether this claim is appropriate. So Knitter says correctly that he is "not questioning *whether* Jesus is unique but only *how*" (*The Myth of Christian Uniqueness*, ed. John Hick and Paul Knitter [Maryknoll, N.Y.: Orbis Books, 1987]).

power. The Son had the power to become incarnate. So then did the Father and the Holy Spirit" (*Summa Theologica*, IIIa, Q. 3, art. 5); and there could have been other incarnations of the Son: "It seems that after the Incarnation the Son has the power to take up another human nature distinct from the one he actually did" (IIIa, Q. 3, art. 7). Aquinas held, of course, that in actual fact there has been only one incarnation, in Jesus Christ. However, if there had been other divine incarnations, they might well have founded other religions which would have been as true and salvific as Christianity. It is therefore perfectly orthodox to affirm the possibility but not actuality of other true-and-salvific religions. And so the traditional exclusivist and inclusivist positions do not preclude what Knitter defines as majority pluralism, that is, apart from the "some" who go beyond possibility to probability or actuality. Pluralism now ceases to be another option in addition to exclusivism and inclusivism. I conclude that Knitter's definition is too permissive to be useful.

In a later note Knitter argues that "it is *probable* that God's love will be found in and through other religions, thus rendering them, at least to some extent, true" (note 15). This is an accurate delineation of Christian inclusivism. Some other religions are, or probably are, to some extent true. But pluralism ought not to be watered down into inclusivism. A pluralism that is worth agreeing or disagreeing with in its own right will hold that we have as much reason to think that the other great world religions are true and salvific as to think this of Christianity. The ground for this lies in their fruits in human life. If it seems to us that Judaism, Islam, Hinduism, Buddhism, Sikhism, and Taoism have shown themselves to be contexts as effective as Christianity for human transformation from self-centeredness to a new centering in the Ultimate Reality that we call God, then we must affirm not merely the possibility or probability but the actuality of their being true and salvific. This is not something to be determined by a priori dogma but by the observation of actual human behavior. Judgements concerning human behavior as reflecting our relationship to the Ultimate are of course difficult, to say the least. I would only claim that we have *as much* reason, on the basis of their fruits, to believe that Buddhism, for example, is true and salvific as we have to believe that Christianity is. This is what I, for one, understand by religious pluralism, that is, the affirmation not merely of a possible or probable but of an actual plurality of authentically true-and-salvific religious traditions.[2]

---

[2] I have no space here to take up the further questions of smaller, extinct, or new religious movements, or of the criteria by which we judge a movement to be an authentic response to the Ultimate. I have done so, however, in Part V of *An Interpretation of Religion* (New Haven: Yale University Press; and London: Macmillan, 1989).

My second misgiving follows from this and concerns something on which Knitter rightly insists; namely, that in interfaith dialogue "if Christians think that they are in possession of the 'fullness' of revelation and the final norm for all truth, then no matter how much they might call for a dialogue 'among equals,' they retain the position of advantage"; or as he also puts it, there must in genuine dialogue be "a level playing field" (thesis 2). But is this position of advantage really renounced in dialogue, producing a genuinely level playing field, when Christians affirm that Christianity is true and salvific but that the religion of their dialogue partner is only *possibly*, or at most *probably*, true and salvific? I cannot help thinking that any impartial observer would judge that Christians here are setting themselves up in a "position of advantage" rather than coming onto a "level playing field." Does Knitter really recommend that we engage in dialogue on this basis?

I applaud Knitter's thesis that God was *truly* at work in Jesus but not *only* in Jesus. This is, I think, an excellent formulation. But my third misgiving concerns his expounding the key word *truly* as meaning that "Christians must announce Jesus to all peoples as God's *universal, decisive*, and *indispensable* manifestation of saving truth and grace" (thesis 3). "Universal," yes, in the sense that God's work in the life of Jesus is relevant to everyone without restriction. Knitter adds that this is *probably* also true of other revelations of the divine. This is a halfhearted or less than halfhearted pluralism. I want to say that we have as much reason to believe that the Buddhist, Muslim, and other messages are universally relevant as we do to believe our own Christian message is. "Decisive," yes, in the sense that, as Knitter says, the Christian gospel "shakes and challenges and calls one to change one's perspective and conduct" (thesis 3). Again, he adds that this is *probably* also true of other gospels; and again I want to say that we have as much reason, from actual observation, to think that the Muslim and Buddhist messages, for example, are decisive in this sense as that the Christian message is. And "normative," yes, in the sense that the Christian revelation is normative for Christians but is, as Knitter says, not "the absolute, final, full, unsurpassable norm for all times and all religions" (note 13). But "indispensable"? Indispensable for what? What is it that cannot occur without this indispensable message having been heard and accepted? Is it indispensable for salvation? This would be the old exclusivism that Knitter has rejected. Indispensable, then, for what? Knitter's answer is that "those who have not known and in some way accepted the message and power of the gospel are missing something in their knowledge and living of truth" (thesis 3). That is to say, non-Christians will be spiritually enriched by hearing and appreciating the Christian message. Knitter adds, again, that it is *probable* that this is also true of the other great religious messages. But if several different messages are all indispensable in the sense that anyone is enriched by hearing and appreciating them, is *indispensable* really the correct word?

I appreciate that it will play well with the traditionally orthodox. But consider an analogy. If your life can only be saved by taking penicillin, then penicillin is indispensable to you in a very clear sense. But if your health will be enhanced by your taking multivitamin tablets, they cannot be said to be indispensable. And if several different brands of multivitamin tablets are more or less equally effective, a particular brand certainly cannot responsibly be advertised as indispensable. In my view, *indispensable* is not the right word, nor is it selected for the right reason.

My third misgiving concerns Knitter's comparative identification of each of the world religions in terms of a single unique feature, with Christianity's unique feature being a concern for social justice, of "the betterment of human beings in this world," the transformation of this world "from one of division and injustice into one of love and mutuality" (thesis 4). Historians of religion are today generally too conscious of the immense internal variety of each tradition to indulge in such one-dimensional stereotyping. But leaving that aside, is the stereotyping being done here in a fair and just way? Surely no impartial observer would pick out as the central and most obvious characteristic of Christianity a loving concern for social justice. Historically Christianity has validated wars, slavery, patriarchy, immense hierarchical inequalities, colonial exploitation, and anti-Semitism—the opposite of what Knitter identifies as the central thrust of the Christian message. And, as he is obviously well aware, Christianity today is still involved in most of these same evils. To define Christianity in contrast to the other world religions as having social and political liberation at its heart is to make a recommendation concerning what it *ought* to be—not an objectively accurate statement of what it actually is. I fully agree with Knitter's recommendation. But to equate the very recent (dating from the 1960s), small, much-contested, and officially condemned movement of liberation theology with the actuality of Christianity in the world today—while ignoring parallel minority movements for social justice within other traditions—seems to me another abandonment of the "level playing field." I think it is clear that Knitter is in fact aware that he is making a recommendation. But must we claim it as an exclusively or uniquely Christian recommendation? Indeed, would not an impartial observer, looking for the most outstanding religious leaders in the service of peace and justice on earth in this century, see above all Mahatma Gandhi[3] and the Dalai Lama?

---

[3] The idea, cherished by some, that Gandhi received his most important ideas from Christianity cannot be sustained in the light of his own speeches and writings. See Robert Ellsberg, ed., *Gandhi on Christianity* (Maryknoll, N.Y.: Orbis Books, 1991), and the discussion by Margaret Chatterjee in *Gandhi's Religious Thought* (London: Macmillan; Notre Dame, Ind.: University of Notre Dame Press, 1983).

The creation of peace and a rational conservation of the earth's limited natural resources in a just and sustainable world economy ought to be the aim of people of all religions. It has, in fact, in recent years been increasingly on the agenda of interfaith dialogue. Recall, for example, the National Inter-Religious Conference on Peace at Washington in 1966, the New Delhi Symposium sponsored by the U.S. Inter-Religious Committee on Peace and the Gandhi Peace Foundation in 1968, the Assembly of the World Conference on Religion and Peace at Kyoto in 1970, and continuing gatherings at Louvain in 1974, Princeton in 1979, Nairobi in 1984, and Melbourne in 1989, as well as very numerous other smaller dialogue occasions centered on the same concerns. This is indeed proving to be the most fruitful area of interreligious cooperation. From a third-world Christian point of view, Aloysius Pieris has said, "The irruption of the Third World [with its demand for liberation] is also the irruption of the non-Christian world. The vast majority of God's poor perceive their ultimate concern and symbolize their struggle for liberation in the idiom of non-Christian religions and cultures. Therefore, a theology that does not speak to or speak through this non-Christian peoplehood [and its religions] is a luxury of a Christian minority."[4] Knitter himself has in another paper endorsed this and spoken of "the liberating potential of Buddhism and Hinduism"[5]—and he could well have added each of the other major world faiths. But the growing interfaith dialogue on peace and justice will not be helped by a Christian claim to a uniquely authentic concern for justice and love. Does Knitter really want us to engage in dialogue on this basis?

A fourth misgiving is triggered by Knitter's statement that "as a pluralist Christian, I can with no difficulty whatsoever announce—indeed, I feel impelled to proclaim—that Jesus is truly the Son of God and universal Savior. The recognition and announcement of Jesus' divinity remains integral and essential to a pluralist christology" (note 20). The point of this language is, of course, that it sounds traditionally orthodox. But if it is meant in a traditionally orthodox sense, it is, in my view, incompatible with genuine religious pluralism. For if Jesus was God the Son, Second Person of a divine Trinity, incarnate, then Christianity is the only religion to have been founded by God in person and must be uniquely superior to all others. And so, presumably, when Knitter speaks of Jesus as the Son of God he does not mean this in the traditional sense

---

[4] Aloysius Pieris, S.J., "The Place of Non-Christian Religions and Cultures in the Evolution of Third World Theology," in Virginia Fabella and Sergio Torres, eds., *Irruption of the Third World: Challenge to Theology* (Maryknoll, N.Y.: Orbis Books, 1983), pp. 113-14.

[5] Paul Knitter, "Towards a Liberation Theology of Religions," in John Hick and Paul Knitter, eds., *The Myth of Christian Uniqueness: Towards a Pluralistic Theology of Religions* (Maryknoll, N.Y.: Orbis Books, 1987), p. 180.

that Jesus is the only source of salvation for all human beings. What he does mean is hinted at when he goes on to speak of Jesus' "divinity" as meaning that he is "the symbol, the story that makes God real and effective for me"—as to all of us who are Christians. But has not Knitter's desire to minimize the difference between Christian pluralism on the one hand and traditional orthodoxy on the other led to an ambiguous use of language?

My fifth misgiving is whether Christian pluralism, as Knitter is here presenting it, is able adequately to take account of the great nontheistic religions—Buddhism, Taoism, and advaitic Hinduism. It is natural and proper for a Christian normally to use our Christian term, *God*, for the ultimately Real. And Knitter does not forget that "God is an unsurpassable Mystery, one which can never totally be comprehended or contained in human thought or construct"(thesis 3). But nevertheless he sometimes writes, like so many theologians, as though he had forgotten this! Perhaps this is allowable in a document that is intended for internal Christian consumption. But in dialogue with, for example, Buddhists, we cannot take it for granted that that which is ultimately real is a personal God, still less a Trinity of Three Persons. We cannot require that the dialogue be conducted in Christian terms. Knitter is, of course, well aware of this, having engaged extensively in the contemporary Buddhist-Christian dialogue.

But there is so much in Knitter's pages that I heartily applaud that I cannot end on a negative note. A short response has only the space to pick out the most debatable points. Knitter has contributed as much as anyone to the development of contemporary Christian pluralism. His chosen mission is within and to the church. This is an entirely legitimate and important—and indeed indispensable—mission. But it carries with it the temptation to resort to easing ambiguities, and I have suggested that Knitter has not entirely avoided this. I nevertheless hope very much that his mission succeeds.

"Faithful" to the New Testament?

Questions in Response to Paul Knitter

KARL-JOSEF KUSCHEL

Paul Knitter deserves, first of all, an acknowledgment for once again raising the issue of christology that for centuries precluded the very possibility of interreligious dialogue, and especially for doing so on behalf of interreligious dialogue. He deserves, secondly, unconditional consent to his thesis that a Christian interreligious dialogue is not merely an option but a "moral obligation" and that witnessing to the Christian truth vis-à-vis non-Christians must be linked to the first and greatest commandment, "love your neighbor as yourself." For in the contemporary world the neighbor is, of course, not only the nonbeliever (atheist) but also the non-Christian. Paul Knitter deserves, thirdly, respect for his own witness to Christ and for his determination to follow Christ. And he deserves, finally, solidarity in his plea both to engage in theological combat against a fatal Christian claim to absolute superiority at the expense of non-Christians and to show a way to make christology—the very center of Christianity—capable of interreligious communication.

The following critical objections to Knitter's theses are therefore not a case of cheap "know it all" but a joint wrestling with the same fundamental problems. In addition, they are not meant to underscore those aspects of Knitter's theses that are persuasive (for example, his demand for a "holistic Christian spirituality") but rather to focus on his "christological" main points in the narrower sense. There I see three critical points.

1. Paul Knitter does not simply wish to speak as a religious person but as "a Christian, who is nourished at the eucharistic table and who feels empowered to live the life of the risen Christ."
2. Knitter asserts that in order to remain faithful to the New Testament witness, "as a Christian," one need no longer insist that Jesus

is "the *only* mediator of God's saving grace in history" or that Jesus is God's *"full, definitive,* or *unsurpassable"* revelation.

3. Knitter asserts that when Christians continue to insist that Jesus is "the full, definitive, or unsurpassable" revelation of God, and that Jesus is also "the final norm," then they are not in the position "to recognize any truth or value in other religions that is genuinely different from what they already have."

How can one respond to these claims?

WHAT IS THE NORM OF "BEING CHRISTIAN"?

Paul Knitter places himself under the criterion of the New Testament. Like other Christians, he wants to remain "faithful to the New Testament witness." And indeed, if one expects to be taken seriously as a theologian and wishes to speak about Jesus Christ "as a Christian," one cannot do so arbitrarily. There are historical presuppositions and fundamental theological conditions, namely, the normative, canonical texts of the New Testament as well as the binding interpretation and reception of this witness by the universal church (creeds, councils, and confessional writings). These documents show that there is certainly no "single way" to speak of Jesus as the Christ; after all, the New Testament already contains various Christ-images. Likewise, there is no "final way" of speaking about Jesus Christ; as long as people search for Christ in the Spirit of God the process of christological interpretation remains open in principle. In this respect there is no cause for dissent from Paul Knitter. There is, however, a right way of speaking about Jesus Christ and a wrong way, in the sense that there are statements about Jesus as the Christ that conform to the New Testament and the tradition of the church and those that fall short of the above criteria and do not come up to the established standard of reflection and use of language. There are christological statements that remain "faithful" to the New Testament "witness" and those that become unfaithful.

Hence we must ask Paul Knitter the following key question: does his christology do justice to the witness of the New Testament (in the sense of the *entire* New Testament)? Scrutiny of his theses in those terms leads to an astonishing finding. Knitter cites directly only a single New Testament passage (in thesis 3, Jn 16:12-13), and then interprets it incorrectly. Of all possible gospel texts, Knitter appeals to John for his "pluralistic" understanding of God as though John's Spirit christology were not in fact the most christocentric theology in the entire New Testament. Knitter interprets the Johannine passage, "When the Spirit of Truth comes, he will guide you into all the truth," as if it did not refer to the spirit and truth of Jesus Christ, but rather to something totally open, as though John's God were the ineffable Mystery which can never be adequately described by any religion and must remain open on principle. In John's gospel we read exactly the opposite.

DOES CHRISTOLOGY EQUAL IDOLATRY?

It is not necessary to cite the New Testament, however, in order to do it justice. There are various ways of making the point. Does Knitter do this? Again, curiously, instead of directly confronting the various christologies of the New Testament—of course on the exegetical level commonly practiced today—we read Knitter's vague generalization:

A growing number of Christians around the world (I found many in India) are suggesting that in order to remain faithful to the New Testament witness and to nurture a true following of Jesus today, it is not necessary to insist that Jesus is the *only* mediator of God's saving grace in history. More precisely, it is not necessary to proclaim God's revelation in Jesus as *full, definitive,* or *unsurpassable.*

What precisely are the meanings of "suggesting" and "not necessary"? Does Paul Knitter only *believe* (along with other Christians) that the New Testament does not demand that we profess Jesus Christ as the full, definitive, and unsurpassable revelation of God? Or is it in fact the case that the New Testament does not demand that profession? Since Knitter has not dealt with New Testament christology he can end up with such an erroneous statement as: the identification of the infinite with the finite is "idolatry"! I have always understood incarnational theology, especially as it appears in John's gospel, to mean that the infinite God reveals himself in a finite human being who is therefore God's Word, Image, the Messiah, the Son. Is this idolatry? Is the entire christology of the Son of God becoming God idolatry? Is it the idolization of the finite? If this is the case, then large segments of New Testament christology can be dismissed as arch-heresy in the biblical sense. Does Knitter intend this?

THE UNREASONABLE DEMAND
OF THE OLD AND NEW TESTAMENT

No, one cannot get around the fact; it is precisely the great unreasonable demand of Christianity that we believe that the infinite God chose for himself the finite in a special way—in the crucified and resurrected Nazarene. Paul himself spoke of the "stumbling block" and the "folly" (1 Cor 1:23) that the one who died on the cross is proclaimed as "God's power and wisdom." Fundamentally the New Testament challenges us with a two-sided position (and I report this not in a spirit of dogmatism but precisely because I am conscious of the serious difficulties this poses especially for dialogue with non-Christians):

1. "In many and various ways God spoke of old to our fathers by the prophets" (Heb 1:1). This is a statement *against a christological exclusivism*; God did not manifest himself for the first time in Jesus Christ. He had already revealed himself through creation and in history through his "prophets." A christological exclusivism which insists on God's self-revelation through absolutely nothing and no one except for Jesus Christ would in fact be unbiblical. Here Knitter is right when he argues against a christological "only." Such exclusivism would undermine the revelation through creation as well as the entire "salvation history" of the Hebrew Bible. There were prophets and revelations of God both *before* Jesus Christ (important in the dialogue with Judaism), and *after* his time, as the New Testament acknowledges prophets who follow Jesus Christ (which is important for dialogue with Islam). This must be maintained against every christomonism. But at the same time we must emphasize just as strongly the following scriptural evidence *against a christological pluralism*: as far back as the Old Testament God did not manifest himself to all peoples in the same manner. While God is the creator of all human beings (Adam is not the first Jew but the first human), promised continued existence to the entire creation (the covenant with Noah), and blessed all the nations (the covenant with Abraham), God also entered into a special relationship with a specific and chosen people, the People Israel, with whom he concluded a third covenant.

Already the Hebrew Bible's (and Judaism's since that time) challenge is precisely that God chose for himself *one* people, revealed his will to this people, and did not do likewise to other peoples: neither to the Assyrians nor the Egyptians; neither to the Babylonians nor the Greeks. If this were not so then the struggle of the prophets for the correct and exclusive worship of Yahweh in the Old Testament would have been utterly nonsensical. We must also add that the God of Israel did not reveal himself in the same manner to the great founders of other world religions or the great religious leaders of humankind—not to the composers of the Vedas and Upanishads, not to the Buddha, to Confucius, or to Lao Tze. Jews and Christians continue to share this conviction. Those who are currently engaged in interreligious dialogue will take offense at it. But individuals who precisely as Christians do not simply wish to set aside the biblical tradition will not be able to dodge this "fact." It all depends on the correct interpretation which respects extra-biblical peoples and does justice to their faith witness. To maintain, however, that God manifests himself in equal fullness and scope everywhere is incorrect according to a scripture-based theology. According to the biblical witness there simply are degrees and steps of divine revelation in human history, and I do not say this without deep apprehension and continued earnest reflection. To this must be added:

2. "In these last days he has spoken to us by a Son, whom he appointed the heir of all things, through whom also he created the world" (Heb 1:2). Christians do not claim to have the first and sole revelation, but they do claim to have *the eschatologically final (definitive and unsurpassable) revelation.* All prophets and revelations after Christ are subject to this factual criterion. This is vexing and problematic for interreligious dialogue. But does diluting or ignoring this christological claim of the New Testament really further this dialogue? As a Gentile Christian of the twentieth century I did not fabricate this claim—I simply encounter it whether I like it or not.

I must admit that I keep pondering this "fact": why did God—according to the witness of scripture—act in this manner and not another? Why are the degrees of the revelations of God in human history so different? I don't know. It remains God's mystery, which I have trusted, just as I am free to reject it. Apparently it pleased God—*sola gratia*—and I can no more argue with him about that than I can about his election of Israel or the election of his Son, Jesus Christ, who had to die on the cross. God is self-justifying. And the position of non-Christian religions in God's plan for humanity is properly "grasped" only in light of the doctrine of justification—actually in the very christological dialectic of understanding and not understanding. In my opinion interreligious dialogue which does not seriously confront the doctrine of justification is superficial. It seems to me that this is the theologically most critical point that one would have to dispute with Knitter.

To put it differently, unless I wish simply to engage in private theology I simply cannot disregard the fact that on all levels of the New Testament such christological statements can be found:

• In the gospel of Matthew, going back to the earlier Christian teaching source (the Q Document): "All things have been delivered to me by my Father; and no one knows the Son except the Father, and no one knows the Father except the Son and any one to whom the Son chooses to reveal him" (Mt 11:27).

• According to Paul: "Although there may be so-called gods in heaven or on earth—as indeed there are many "gods" and many "lords"—yet for us there is one God, the Father, from whom are all things and for whom we exist, and one Lord, Jesus Christ, through whom are all things and through whom we exist" (1 Cor 8:5-6).

• According to John: "No one has ever seen God; the only Son, who is in the bosom of the Father, he has made him known" (Jn 1:18).

• In Colossians: "He is the image of the invisible God, the first-born of all creation; . . . For in him all the fullness of God was pleased to dwell" (Col 1:15, 19).

• In Hebrews: "He reflects the glory of God and bears the very stamp of his nature, upholding the universe by his word of power. When he had made purification for sins, he sat down at the right hand of the Majesty on high, having become as much superior to angels as the name he has obtained is more excellent than theirs" (Heb 1:3-4).

I do not wish to be misunderstood as though I were pandering here to the vice of proof-text exegesis. Even less do I wish to allow christological dogmatism to torpedo interreligious dialogue. I have dealt thoroughly with this particular christological New Testament evidence in my book *Born before Time? The Dispute over Christ's Origin,*[1] not only by applying contextual hermeneutics but also *on behalf of interreligious dialogue.* The present discussion presumes that work. But I would like to know what position Knitter takes, "as a Christian," vis-à-vis these christological assertions? How does he interpret the New Testament passages affirming Christ's mediation in creation and the preexistence of God's Son? He does not say a word about these passages in his Five Theses. He acts as if they did not exist. We cannot appeal here to historical selectivity according to the motto "None of this has to do with the historical Jesus." This attempt foundered back with the liberals (Adolf von Harnack and followers) and provoked the justified ire of dialectical theology (Barth and Bultmann).

Why is their ire justified? Simply because for Christians the "Word of God" is the entire New Testament and not only a historically reconstructed Jesus. Fortunately Knitter does not argue in that direction. But he says nothing concerning the New Testament creeds, the oldest of which is *"Jesus* is Lord and none other," or about the other New Testament christologies. That is astounding. Knitter could have explicitly rejected these christological statements. Scholarly analysis of specific New Testament subject matter is legitimate. Such christological assertions are indeed out of step with the contemporary spirit of relativism and pluralism. But he does not do this either. Rather, he engages in what seems to me an internally inconsistent process: he announces that he is doing christology "as a Christian" without grappling in any way with the basic creeds and christologies of the New Testament (not to mention the councils of the early church).

THE NEW TESTAMENT UNDERSTANDING. OF THE "MYSTERY OF GOD"

If, however, as a Christian I accept the New Testament as the normative original document, it is my duty to affirm it, whether I like it or not.

---

[1] Originally published as *Geboren vor aller Zeit? Der Streit um Christi Ursprung* (1990). Published in English as *Born before Time? The Dispute over Christ's Origin* (London: SCM; New York: Crossroad, 1992).

Christians simply do not merely believe in God as "an unsurpassable Mystery, one which can never totally be comprehended or contained in human thought or construct," as Knitter contends. As he had already done in his earlier works, Knitter here proposes an *anthropological-epistemological notion of mystery* that is alien to the New Testament. The New Testament posits instead an *"anthropos-critical" christological notion of mystery*, according to which no human (*anthropos*) has ever seen God (this is "anthropos-critical" insisted upon) except Christ, the Son, who is "in the bosom of the Father" (Jn 1:18). For Paul as well, the "depths" of God are unfathomable, but at the same time the Apostle leaves no doubt that God revealed his mystery in Jesus Christ, who may therefore be called "the mystery of the hidden wisdom of God" (1 Cor 2:7). According to the New Testament, Christians who depend on Jesus as the Christ may trust that this God does not want to be an impenetrable, unfathomable riddle; that God has revealed his secret, and has done so in Jesus Christ. To say that "Jesus is not God's total, definitive, unsurpassable truth" does not do justice to the New Testament (not to mention the creeds of the early church).

Undeniably these christological statements are awkward for interreligious dialogue and difficult to communicate. But I would also expect my non-Christian dialogue partners to express those core beliefs that are most deeply theirs even if these beliefs should be in glaring contradiction to Christian claims and demands. As Jesus Christ is for a Christian "the way, the truth, and the life," analogously for a Jew it is the Torah, for a Muslim the Qur'an, and for a Buddhist the Buddha's Eightfold Path. Why should dialogue become impossible if the partners set out from such opposed starting points, even if such firm claims at first appear to subordinate the other to one's own truth claims? This does not mean that the non-Christian partner is thereby rendered an unequal partner, as Knitter contends, as if all participants in the dialogue did not have the same rights. As a Christian I must put up with the possibility that a representative of Hinduism (for example, someone from the Vedantic tradition) might call me naive and superficial in my understanding of God, or that a Buddhist might tell me that the Christian image of God is far too anthropomorphic (in comparison with *Sunyata*, the Buddhist notion of Ultimate Reality). This would not make me feel in any manner discriminated against or unequally treated. According to my understanding, of course, witnesses to the truth and respect for contrary witnesses to the truth are not mutually exclusive. The decisive question is whether there is the *will to dialogue*, that is, a will to engage one's own truth claims in conversation with competing truth claims of others. Whoever enters an interreligious dialogue must be prepared to do this.

Knitter, however, disputes precisely this connection: he portrays as incapable of dialogue those who want to find ways of communicating their witness to the truth. This is unfair and does not even correspond to the facts. It is not the case that my confession of Christ prevents respect for other confessions of faith, even if I am of the opinion that other faith witnesses do not reveal the same encompassing depth of truth as does the Christian. Non-Christians will not be denied the "right" to bring their truth witness to the dialogue. And non-Christians will surely have enough self-confidence critically to examine my truth claim. Interreligious dialogue does not presuppose the suspension of the truth question but a wrestling for the truth, which I hope to grasp with greater depth and comprehension through dialogue.

IS CHRISTOLOGY CAPABLE
OF INTERRELIGIOUS DIALOGUE?

But is New Testament christology even capable of dialogue? I am convinced that it is, if it is developed concretely out of the New Testament. For just as it is inappropriate simply to trivialize or ignore the christological claim of the New Testament it is equally inappropriate—as is traditionally done—to interpret it in a superior or absolutist manner. The universalist-cosmic New Testament statements about Christ as the mediator in creation (often extolled in hymns and preserved in Christian creeds) can and must be interpreted within the framework of contextual exegesis in a non-absolutist and non-superior way as the faith witness of human beings who are willing to wager their very living and dying upon the reliability and trustworthiness of God. To base the presumption of the superiority of the Christian over the non-Christian on these frequently bold, even reckless and therefore hurtful faith statements is a betrayal of the very thing one seeks to defend as the spirit of Christ. And the spirit of Christ—Knitter is right—is the spirit of the Great Commandment: all-encompassing, unconditional love. Intolerant exclusivism, absolutism, and triumphalism which seek to define the characteristic features of one's theology and the superiority of one's own religion *against* all other religions lacks love and is unchristian. It cannot be justified on the basis of the New Testament.

We urgently need a biblical theology of interreligious dialogue. Christian theologians who are engaged in interreligious dialogue have too frequently ignored or only selectively interpreted the Old and New Testaments. On the other hand, Christian fundamentalists have done everything possible, Bible in hand, to discredit interreligious dialogue as enticement to syncretism. Such a situation is unbearable from the perspective of the history of theology. Theologians who are engaged in interreligious dialogue must not simply surrender the Old and New Testaments to the fundamentalists. They must resolve to take up the battle for the hermeneutic of key christological passages in order to determine whether they exclude interreligious dialogue or whether they actually promote it.

I am convinced that we can take a *middle path*. In the interest of interreligious dialogue the christologies of the New Testament (including the christologies of pre-existence, mediation in creation, and incarnation) need not be watered down, historically faded out, or pluralistically ignored. If read within a contextual hermeneutic, they can be interpreted in terms of interreligious dialogue and rendered fruitful. The christologies of the New Testament are no obstacle for interreligious dialogue but rather its legitimation and incentive.

To sum up, Paul Knitter deserves recognition, consent, respect, and solidarity for his venture. His key points, however, if I read them correctly, fail to do justice to the New Testament, not to mention the tradition of the church. The conversation concerning the function of the christologies of the New Testament and church tradition in interreligious dialogue must be reopened. Paul Knitter's Five Theses may provide the needed spark.

—Translated by Ingrid Shafer and Paul Mojzes

Revisiting the Christological Dimensions of Uniqueness

JOHN MACQUARRIE

I find myself in general agreement with the views advocated by Paul Knitter in his Five Theses on the uniqueness of Jesus Christ in the spectrum of savior figures presented by the major religious faiths on this planet and claimed to be mediators between God and the human race. Indeed, for about thirty years, beginning with the article "Christianity and Other Faiths" in the *Union Seminary Quarterly Review*,[1] I have been teaching views which, I believe, are quite close to those of Professor Knitter, though I have used different terminology. I have urged the case for a combination of "commitment" and "openness" on the part of the religious believer, that is to say, a full commitment to one's own faith and to its mediator (in my own case, this would be to Christianity and Jesus Christ), yet at the same time an "openness" toward other faiths and other mediators, in the sense of acknowledging that God has made himself known and has made salvation available through these other channels also.

Of course, I never pretended that it would be easy to combine these attitudes of commitment and openness. To many people, it may seem like an attempt to serve two masters in a situation where loyalty can be given only to one. How, they will ask, can one have the total commitment that seems to be demanded in a religious faith without making that commitment exclusive? Or, from a different point of view, how can one lay claim to openness if one already has a quite special attachment to a particular savior figure? It is hard to work out a consistent position, but in spite of the difficulties, we surely have to strive for some such position rather than remain content with the religious rivalries of the past. Now that we all have to live much more closely together in the so-called global village, we realize that we can no longer afford these old rival-

---

[1] "Christianity and Other Faiths," *Union Seminary Quarterly Review* 20:1 (November 1964), pp. 39-48. There were responses by Paul Tillich, Roger Shinn, J. R. Chandran, Seymour Siegel, and Paul Lehmann in the next issue of the journal (January 1965).

94

ries. More than that, we see that they brought discredit on the several religious faiths and were in fact in contradiction to some of the central truths taught by those faiths.

Having indicated my general agreement with Paul Knitter's Five Theses, let me now consider each of them in turn.

THESIS 1

Previous understandings of the uniqueness of Jesus **can** *be reinterpreted.*

This thesis, I think, is true, but I believe one might go even further and say that these "previous understandings" have never spoken with a single voice, and that the view that there is a multiform revelation of God has had a place in Christian teaching from the beginning. The New Testament itself does not give us unambiguous teaching on the question. Even within individual books we may find more than one point of view seeking expression. In Acts, Peter tells us (ch. 4) that "there is salvation in no one else" except Jesus, but Paul at Athens (ch. 17) seems to find at least some common ground between himself and the Greeks. John certainly introduces the expression "only begotten" and claims that "no one comes to the Father" except through the Son (ch. 14). But the words reported in John's gospel are not just the words of Jesus of Nazareth but of the Word or Logos himself, who has been with God since the beginning, and is "the true light" (ch.1) that in some sense and to some degree enlightens every human being—including, we must suppose, the teachers and savior figures of the non-Christian religions. The epistle to the Hebrews certainly assigns a unique priestly role to Jesus Christ, but in the great pageant of the men and women of faith (ch. 11) the line is traced back not just to Abraham and the Hebrew patriarchs, but to Abel and Noah, mythological figures who belong to the whole human race. John Baillie commented that this passage in Hebrews shows us "the earliest Christian way of recognizing and explaining the common elements that pervade all the religions and therefore all the moral traditions of mankind."[2]

The two views, already present in the New Testament, reappear in the patristic age. As early as 150 C.E., Justin Martyr was recognizing that the Logos had spoken also to the Greeks, through such thinkers as Heraclitus and Socrates. Though an exclusive claim for Jesus Christ was perhaps dominant, an alternative view was never suppressed. It is sometimes said that the doctrine of incarnation does draw an absolute dividing line between Jesus Christ and other savior figures. John Hick, for instance,

---

[2] *Our Knowledge of God* (Philadelphia: Scribner, 1939), p. 18.

regarded this doctrine as a barrier to dialogue. But I myself would say that from creation onward, God (or the Logos, if one prefers) has been incarnating itself in the world in many ways and in many degrees. To quote Teilhard de Chardin, "The prodigious expanses of time which preceded the first Christmas were not empty of Christ." It is in some such way that we have to interpret something that was said to me when I was holding a seminar on christology in India more than twenty years ago. A member of the group, who had grown up as a high-caste brahmin, declared: "In India, christology is possible only as krishnology." I would not quarrel with that assertion. It is very much in the spirit of Raymond Pannikar's book *The Unknown Christ of Hinduism*. If it is not insisted that incarnation is an event uniquely and exclusively associated with Jesus Christ, then the idea of incarnation, so far from being a barrier, can be a most valuable topic for dialogue.

So I think that as far as thesis 1 is concerned, I am simply saying that while some previous Christian understandings of the uniqueness of Jesus need reinterpretation, one can also say that when we search in the traditions of christology, we find already extant interpretations of Jesus which need to be rescued from the obscurity cast over them by the dominant emphasis on the notion of the "only begotten."

THESIS 2

Given the ethical imperative of dialogue, previous understandings of the uniqueness of Jesus **must** *be reinterpreted.*

It seems to me that Knitter's second thesis is again one that will command wide assent. There is, however, an irony in the way in which the thesis has been stated. The first reason given for the need of dialogue is the fact that we have been forced to recognize our interdependence and the need for cooperation because of the threats to the future of the human race. The irony is that not the visions of savior figures, not the sacrifices of their disciples in spreading the vision, not the wisdom of philosophers, have brought about a consciousness of human solidarity, but rather the deterioration of the earth through human exploitation, the oppression of some through the aggression of others, the threat of war in a destructive form without parallel, the sheer aggregation of numbers forcing us closer and closer together. This may well suggest a pessimistic view of the future, with Jesus Christ, the Buddha, Muhammad, and all the other mediators fading out of the picture, while the course of history is determined by purely material forces. This is an irony that was well portrayed by a British scientist some years ago when he wrote a novel in which the appearance of a dark cloud from space caused an immediate cessation of national rivalries as earth's peoples faced the common threat. When the cloud eventually receded without having revealed any hostile intent or inflicted any damage, the earthlings promptly returned to their former nasty ways. Or could it happen that the accumulated threats that are driving us together may awaken deeper desires for a salvation such as the religions have long promised?

At any rate, we can agree with Knitter that verbal proclamation in itself will hardly be enough, and perhaps past failures have been in large measure due to proclamation not backed up by obedience to an ethical imperative. The question is one of mission. What does that word mean for Christianity today and for other religions that are also missionary in outlook?

I do not say that proclamation is simply a thing of the past. There probably is still a place for the old-fashioned type of missionary proclamation, especially in the secularized nations of Europe and North America.

As far as Christian mission in other parts of the world is concerned, I fully agree with Knitter that it should take the form of open dialogue rather than proclamation. I have learned the lesson taught me by my Indian friend—in India, christology must take the form of krishnology.

But I suggest that even dialogue does not go far enough, and I don't think Professor Knitter would disagree. If we are asked, "Who is the great Christian missionary of our time?" I think most of us might answer, "Mother Teresa!" So far as I know, she doesn't hire the city stadium for a preaching session, she doesn't engage in profound dialogue with Indian professors at Benares, but she tends the sick and dying on the streets of Calcutta. Could anything communicate more clearly than that the meaning of Jesus Christ?

THESIS 3

Jesus' salvific role can be reinterpreted in terms of **truly** *but not* **only.**

Here again I would have no basic disagreement with Knitter, though I would wish to use a somewhat different vocabulary. He is correct in saying that in Jesus there is not, and indeed cannot be, a *full* revelation of God, for the infinite cannot be fully comprehended in the finite. But Christian dogma has never claimed that the whole of God was incarnate in Christ. It was the Word, the Second Person of the Trinity, who is said to have been incarnated. Even at that, Calvin maintained that something of the Logos remained outside of Christ—a doctrine known as *illud extra Calvinisticum*, intended to counter the Lutheran tendency to maintain that the Logos was wholly contained in Christ. On the other hand, I do not go along with Knitter in rejecting the word *definitive*. It seems to me, this word always implies definitive *for* someone (or some community). I confess that Christ is definitive for me, both in the sense that he defines *for me* (and presumably for Christians generally) the true nature of a human being, and also the nature of God, whose image (Col 1) is revealed in him.

In this connection, I think we must notice that the same finitude which prevents us from saying that God is wholly revealed in Christ also prevents us from embracing an unlimited pluralism. Though I can be open to the truth in other faiths, both my life and my intellectual powers are too limited for me to reach even a moderately adequate understanding of all the religions that might bring spiritual enrichment. Those of us who are Christians recognize that there is much in our own faith and much in Jesus Christ with which we have failed to come to terms. Some people do acquire—through long study, dialogue, and social intercourse—a living knowledge of perhaps one religion other than their own. A good example is Kenneth Cragg, who has entered probably as far as a Christian can into a sympathetic understanding of the mind and heart of Islam. But that accomplishment is exceptional.

So when I say that Christianity is definitive for me, I am not, as Knitter seems to think, making a boastful or arrogant claim. I am not making a comparison with another faith. I am simply saying that within my limited faith and experience, Jesus Christ is *sufficient*. Through him I think I have been brought into relation to God. I have, of course, learned something about other faiths and even studied some of the languages in which their scriptures are written. I hope to enter further into their treasures. But perhaps I would do better to work at deepening my own faith, or I might find myself in danger of becoming a dilettante.

THESIS 4

Today, the uniqueness of Jesus can be found in his insistence that salvation or the Reign of God must be realized in this world *through* human actions *of love and justice.*

Perhaps this is not saying anything very different from what I wrote above about Mother Teresa as one who in an eminent way communicates the meaning of Jesus Christ in our world. But I think we must always remember something that Reinhold Niebuhr never tired of teaching: the Reign or Kingdom of God is an eschatological ideal which will never be fully achieved in this sinful world. We may prepare for it and work for it, but it remains a "transcendent norm," in Niebuhr's language, and he claimed that the error of regarding it as "simple possibility" is one to which American liberalism has been peculiarly prone.[3]

Maybe it will seem incredible to twentieth-century people that the Reign of God lies beyond history, but it can hardly be denied that Jesus and the New Testament writers thought of it in that way.

---

[3] *The Nature and Destiny of Man*, II, p. 90.

THESIS 5

The orthodoxy of this pluralistic reinterpretation of the uniqueness of Jesus must be grounded primarily in the ability of such a reinterpretation to nurture a holistic Christian spirituality. . . . The proposed understanding of Jesus as God's truly but not only saving word does meet this criterion.

Here Knitter comes back to a point he made in the course of expounding thesis 1—that the "*lex credendi* (norms for belief) must resonate with and foster the *lex orandi* (norms for spirituality)" and that such norms "are dangerously inadequate if they are not linked to the *lex sequendi* (norms for discipleship)." But here a new point turns up and will call for further discussion. Both Gabriel Moran and William Burrows are quoted for the point that in Christianity (and presumably in other faiths) there is a distinctness which need not be interpreted in terms of better or worse but which certainly makes them different. To quote Burrows: "The uniqueness of Christ and Christian life lies in a distinct structure of existence; the Christian manner of being a saint . . . is unique."[4] What is "a distinct structure of existence?" Is there more than one "archetype" (to use Kant's expression) of human existence? Has Knitter sufficiently taken into account the differences among the religions and their ideals for humanity? What does this say about ethical norms? Or about how one might conceive the Reign of God? Are Christian, Buddhist, and Islamic ideals compatible? For instance, recently a Christian bishop in the Sudan was publicly flogged for (alleged) adultery. No doubt this was sincerely understood as a realization of Islamic teaching in society, but even if we deplore adultery, we may think the punishment was not appropriate. We might even remember the interpolated passage in John's gospel about the woman taken in adultery (8:3-11).

---

[4] In a letter to Paul Knitter, quoted by the latter in connection with thesis 5.

Asian and African Voices on the Uniqueness of Jesus

JOHN MBITI

In preparing my response to Paul Knitter's Five Theses, I felt annoyed with myself for agreeing to respond because (a) I do not find the issue of *the uniqueness of Christ* discussed in the Bible. (b) My encounter with this term has been largely among people who use it with aggressive undertones toward followers of other or no religions. (c) Besides teaching at the University of Bern I have worked in a large parish (12,500 members) of the Reformed Church of the Canton Bern for over twelve years and have not heard even one reference to the uniqueness of Christ in the parish and rarely at the university. (d) I get the impression that, apart from some (older and evangelical?) missionaries and a few theologians in Asia and Africa, the issue is not being discussed there, at least not in the literature I could find. It seems as if Christians and others there who pay attention to Jesus are wrestling with more burning questions (for them) concerning who Jesus Christ is and what he means to them.

Nevertheless I am grateful for the Five Theses of Paul Knitter. They are stimulating and provocative. He reminds us that there are some circles where the uniqueness of Christ is being or should be raised and reexamined. Thus we cannot ignore the issue.

I have chosen to address myself particularly to thesis 4, which deals with a reinterpretation of the uniqueness of Christ. As Knitter's thesis draws heavily from America and Europe—and nobody can embrace the whole globe—I confine myself to what is currently being said about Jesus Christ in Africa and Asia.

I hear voices which are articulating loudly or feebly how Jesus encounters people in their different situations in Africa and Asia. It is at the point of these encounters that I find meaning in talking about the uniqueness of Jesus. Somehow he penetrates into their being, into their concerns, into their joys and problems. He becomes a companion in the wide sense; they feel his presence in what he was and did during his earthly life. He does not necessarily perform wonders out of the blue to rescue them, but he is with the people, understands their situation, shares their concerns, and gives them hope for the future. This is not a theoretical uniqueness, but a genuine presence at the historical level in which Jesus shares our life. It is down to earth. At the same time, in that awareness of him (through different images) there is a deeper and spiritual presence which uplifts human life and sets it reaching toward a higher ground—whether one of hope, freedom, justice, dignity, harmony, or being oneself.

There are many examples of this multiplicity of experiencing, responding to, or reinterpreting Jesus Christ in more ways than, and besides, the traditional images. Naturally, some of those inherited christological images or symbols remain meaningful, but they are also being recast, reinterpreted. The uniqueness of Jesus cannot be isolated from traditional and new images of Jesus because, in the final analysis, it is probably their sum total which makes Jesus so unequivocally unique.

In the Asian situation characterized by, among other things, poverty and religious plurality, we hear that

> God addresses the experience of suffering through a "gravity-bound" love that draws God into human history and into the historical lives of human persons. . . . This is not God's suffering "on behalf of" in order to solve the conundrum of human suffering; rather, God suffers "with" humankind. Here vicariousness is replaced by identification. The crucified God is the God who identifies all the way with us in our suffering and death. He suffers with us and dies with us.
>
> God's love for humanity and God's suffering with humanity coalesce in the term "pain-love." This suffering God feels pain-love; that is, God loves people to the extent of feeling their pain, as a mother feels pain in childbirth for the child whom she loves. Jesus was the pain-love of God in his earthly life.[1]

Consequently, new images of Jesus are emerging from Asian women's movements for self-determination and liberation, as the Korean woman theologian Chung Hyun Kyung tells us:

> The freer Asian women become from the patriarchal authorities of their family, church, and society, the more creative they become in naming their experience of Jesus Christ. Sometimes the images of Jesus are transformed to the degree that they show the radical discontinuity between the ones found in the Jewish and Christian cul-

---

[1] Priscilla Pope-Levison and John R. Levison, *Jesus in Global Contexts* (Louisville, Ky.: Westminster/John Knox Press, 1992), p. 67. In this and other observations the authors cite Asian theologians.

ture and those from the Asian women's movement. Some Asian women have become confident enough in themselves to name the presence of Jesus Christ in their own culture, indigenous religions, and secular political movements, a Christological identity that is not directly connected in the traditional sense with Christianity. They use religio-political symbols and motifs from their movement in order to describe what Jesus means for them in today's Asia. This is a *Christological transformation* created out of Asian women's experiences as they struggle for full humanity. The old Christological paradigms are transformed, new meanings are achieved, and diverse images of Jesus Christ emerge. Asian women as meaning-makers jump into an unknown open future shaping a new Christianity out of their own experience that never before existed in history. The following are examples of new, emerging images of Jesus Christ derived from Asian women who believe in their historical lived experience more than imposed authority.

Chung goes on to consider Jesus as Mother, Woman, Shaman, Worker, and Grain. She explains, for example, how

many Asian women portray Jesus with the image of mother. They see Jesus as a compassionate one who feels the suffering of humanity deeply, suffers and weeps with them. Since Jesus' compassion is so deep, the mother image is the most appropriate one for Asian women to express their experience of Jesus' compassion. . . . Like a mother who laments over her dead son who died in the wars in Indochina, like many weeping Korean mothers whose sons and daughters were taken by the secret police, Jesus cried out for the pain of suffering humanity. . . . According to Lee [Oo Chung] . . . Jesus took on himself the pain and suffering of all his neighbors even of all humankind.[2]

The emphasis on the suffering of Jesus is not a new idea, as such. But it is put into the context of Asian realities and these clothe it with a burning urgency. Suddenly the events of nearly two thousand years ago in Judea and Galilee, an entirely different cultural setting, become alive and Jesus is very much present in them. In Galilee, Jesus

felt that one by one the griefs of all the people in the world were coming to rest on his shoulders. The sorrows began to weigh on his back with an onerous crunch, like the heavy cross that he himself would have to carry sometime in the future. . . .

---

[2] Chung Hyun Kyung, *Struggle to Be the Sun Again* (Maryknoll, N.Y.: Orbis Books, 1990), pp. 62ff.

Jesus had to go through every misery and pain that men and women go through because otherwise he could not truly share in the misery and pain of humankind, and because otherwise he couldn't face us to say: "Look, I am at your side. I have suffered like you. Your misery—I understand it; I went through it all myself." The burdens he had carried throughout his life fell on him with a final crashing weight. On the cross, there could be no mistake that he was now one with the suffering masses. And, as in life, so in death and beyond death, he remained the "Eternal Companion of those who suffer."

After the resurrection, the disciples realized the import of Jesus as a suffering messiah. If all of life is suffering, then suffering is the one experience that unites all people together, regardless of status or class. Therefore the disciples "realize that a messiah with a gold crown on his head" might save a nation but cannot redeem suffering humanity. And it is humanity in suffering that longs to be taken into the bosom of God laid open in the suffering of Jesus the messiah.

In the resurrected community of Jesus, the Church, there can be no talk of love without pain. . . . The distance between love and suffering is very short indeed. With this depth of identification with suffering, the Church embodies the pain-love of Jesus. His singular pain-love becomes communal compassion, "together-loving and together-suffering."[3]

Another voice links traditional Chinese thinking with Christ, through the image of *yin* and *yang*.

Yin presupposes the necessity of *yang* and *yang* cannot exist without *yin*. . . . Such concepts as the nature of divine transcendence and immanence, God as personal, Jesus as the Christ, or the relation of body and spirit can all be illuminated by the *yin-yang* mode of thinking. Jesus as the Christ, as both God and man, cannot really be understood in terms of either/or. How can man also be God? . . . In *yin-yang* terms, he [Christ] can be thought of as both God and man at the same time. In him God is not separated from man nor man from God. They are in complementary relationship. He is God because of man: he is man because of God.[4]

Let us move from Asian to African voices and take only a limited number of examples. The Ghanaian-Nigerian theologian Mercy Amba

---

[3] Pope-Levison and Levison, p. 68.

[4] Anton Wessels, *Images of Jesus*, English trans. (Grand Rapids, Mich.: Eerdmans, 1990), pp. 156f.

Oduyoye, like many other women theologians concerned about patriarchal domination in church and society, focuses on the liberating work of Jesus. She writes: "The Christ of Christianity touches human needs at all levels. . . . We find Jesus in the New Testament snatching women and men away from all domination, even from the jaws of death."[5]

Another understanding of the saving presence of Jesus comes from the East African Revival Movement, which started in Rwanda and Uganda in 1929 and spread widely all over eastern Africa and beyond. Its emphasis is upon a brokenness of heart before Christ, who removes barriers, according to Colossians 3:11.

> That Christ is a revolutionary who over-turned man-made structures, obliterating racial, ethnic, sectarian and other barriers is a message the East African Revival has taught and upheld. . . . It challenged the status quo in the African mission field. . . . Due to its vision of brokenness at the foot of the Cross the story of the Revival is a testimony of how the Revival vision of Christ and His achievement at the Cross has brought down blockades of colour, class, status, ethnicity, sex and education, and how it has merged pulpit and pew.[6]

In other African theological circles the image of kinship relationship with Jesus is taken up. He underwent the necessary "rites" of being initiated into humanhood. So we hear that,

> Jesus, as elder brother, developed as a mature member of his community through rites of passage. Genealogies clarify his tribal affiliation (Mt 1:1-18; Lk 3:23-38). Attended to at birth with the required offerings and period of maternal purity (Lk 1-2), he went on to join in solidarity with his people at his baptism. Following a period of seclusion in the wilderness, he entered public life, healing and teaching among his brothers and sisters. His life ended in the final rite of passage, death on the cross, which symbolized completeness rather than shame. "He died on the cross because he was a perfect, complete, entire, mature and responsible Man."

As elder brother who undergoes communal rites of passage and cares for his younger brothers and sisters, Jesus can find a place in the kinship ties of Africa. "Our Brother Christ is walking through

---

[5] Mercy Amba Oduyoye, *Hearing and Knowing* (Maryknoll, N.Y.: Orbis Books, 1986), pp. 97ff.

[6] Hannah W. Kinoti, "Christology in the East African Revival Movement," in *Jesus in African Christianity*, ed. J. N. K. Mugambi and Laurenti Magesa (Nairobi: Initiatives, 1989), pp. 60ff., esp. pp. 73ff.

the copper mines of Zambia and the forests of Zaire; Our Brother Christ is walking through Africa, Alleluia."

Yet this interpretation, on its own, accentuates the human component of the incarnation without incorporating the divine-vine element. But while it was "as an ordinary man that Jesus died . . . the great Christian differentia comes obviously from the fact of the Resurrection by which the Christian faith stands or falls." The centrality of the resurrection raises the further possibility that Jesus is firstborn both of the living and of the ancestors or living dead.[7]

A further elaboration on the image of kinship regards Jesus as our Ancestor. Among exponents of this image is Bénézet Bujo from Zaire, who writes: "Modern Africans can only follow in the footsteps of Jesus Christ if they see in Jesus, not some proud tyrant, but rather the Proto-Ancestor whose last will was an appeal for human love and for untiring effort to overcome all inhumanity."

Bujo concludes:

All our considerations on Jesus Christ as Proto-Ancestor bring us finally to the one reality which constitutes the real framework of these short reflections: the Cross. To understand Jesus as Proto-Ancestor means accompanying him on the way of the Cross. It is not enough to stand at the foot of the Cross or to gaze upon the scene at Golgotha from a distance. We are called to nail ourselves to the cross with Jesus and to suffer with him. This cross will always remain a scandal and a folly. Only the African who has been converted and has faith will see in the Crucified Jesus the Proto-Ancestor with whom he or she can identify.

Jesus is Proto-Ancestor, the eschatological Adam, life-giving Spirit (1 Cor 15:45), only because he passed through death on the Cross. It is the remembering of this event, and the retelling of it, that is both liberating and challenging. This it is which humanizes and purifies the African ethos.[8]

Among the Gbaya people of Cameroon in western Africa, a tree known as Sore is used for virtually all activities of people's lives: celebrations and rituals, such as birth, naming, circumcision, marriage, and burial rites; drawing up peace and reconciliation agreements; treating some illnesses; cooling fights and settling disputes; hunting and establishing new villages; and more. It is regarded as "a tree of life." The Gbaya

---

[7] Pope-Levison and Levison, pp. 103f., citing several African theologians.

[8] Bénézet Bujo, *African Theology in Its Social Context* (Maryknoll, N.Y.: Orbis Books, 1992), p. 91 and passim.

Christians look at and interpret Jesus Christ as their "Sore." He fits beautifully into this symbol, which is so meaningful to their traditional thinking and daily life.[9]

In considering the Christian encounter with African religion, there are those who seek the presence of Jesus Christ in African religion. He is not named as such in the traditional religion of African peoples, which dates back to prehistoric times. But these interpreters find his presence at work in African religion as men, women, and children practice values such as "peace, justice, joy, harmony, love, fight against evil; in fostering fellowship with one another and maintaining harmony with nature; in celebrating birth as victory over death and in renewing community life through rites of passage . . . ; in praying, praising and giving honour (glory) to God."[10]

These are but a few among many serious voices depicting Jesus Christ in Africa and Asia. What do they attempt to say concerning him? They are partly reinterpreting his uniqueness. At the same time they are pointing to a complexity of christological dimensions, some of which are treasured as ancient images, some of which are largely or entirely new, and others which had apparently been neglected by the church at various times in its history but are being rediscovered. All these add up to the many faces of Jesus Christ, to his "flexibility" to be all things to all people, in all places, and at all times. He is unique in that he cannot be possessed or monopolized by any one set of images or symbols; he cannot be contained in his entirety in one place; and he cannot be exhaustively interpreted or understood. He is unique in that it is possible for him to be and not to be, to appear and to disappear. That is the unique nature of Christ, which spans time and space—yet makes him present everywhere. He may be briefly or indefinitely "hidden," as he was from the followers who walked with him on the day of the resurrection from Jerusalem to Emmaus (Lk 24:13-35). But in that encounter he may also be recognized and named, especially at the breaking of bread, which he gives to all.

---

[9] See the fuller exposition by Thomas G. Christensen, *An African Tree of Life* (Maryknoll, N.Y.: Orbis Books, 1990).

[10] John S. Mbiti, "Is Jesus Christ in African Religion?" in *Exploring Afro-Christology*, ed. John Samuel Pobee (Bern and New York: Peter Lang, 1992), p. 28. Cf. Judith M. Bahemuka, "The Hidden Christ in African Traditional Religion," in Mugambi and Magesa, pp. 1ff.

The Uniqueness of Christ and the Plurality of Humankind

JOSÉ MÍGUEZ BONINO

It is impossible to address Knitter's Five Theses without beginning by recognizing the enormous debt that we owe the author. Those of us who have frequently had to work and teach in the area of comparative theologies have found in works like *Doing Local Theologies* a wealth of analyses and insights; a wise and fruitful organization of models and patterns; and a constant resource of bibliographical information that has made his work invaluable. Now he again opens a very suggestive and convincing path for dealing with a question that has become central in ecumenical theology. As I look back to the 1992 debates at the last Assembly of the Ecumenical Association of Third World Theologians (EATWOT) in Nairobi, I find in Knitter's theses an excellent guide for tackling the issues that were central in that meeting.

With some queries here and there I would not have problems in accepting most of the theses. Knitter seems able to hold what is central to the Christian faith and at the same time to make possible a free and grateful recognition of God's presence and action in the variety of the ways in which humankind has recognized, celebrated, lived, and reflected its relation to the divine. At the same time, his constant reminder of the varying and changing ways in which Christians themselves have expressed their faith and interpreted Christ makes us aware of the historical and conditioned character of our christologies and utter the necessary caveat against confusing the Christ with our christologies. It is only as the Christ is seen, received, recognized, and interpreted through time and space that we begin to learn "the riches of grace and wisdom" hidden in him. And who can doubt that the religious, philosophical and ethical insights of the different peoples and cultures have revealed to us that richness?

In fact, Knitter could well have—in terms of Christian theology— framed his interpretation in terms of a doctrine of the freedom of the Holy Spirit. I suspect that much of our inability to deal with this kind of issue is a theology of the Holy Spirit which has so unilaterally "restricted" the role of the Spirit to the work of the Son that any operation of God in the world had somehow to be justified exclusively in relation to creation and was thereby devoid of dynamism and historicity. One wonders whether this restriction has resulted in an ecclesiastical "monopoly" of the Holy Spirit or whether the "ecclesiastical monopoly of salvation" inspired this limited doctrine of the Spirit. Particularly in the West we have been so obsessed with the *filioque* that we have forgotten that, in any case, the Creed says that the Holy Spirit *ex patre . . . procedit* (proceeds from the Father). Societies, cultures, and religions—including Christianity—are not static; neither do they evolve, particularly in our world today, as isolated streams. They reinterpret themselves as they face new questions and challenges, including the religious and theological questions and challenges that they meet as they rub shoulders in our plural conditions. Why can we not recognize that the Holy Spirit, who moved over the waters in creation, who anointed Cyrus, who begat Jesus in the womb of the Virgin, and who descended at Pentecost causing people to hear the message in everybody's "own native language" has also been active in the history, culture, and religious life of others as well as in ours, and continues to move us today? To be sure, such recognition would not end all theological problems. Still, as a Western Council put it in 1274, the Spirit proceeds from the Father and Son "not as from two principles" (*non tanquam ex duobus principiis*) but "as from one principle" (*tamquam ex uno principio*). But that unity cannot simply operate as a christological "control" of the work of the Spirit, but also as a pneumatological universalization of the presence of the Christ. The points the author makes in his first thesis would gain, I think, in theological force by placing christology in a Trinitarian framework and developing its pneumatological dimension.

As a Protestant I would have some quarrel with *the* criterion of christological legitimacy formulated by Knitter in his first thesis, that the *lex credendi* must "resonate with and foster" the *lex orandi* and be linked with the *lex sequendi*. "In other words," he summarizes, "any new understanding of Jesus . . . must flow from and nurture a saving experience of and commitment to Jesus . . . and a resolute following of him in the world." I could not agree more wholeheartedly with this formulation, but I miss the reference to scripture, not as a repository of dogmatic definitions, but as a "story" that has to be constantly read, heard, repeated, and received as we reinterpret new ways of praying and following with which doctrine must "resonate." In fact, I am tempted to say that the best way Christians can participate in the dialogue is constantly to retell *the story* without much interpretation, and let it create its own "resonance."

My main concern, however, is not about the theological articulation. Rather, I suggest that there is a previous step that has to qualify our total assessment of the "dialogue situation." My question about Professor Knitter's approach, or rather about the prioritizing of this discussion, lies in a different direction. I wonder to what extent the problem of the Christian's relation to people of different faiths is primarily a christological question, or, indeed, a theological question, or even a religious question. Christians, to be sure, have to try to clarify for themselves the theological issues that arise out of their dealings with peoples of other faiths. In fact, we should be equally concerned with theological issues which arise in our dealing with peoples of our own faith. But is it not really a prior question to try to understand the conditions in which we meet this people? It is the danger of abstracting the christological question from the context of the totality of our relations that makes me uncomfortable. I'll try to explain what I mean.

1. It is an obvious fact that we do not meet religions but people. In that sense a human encounter precedes and conditions any dialogue. In Knitter's theses—perhaps with the exception of the fourth one—the dialogue on who Jesus Christ is seems to be "abstracted" from the conditions and the manner of the encounter. Thus, it takes the nature of a conversation between religions rather than a dialogue between people. Naturally, abstraction is a necessary step as we look back to understand any human encounter or as we look forward to it. But the abstraction, to be useful, has to abstract from the totality of the experience, including its personal, historical, cultural, and sociological elements.

2. The encounter takes place in the framework of some context which we share. Even in a very elementary—but not insignificant—sense, we meet to dialogue in a room, in a place, at a time. More profoundly, though, we "theologians" of one or another faith or religion carry with us a "people" who confess that faith, who carry its tradition, who have inculturated that faith, and who live it every day—consciously or unconsciously—in their habitual ways. More and more, these different "constituencies" live in the same continents, under the same governments, within a social and economic structure, and in fact they shape and are shaped by all these factors. Increasingly, the context and its problematics are global. From such situations different kinds of issues and problems become central and crucial for all. A common context, therefore, is not an external reality but a commonality that—at least in part—is constitutive of encounter and consequently enters into any dialogue in which these people may engage. Should not any religious dialogue begin by examining these common contexts and problematics? Do we not learn more about ourselves and our interlocutors, about our faith and theirs, by understanding how we and they live, interpret, and act out this common locus that we all inhabit than by merely comparing in the abstract our "religious views"? People unemployed in Spain or Brazil, a middle class alarmed by mass immigration from outside, "yuppies" in the new "economic aristocracy" in Japan or Argentina—

these may be Catholic, Moslem, Pentecostal, Umbanda, Shintoist, or agnostic, and no doubt this will make a difference, but it will make it most significantly in relation to the common problems they all face. Is not that the best place to begin understanding ourselves and others?

3. For us Christians the point has to be pushed one more step. Ever since the fourth century almost all of our religious encounters have taken place from one place: the place of power. Whatever we say about "our" Christ, even in the most modest and conciliatory ways, is said by those who have the power—economic, political, military—to make their claim stand! It is not so much the uniqueness of Christ, or Christ's universal claim that offends and repels: it is our uniqueness, our universal claim. Early Christians were able to make extraordinary claims about Christ because they made them "from below" and supported them by their martyrdom and not by their legions. Whenever a poor Pentecostal cleaning woman in my country "testifies" to her faith to her employer, however extreme and exclusive her claims may be, she opens a free conversation, because it stands simply on the confession of her faith and not on her cultural, social, or economic superiority. It is not theological concessions that make dialogue possible, if the concessions are inevitably seen as—and in fact objectively are, whatever the intentions—instruments (in fact, crafty ways) of the powerful.

Certainly we cannot walk out of our own skin. We cannot unwrite the history of Christianity in the world and begin again as a small, persecuted sect. Sometimes people have called for a moratorium on all missionary and evangelizing activity. It might not be a bad idea to stop all organized—ecclesiastically planned and strategically directed—mission and evangelization and let the faith of Christian people in the world move freely "as the Spirit." But we cannot realistically expect such a thing. What I think *is* possible is that we take seriously the nature and conditions of the encounter and try to relate dialogue to these conditions. In that context, the theological orientations that Professor Knitter offers us could perhaps be much more fruitful.

Whose Uniqueness?

RAIMON PANIKKAR

History has given us enough examples of hotly debated issues, allegedly vital, that turned out *later* to be seen as pseudo-problems: nature and grace, predestination and free will, the Almighty and the reality of evil, creation in time or for time . . . up to the chicken and the egg.

Could we not be facing a similar case here? The question of the uniqueness of Christ arose from the idea of Christianity being the only one and true religion, the unique and fully saving religion. Christianity was supposed to be unique because it alone saves. This may be right or wrong, but it is not incoherent, it makes sense. Once this idea has been given up by a good number of theologians, a strategic retreat has shifted the question to Jesus: is Jesus unique? My submission is that this uniqueness may prove to be yet another pseudo-problem.

I have dealt with this specific issue for the last forty years. I am glad it comes again to the fore, because it will certainly help to purify Christian self-understanding from the stink of fanaticism.

Paul Knitter sticks to the uniqueness of Christ, and I do as well, but perhaps for a different reason. For him the criterion is discipleship—and for me also, but perhaps from different motivation. The person of Jesus enkindles in him a divine love for the neighbor and thirst for justice in the world—and so it does for me. But I will speak from now on for myself.

If I love my neighbor it is because I find my neighbor lovable. I cannot love out of an extrinsic command to love. The Christian theologian in me tells me that I find my neighbor lovable because the grace of Christ is poured on her, and so I discover his face. But the Buddhist mind, which I also have, tells me that I love her because we all have Buddha-nature. The Hindu in me leads me to discover karma as universal solidarity, and this links me with my neighbor as to myself. The secular person, which I also am, makes me ponder the fact that all those (and also other) traditions, in spite of their lofty words, have pretty well forgotten to love their neighbors in deed, and leads me to suspect that there is a *Zeitgeist* (not uniquely Christian), an actual *mythos*, I would rather say, which makes us realize that without such a passion for justice the world faces disaster and we harm our own humanness.

It is significant, not to say suspicious, that precisely now Christians (as well as many others) speak of salvation to "be realized *in this world* through human actions," when for centuries they (and others as well) have given the impression that their "reign is not of this world" and that faith rather than works has saving power—not to speak of connivance with the powers that be in order to preach resignation, patience, and postponement of justice until the coming world.

It is a telling "sign of the times" that we all now seem to stress the "Unknown Christ," the "Universal Buddha-nature," the "Cosmic Karma" and the "Humanum." Where is the uniqueness here? Are some more unique than others? Do we not mean perhaps distinctiveness?

For too long theologians have entrenched themselves in a specialized fortress and neglected philosophy, from which they did not want to be contaminated once the handmaid of theology came of age—so the Enlightenment saga goes.

To put it all in one sentence: *identity* is not synonymous with *identification*, nor *uniqueness* with *distinctiveness*. Christ's identity is not our identification of him, nor is his uniqueness his distinctiveness.

The uniqueness of Christ has been interpreted as meaning a *unique* person (Jesus, the son of Mary), with a *unique* message (say, the Beatitudes or love for all, including enemies), eliciting a *unique* praxis (helping the other or striving for justice), and with a *unique* function (salvation or liberation of humankind).

Now, the fourth uniqueness cannot be defended unless one condemns all the "non-followers" of the unique Christ. The third and second uniquenesses are simply not the case. Many saints, prophets, and traditions have uttered and practiced all those sublime doctrines—independently and even before Christ. There remains only the first uniqueness, which is an obvious truth: everyone is unique.

Perhaps our usual philosophical instruments are not adequate to tackle the problem. This would not be the only such case. Statements like "I and the Father are one," "before Abraham I am," "He that loveth his life loseth it," and similar utterances are incomprehensible, to say the least, to mainline Western thought. Let us recall, not so incidentally, that simple events cannot be the subject matter of modern science, and that modern science has shaped our modes of thinking. Jesus Christ as a *person* is unique, as is everybody else. Christianity as *religion* is not unique; it is one religion among many. The unique *saving function* of Christianity (as the only religion that can save) can hardly be defended. Where is the uniqueness?

Does the uniqueness lie perchance in the conjunction of the three? In the confluence of the three *leges—credendi, orandi, sequendi*? Curiously enough, some scholastics seemed to imply this when they were defending that to be a Christian was the easiest (and thus ordinary) way to go to heaven. Christianity spreads the means to salvation, as it were, making them available to the common folks. They spoke of extraordinary ways outside of Christianity. With the geographic expansion of Christianity and an increased intercultural awareness this answer lacks convincing power. Yet, I detect distant similarities in the positions of Küng, Knitter, and others: the Christian has some advantages, after all.

Another modern trend emphasizes the personal aspect of the experience of uniqueness, thus liberating the Christian from the blame of intolerance. It is the position of "Jesus is my Savior; take it or leave it." To be sure, my mother is unique to me. She has given birth to me. Similarly, Christ is unique to me. He has given life to me. But the simile breaks down here because the one function of mothering is hypostatized in many subjects, while the christic function is attributed to one single subject called Jesus-Christ. Mother is a common noun, Christ a proper noun. If it were also a common name (the anointed), it could not claim to be unique.

This means that we cannot avoid the question: in what is Jesus unique? If we want to say something more than the old *individuum ineffabile*, we must add some qualification to Christ. If each individual is unique, we must find a unique adjective to that individual to spell out the specific meaning of uniqueness. Knitter makes it plain when he writes: "The content of Jesus' uniqueness." He assumes that the operative uniqueness lies not in his person but in some content. He argues that this content today lies "in his insistence that salvation" is realized through inner-worldly actions of love and justice. He shifts from a uniqueness of theory to one of praxis. I cannot agree more, except that I do not see any uniqueness in this.

Christian scripture puts it more pointedly: "The Man Jesus Christ is the one Mediator" (1 Tm 2:5). But we discover then that the simple sentence "one God and one mediator between God and Men" introduces a whole ideology. It implies an entire theology, anthropology, and cosmology. We realize then that the problem of Christ's uniqueness is no problem at all. It arises only when we link up this concept with another one: universality. My mother is unique (to me), but she is not a universal mother. Christ is unique (to me). But this does not mean that he is the universal savior. Nor does it mean that there are many Christs. Would not my mother cease to be unique to me if there were many mothers identical to her?

Here we face a dilemma. Either we defend the universality of Christ above, behind, or through all cultures, or we bestow universal and absolute value to one single culture or group of cultures, namely, that doctrinal world for which the statement makes sense.

In the first case we should fall into utter silence and cannot speak of uniqueness, because the moment we utter a word we do it within a particular culture. A kenotic Christ is neither unique nor not unique, because "it" does not admit any qualification. In the second case the uniqueness has been transferred to an entire cultural set. And this, in fact, was a common belief during many centuries. It is the very nature of colonialism: cultural monism.

Indeed, we may find a transcendental relationship between what Christians call Christ and what other cultures and religions may express with a set of homeomorphic equivalents. But in this case the uniqueness of Christ has been relativized and brought into the field where it has an accepted meaning. Christ is then the logotype, as it were, of the Christian language. May I recall that the relativity I am espousing has nothing to do with relativism?

I insist, because apparently I am often either not heard or misunderstood. Pluralism, for me, is not an attitude which posits that there are many true religions or many authentic Christs—albeit with different names. Truth itself is pluralistic, not plural. The pluralistic attitude is fruit of the experience that we are not the masters of truth and can thus only decide (about truth) in each particular case through dialogical discourse. Even in law courts one does not judge the other by sheer hearsay. This is the flaw of any *single* theo-*logy* of religions with the claim to universal validity. Even the one Christian *logos* has spoken many *logoi*, as Christian scripture itself (and tradition) asserts. We may understand some languages of others (not all), and hear new tunes of the symphony or eliminate others, but we cannot say that all languages (religions) say the same until and unless they actually say it. The abstract "sameness" of a "thing in itself" is extrapolated cryptokantianism.

I have been asked to react to the question put to me. Although I submit that philosophically it is a pseudo-problem, there is a real and legitimate concern lurking behind the question. It is a question of faith, and therefore it touches an ultimate concern. I shall not hesitate to make my confession.

The philosophically awkward question about the uniqueness of Christ expresses in this inadequate way an utmost serious concern about something ultimate. And because it is ultimate, it cannot but be a tautology—otherwise one could proceed further (to a contradictory meta ultimate). This is probably what it means to utter a confession of faith and not a statement of fact. We are not so much interested in the uniqueness of Don Pelayo, in spite of his historical significance (for some, of course).

In short, the question of the uniqueness of Christ entails deep down a tautology. But as all important ultimate questions, it is a qualified tautology. It is not a barren one. The question about "what is being" is undoubtedly a tautology. But its qualifications have provoked some of the greatest creations of humanity. Here then is my answer.

When I put to myself the question of Christ's uniqueness I do not ask about his distinctiveness; I do not enter into competitiveness—this virus of modern life. Nor do I confuse his identity with my identification (of him). Nor, for that matter, do I confuse the (objectifiable) principle of singularity with the (non-objectifiable) principle of individuality—as I have repeatedly elaborated elsewhere.

Christ's uniqueness lies, for me, in the lived experience that I am at once finite, infinite, and on the way. This is a threefold but single experience, which by a thinking process I would apply to any human being. We all experience ourselves as finite, limited, even contingent. We also feel and are convinced that we are not finished, finite, that we are capable of growth without any preestablished limit, that we are in this sense, infinite. We also are directly aware that there is a link between the two, without which we would neither experience finiteness nor infinitude.

Now the Christian, but *only* the Christian, name for this link, for such a mediator, is Christ. After all, Christian scripture also tells us that his real but hidden name is a supername (Phil 2:9). For this reason my concrete Christian belonging to a community (I am not uprooted) does not segregate me from any being, human, material, or divine. Yet the Christian language is unique but not universal; it is different, specific—and enters into dialogue with other languages: complementing, correcting, contradicting . . . each other. Meanwhile, the uniqueness of Christ is a unique opportunity to keep one's own identity.

I feel that Knitter had an inkling of that uniqueness when at the acme of his christology he declares that Christ himself will lose his uniqueness (the kenotic Christ), so that ultimately "God will be all in all" (1 Cor 15:28).

An Evangelical Response to Knitter's Five Theses

CLARK H. PINNOCK

The uniqueness and universality of Jesus Christ in the order of salvation have always been cardinal issues for Christian theology. I am delighted that Paul Knitter addresses this issue in a positive way and does not abandon it. I had come to expect pluralists to belittle the category in the interests of interreligious dialogue and to speak of the myth of uniqueness as if it were an outworn idea. Not anymore it seems. Knitter does not wish to hand uniqueness over to nonpluralists to defend but wants to redefine and defend it himself.

I suppose that the pluralists have realized that denying (or appearing to deny) the uniqueness of Jesus puts them in a weak position with almost everybody. Both Christians and not-yet Christians know that historic Christianity has always claimed that Jesus is the one mediator between God and humanity; to deny this simply puts a question mark over pluralism as a form of Christian theology. How many Christians would respect them as caretakers of the tradition, and how many Muslims or Buddhists would want to dialogue with such a watered-down faith? For me, the primary significance of Knitter's essay is that this pluralist at least realizes that treating the uniqueness of Jesus negatively is a bad idea.

How then is Jesus unique according to a pluralist vision? From Knitter's theses 4 and 5 we learn that Jesus' uniqueness lies not in being a metaphysically singular individual, but in symbolizing and embodying a new communal ethos which enhances humanization. Jesus is important for the world in supplying a fruitful norm for orienting life, for calling all humanity to inclusive communities which embrace all the divers ways of being human. Jesus' uniqueness (that which gives him universal meaning) is the power of his story to help people orient their lives in more redemptive ways. I agree with this as far as it goes—indeed I celebrate it.

Knitter now places more emphasis on lifestyle (salvation) than on God (theocentricity) than he did previously. This shift needed to be made in the interests of inclusivity, since belief in God (vague though it was) was a limiting condition when it to came to non-theists. Knitter now wants to espouse pluralism in a liberationist mode, where the uniqueness of Jesus is focused on a mode of worldly engagement, a following of Jesus which promotes peace and justice in the world. Orthodoxy is to be measured not by adherence to creeds but by radical discipleship. Jesus is a unique saint for the world rather than only the savior of it.

I am in agreement with Knitter about the propriety of reinterpreting Jesus' uniqueness (thesis 1). The subject is inexhaustible and its interpretation is never finished. There are many ways to characterize uniqueness, and I am eager to acknowledge each one. Specifically, I appreciate what Knitter says about the lifestyle implications of christology, how Jesus calls us to repent and live according to the norms of God's Reign. However, we must say more than that, because ethical uniqueness is part of a larger package. The affirmation of ethical uniqueness does not go far enough. Though revolutionary in itself, it rests upon deeper ontological foundations.

The New Testament and the broad Christian tradition displayed in theology and liturgy have always maintained that the incarnation of the Word of God in Jesus of Nazareth has universal significance for more than ethical reasons. We have always claimed that in Jesus an event happened which is salvific for the whole human race. This conviction is ultimately rooted in Jesus' claim to divine authority. He claimed to supply the true meaning of Torah, because he enjoyed supreme authority in relation to it. He proclaimed God's coming Reign as already present and active in his ministry. He cultivated a unique relationship with God his Father and understood himself to occupy a position of unique mediation between God and humankind. By the claims he made about himself and in the central position he assigned to himself in the accomplishment of God's purposes, Jesus assumed unparalleled authority.

This helps explain how, after the resurrection, the apostles preached much about his death reconciling the world and his resurrection inaugurating a new creation. They present Jesus as Israel's messiah and the medium of eschatological salvation. They speak of him as the Father's only Son, the lord of creation, and the savior of the race. In his name the church has felt constrained to make disciples of all nations, since Jesus is lord of all people, not only of some. It seems to me that every document, every title, every tradition of the scriptures in one way or another lifts up Jesus as risen lord and savior of the whole world. Jesus is the particular man, the incarnate One in whom resides the possibility of salvation for the whole world. According to the gospel, in Jesus Christ, God made an irrevocable commitment to humanity, by becoming God for us in a human way, inserting himself deeply into history, and calling all men and women to share in the divine life. The uniqueness of Jesus is much grander than Knitter acknowledges. More than an ethical norm, more than God's love in action, Jesus is God's presence in history according to our canon and tradition.

Arguing in this manner, I am making an assumption about theological method. I am assuming that Christian theology ought to be a faithful rendition of the canonical symbols and not free-wheeling doctrinal construction. While there is room under this method to reenvisage categories like the uniqueness of Jesus, our freedom does not extend to straying beyond limits or ignoring central canonical emphases. Not just for evangelicals, the canon establishes the field of play for theology and the boundaries of negotiation. However richly diverse the canon on christology, the writings encourage some moves and warn against others. The center of New Testament christology is the crucified Jesus, now risen and exalted as Lord. Knitter's first thesis is sound but his second is not. Any valid reinterpretation of Jesus' uniqueness must be canonically permissible and not ruled by norms from modernity and relativism. His theological pluralism has a tenuous hold on the status of Christian theology. If I were a pluralist, I would argue more forthrightly and say that although the Bible thinks mythically about christology and reifies the uniqueness of Jesus, we cannot do so today. I would not attempt to deny what the Bible clearly says but make a break with the Bible. I can understand why many pluralists do not want to say that—it would force them to break with canon and tradition and threaten to marginalize pluralism as an influence on the church and culture. But it would be better to come out and say exactly what they mean and not hide it.

I sympathize with Knitter's desire for a universal vision arising from a responsible understanding of Jesus' uniqueness. I want the same thing myself. But it may be that there are moves more viable for Christian theology. First, we can acknowledge the remarkable universality of the biblical message as it stands. Paul says that God was reconciling the whole world in Jesus Christ (2 Cor 5:19). John sees a rainbow overarching the throne of God, reminding readers of God's covenant with all humankind (Rv 4:3). We are told that God desires all to be saved and know the truth and that Jesus died for the sins of the whole world, not just our own (1 Tm 2:4; 1 Jn 2:2). The biblical message is not lacking in universality and hopefulness. God loves all people and grace is being brought to bear upon the whole world. Contrary to the pluralist assumption, traditional biblical christology does not have to entail narrowness on the part of believers toward other people. I think that Vatican II was right in its repeated insistence that belief in incarnation does not deny that God's grace is global.

Second, interreligious dialogue is imperative—we cannot be said to love our neighbors if we are unwilling to dialogue with them. But holding to the metaphysical singularity of Jesus as the unique Son of God does not threaten dialogue, in my opinion, because in dialogue we not only share what we have learned about God but also pursue the truth.

There are truth claims, which all the religions make, that need to be tested. Is Mohammed seal of the prophets or not? Was God with us in a human way in Jesus or not? Is the Buddhist reading of the human condition redemptive or not? These are not awkward traditions to be swept under the rug but serious proposals and topics for discussion. The fact that various physicists or biologists have differing theories about nature does not prevent dialogue—on the contrary, it makes it crucial. Interreligious dialogue does not require theology to be noncognitive or reduced to the business of social construction. We pursue religious truth in dialogue because we want to worship God and not idols.

There are different kinds of dialogue, and one sort of dialogue needed is truth-seeking dialogue, dialogue that sifts through the disparate claims of religions in regard to God, humanity, and the world. Our goal should be to discover where the truth actually lies in these matters, as happens when philosophers of different persuasions meet each other and converse about their pluralism of convictions. Of course we must pursue the truth in a humble and modest way. We are dealing with mystery and cannot expect to demonstrate the truth conclusively in advance of the eschaton, a moment before which our knowledge is incomplete (1 Cor 13:12). Demonstration must await eschatological verification. But the eschatological perspective is better than a pluralistic reduction that evaporates the specific claims not only of Christianity but of every other proclamation as well. Reductionism neither respects the convictions of other people nor serves the truth.

The fact that God has a witness in every nation does not exclude the possibility that Jesus was a unique incarnation of surpassing value for the world. "God" is a vague category unless there exists a decisive clue about its nature that can give it specificity and definiteness. We need what the New Testament declares there to be in Jesus—a visible image of the invisible God. I see in Knitter a confidence about a personal God in love with the human race, but this is a belief surely grounded in a high christology. It is not a belief picked up from Buddha or Mohammed. It is christologically grounded. We know that God loves the world because of the incarnation of Jesus Christ. One cannot assume the universal salvific will of God, as Knitter does, without acknowledging the centrality of Jesus in which it is grounded.

Third, regarding other faiths, we cannot say (just to be charitable) that all religions mediate God's grace and truth. Knitter refers to Ogden's hesitancy to admit that there actually are a number of true religions. Surely Ogden is right to be hesitant. The Bible is dialectical on this question, as is human experience. On the one hand, it praises the faith of pagan saints such as Noah, Job, Melchizedek, and Abimelech; on the other hand, it castigates the religions of Canaan and aspects of Israelite religion as well. We cannot assume from the fact of God's love for the world that every person on earth has been supplied with a true religion.

A good deal of religion is wicked and deceptive, according to the Bible and experience, and God is not bound to work through religion in mediating grace to the world, though God may do so. We ought to hesitate and not be too hasty to conclude that religions mediate God's grace and truth. Religions are a mixed bag, and we should not be naive about them. Pre-axial religions that do not advance human salvation are still plentiful. Some religions facilitate an approach to God, while others are a means of escaping.

Knitter rightly says that the church cannot obey the last commission of proclaiming the gospel to the nations unless and until it obeys the first commission of loving the nations as our neighbors. I agree, but the reverse situation is also true. The church cannot be said to be loving the nations as her neighbors unless and until it seeks to disciple them and bring them to faith in the triune God. The great commission gives the love commandment a new dimension. Those who truly love their neighbors will no doubt want to share the good news of Jesus as God's word with them. Can we accept the sincerity of pluralist neighbor love if it does not lead to world evangelization?

Idolater Indeed!

JOHN SANDERS

Professor Knitter comes across as a very sensitive person concerned about the well-being of others. His call to put our faith into action is admirable. His willingness to dialogue with people from other traditions, including evangelicals such as myself, shows him to be open-minded. Yet he definitely has strong convictions; he accuses others of being imperialistic, intolerant, and idolatrous. According to Knitter, it is idolatrous to affirm the unsurpassability of Jesus, for nothing earthly (including human language and thought) can contain God. In order to make his criticism stand, Knitter assumes certain points I wish to call into question. I am particularly interested in how he knows and can speak about what this God is like who so transcends human language, and his use of that understanding of divine reality to revise the gospel.

Knitter defines God as an "unsurpassable Mystery, one which can never totally be comprehended or contained in human thought." Since Jesus was human he could not possibly contain God, so God remains much more than Jesus. Hence, we should be open to revelation that surpasses Jesus. This procedural move, in which God is first defined by the canons of natural theology and the biblical revelation is then made to conform to it, has a very long pedigree. The method was forged by the Greek philosophers, who did not, overall, reject the Olympian gods but subordinated them to the ultimate metaphysical principle—a rational explanation of all reality to which even the gods must conform. This method of *theoprepes* (that which is appropriate for a god to be) was used by the pre-Socratics, Plato, Aristotle and the Stoics to arrive at a conception of ultimate reality that provides a rational explanation for the cosmos. Above the personal gods there exists the impersonal, timeless, immutable, utterly transcendent "god." The ultimate deity, in this sense, though incapable of being contained in human thought, is, nonetheless, the necessary presupposition for the explanation of the world. The ultimate god functions as a metaphysical principle needed to explain temporality and change.

Philo of Alexandria adopted this method for his reading of the Bible and became the first to begin the development of the biblical-classical synthesis whereby the biblical language about God is made to conform to the canons of Greek philosophy. This synthesis, which came to dominate Jewish, Christian, and Islamic thought on the divine nature, understood God to be timeless, impassible, and immutable. According to *theoprepes*, the biblical language about God repenting, having feelings, planning, and so on, is seen as inappropriate for a divine being and therefore it must be reinterpreted. Such expressions are anthropomorphisms that do not genuinely communicate the divine essence. The biblical text is read through the lenses of a foreign world view and is only allowed to speak that which does not conflict with that world view. In the Christian tradition a shift of emphasis gradually occurred from the God of salvation history (*oikonomia*) to the abstract being of God in Godself (*theologia*). What was sought was the "true" nature of God behind the biblical witness—the God beyond the God of the Bible. This quest deeply affected the discussions of christology in that the early church had to solve the problem of how the timeless and immutable divine Son could function in an incarnation involving time, suffering, and change. Generally speaking, the incarnation was not used to call into question the understanding of God arrived at by *theoprepes*. The "correct" understanding of the divine nature continued to be derived from metaphysics and the biblical revelation was made to conform to it. Hence, instead of allowing the biblical message to critique the prevailing plausibility structure, the God beyond God was allowed to stand, which led to the Hellenization of the gospel.

Knitter, very Greek in this regard, uses the same method that Hellenized the gospel in order to achieve the pluralization of the gospel. Accordingly, a particular understanding of ultimate reality and how we should live are used to filter the biblical message in order to determine what may be said. For Hellenism, God was a metaphysical necessity needed to explain reality. For pluralism, God is a soteriological necessity needed to provide a purpose for living. Knitter relies on process and liberationist thought, both of which begin with the analysis of human life, to show the necessity of religion. It is humanity in search of meaning. In this method it is *we* who establish the ground rules into which God must fit.

One of these rules is that the universal principle of meaning must be immediately accessible to all people (hence the scandal of historical particularity). Furthermore, this unifying principle is valid for all religions. In other words, it is a meta-theory establishing the God beyond the God of the religions. Moreover, this ultimate metaphysical principle is an absolute undifferentiated unity (doctrine of simplicity) which makes definitions impossible. Knitter seems to agree with both Greek and Eastern thinking that ultimate reality is formless (non-dualistic).

What Knitter adds to this metaphysical abstraction is the notion that there is a unifying set of works (*praxis*) valid for all religions. Whereas Troeltsch and others reduced Christianity to a set of ideas (timeless truths), Knitter reduces Christianity to a set of practices (timeless works). In either case the accidental truths of history fade in importance, as does our need for a personal relationship with the Father based on the reconciling work of Jesus. Furthermore, Knitter's timeless works are an ever-present reality, so there is no need to look forward to the future event of God as judge and redeemer (2 Cor 5:10; Heb 9:28).

But Christians do not admit a reality more ultimate than Yahweh. The Christian God comes to us in concrete history and language, especially in the person of Jesus, and that is how we know what ultimate reality is like. Claiming that Jesus is the unsurpassable revelation of God is, according to Knitter, idolatrous. In this light, has Knitter caught me in the act? Should I come forward and confess my idolatry before the tribunal of soteriocentrism? Am I guilty as charged? Yes. Yet I feel no need to repent of this "sin." After all, I am only following the example of the Bible. Using Knitter's understanding of idolatry, the New Testament writers "sinned" when they said that Jesus is the exact representation of the divine nature (Heb 1:3); that in Jesus the fullness of deity dwelt in bodily form (Col 2:9; 1:19) and that the one who has seen Jesus has seen the Father (Jn 14:9). These are very "arrogant" and "idolatrous" remarks, unless, of course, Jesus does reveal the essence of God because he is God. There is no God beyond God we must try to grope after. In Jesus we meet God himself coming to us and revealing himself to us. The seeking is over, for God has found us.

Knitter has, in the past, sought to bypass this problem by claiming the New Testament writers were part of a "classicist culture" which held to exclusivistic truth or that they were speaking the "language of love." Such patronizing language is unfounded, however, as they were well aware of the dangerous game they were playing. Those Christians lived in a pluralistic world where they knew such exclusivistic claims meant persecution from both their fellow Jews and imperial Rome. In spite of this, the early Christians stated what they believed was true, disturbed the peace, and accepted the consequences.

Several other observations about Knitter's charge of idolatry are worth mentioning. First, the New Testament writers, according to Knitter, are idolatrous, but those who literally worship idols are not idolatrous so long as they admit that their idols are surpassable. A curious situation indeed.

Second, Knitter says I am idolatrous because I place the constraint of unsurpassability on Jesus. Yet, Knitter places constraints on his "unsurpassable Mystery" when he argues that it *cannot* reveal itself in such a way as to be unsurpassable. Whence did he get such information that he can pronounce a priori what God cannot do? In the Bible God created us in the divine image, so idols are ruled out because God had already made the only legitimate "idol" (humanity). In the incarnation Jesus became the idol of idols. It is *hubris* to claim that God cannot do such a thing and to deny God the freedom to define Godself and declare that definition unsurpassable. The making of idols may be illegitimate for us but may be quite legitimate for God.

Third, Knitter says God is "unbounded love" who "communicates" and "wills." This sounds like a personal God. Is this understanding of God surpassable? It would seem so, since he says we must accept the insights of non-duality. Is the insight of non-duality surpassable? Surely it is. Then why does Knitter claim that ultimate reality is "one"? How does he know it is not plural or polytheistic? His response may be that Jesus revealed the "true" but surpassable notion that God is one, since he says there will be no revelation that contradicts the "central ingredients" of the truth *we* find in Jesus. What are these central ingredients? He does not say, but it would seem that they are only the this-worldly practice of love and justice. The central ingredients of the truth we find in Jesus are not that God is personal or that we have sinned against the Creator or that Jesus provides the atonement bringing reconciliation between God and humanity and providing the grace for human to human reconciliation. Knitter's unsurpassable criterion that he finds in Jesus is that we should seek love and justice (appropriately defined in Western terms).

Is this the only unsurpassable truth? Moreover, how did Knitter arrive at this criterion? It seems by his desire that all dialogue partners have "equal rights" on a "level playing field." Hence, no one has truth above anyone else's. What is going on here is the placing of a criterion above the God of salvation history, which is then used to filter out the surpassable, initial revelation from the biblical message. What is left, then, is the one goal of life on which all major religions can agree: soteriocentrism. But the religions will not agree to this placing of something more ultimate above them. Christians need not apologize for what God decided to do in salvation history. If Yahweh chooses to work through the particularities of history in order to bring salvation for the entire human race and provide an unsurpassable revelation of self through the incarnation of the Second Person of the Trinity, then who are we to say that God cannot do this? On what grounds do we place a criterion above God? Who is the real idolater here? I suggest that the idolater is the one who places a god above Yahweh in order to constrain Yahweh's freedom.

The criterion, derived according to that which is appropriate for salvation to be (*soteriaprepes*), is used to reinterpret the uniqueness of Jesus so that he becomes a teacher of love and justice. Presumably other religions need to be reinterpreted also in light of the criterion. Hence, one who views salvation as release from the karmic cycle, or who understands those suffering from poverty as getting what they deserve, or who views evil as *maya*, must reinterpret these doctrines according to *soteriaprepes* and become a social activist. Moreover, what of the humanist who agrees with the goal of social justice but denies any ultimate reality beyond the cosmos? Is such a view religious? Does it need any further reinterpretation? If not, then it seems that soteriocentrism is little more than a warmhearted moralism. If there is more to religion than moralism and praxis, then what is it?

Another problem with Knitter's analysis is that though it is correct that all religions seek to answer questions about, for example, why some people are more privileged than others (a purely formal category), it is not correct that all religions seek liberation from poverty, oppression, and social injustice. In order to get the religions speaking the same language we must use purely formal categories apart from a specific content. Knitter, however, uses a specific content that entails a Judeo-Christian valuation on material well-being. But this will always entail taking a stand—being exclusivistic. Knitter now admits to being an exclusivist in this sense: that all religious beliefs and practices must be judged *soteriaprepes*. But is this criterion unsurpassable? If surpassable, then perhaps love and justice (at least the way Knitter defines them) are not ultimate and further revelation will pass them by. If it is unsurpassable, then it is an idolatrous practice. So it seems that all of us are idolaters, according to Knitter, and the question becomes what our idols shall be.

For me, as a Christian, the "idol" can be none other than the triune God, whom the Son revealed to us in the person of Jesus. According to this revelation any sin against another human is first of all a sin against God, for sin is anti-creational. Accordingly reconciliation needs to take place first of all between humans and God. This is the message Knitter either leaves out or subordinates to the task of earthly betterment. For me, Jesus is much more than an exemplary figure of what each of us can attain. He is Yahweh's decisive, unique, normative, and unsurpassable revelatory action that has changed human history forever. He is the light of the world, which enlightens every person. There is no "greater light" of soteriocentrism above him.

This, of course, is "foolishness to the Greeks." But seeking to remove the foolishness by placing a rule (*arche*) above Jesus and develop a revisionist gospel palatable to its cultured despisers is idolatrous. For Jesus is the *archon* above all rule (Eph 1:21) and is the author (definer) of God, love, salvation, justice, and faith (Heb 1–2). Jesus, as the universal and unsurpassable cornerstone, is a cause of stumbling. Whereas my evangelical brethren sometimes stumble over the scandal of universality[1] (that is, that God makes salvation universally accessible), the pluralists stumble over the scandal of particularity. It is Jesus, the only savior, the great shepherd who seeks all the lost sheep, desiring that all come to a personal relationship with the living personal God. In this "idol" Christians trust.

---

[1] See my *No Other Name: An Investigation into the Destiny of the Unevangelized* (Grand Rapids, Mich.: Eerdmans, 1992).

The Incarnation as Koan
or
The Unique Universal Ultimate

A Personal Midrash on Paul Knitter's "Five Theses on the Uniqueness of Jesus"

INGRID SHAFER

Especially in the Western cultural sphere, with its extensive rootedness in ancient Greek thought, the interplay of two contending, coherent, and internally consistent theoretical paradigms determines, or at least affects, the way people understand their worlds, including Ultimate Reality (God by a number of names), Jesus, the church, the interaction of various Christian denominations, and the relationship of Christianity and other religions. In practice these two models are usually mixed, generating a plethora of gradations along a sliding scale between extremes. Nevertheless, most thinkers tend to follow one approach more than the other. These models are as ancient as Parmenides and Heraclitus, a static, one-dimensional, absolutist, closed either-or model that values perfection, completion, permanence, convention, and unity; and a dynamic, non-absolutist, multidimensional, open "both-and" process model that values growth, evolution, change, novelty, and diversity. The former operates primarily through vertical monologue and criticism. The latter operates primarily through horizontal dialogue and empathy. The former insists on sharp boundaries and by definition excludes the other by any name. The latter has permeable boundaries and can include the former.

These paradigms are closely related to David Tracy's two master modes of religious interpretation that can be traced throughout the history of Christianity: the "analogical and dialectical languages."[1] The analogical imagination (of manifestation) sees, seeks, and expresses "similarity-in-difference" (413). It originates in the experiences of "trust, wonder, giftedness," albeit not as the "cheap grace" of dead univocity but the genuine grace of emergent—and hence uncertain—possibility: the "radical mystery empowering all intelligibility" (413). The dialectical imagination (of proclamation) sees, seeks, and expresses difference-in-similarity[2]; it is rooted in the experience of "prophetic suspicion" (416), the Word of Jesus Christ as "disclosing the reality of the infinite, qualitative distinction between that God and this flawed, guilty, sinful, presumptuous, self-justifying self" (415). The dialectical imagination denies "all claims to similarity, continuity, ordered relations" (415).

The interplay of these two hermeneutical modes constitutes the cultural matrix of the West. Until the Reformation both paradigms were part of the Catholic tradition. After the Reformation, Protestants and Catholics have tended to separate along analogical and dialectical party lines, even though both modes are still found across the Christian spectrum, and ironically the Catholic hierarchy, in contrast to the majority of the laity, has tended to follow the absolutist and dialectical paradigms. In this essay I apply the non-absolutist, open-ended, dynamic, dialogical (dia[lectical ana]logical) hermeneutical model to the question of the uniqueness of Jesus. I will cite a number of passages from Knitter's essay, followed by my interpretation and commentary.

Precisely by reinterpreting Jesus' uniqueness, Christians can reaffirm it with greater relevance for our contemporary world (thesis 4).

If we go beyond the original understanding of Yeshua as teacher and prophet (reflected in the synoptic gospels) and call Jesus the Word become Flesh, the Light of the World, God Incarnate, Son of God and Son of Man, the Infinite Finite, or the Ultimate Paradox, then we already possess the key that will allow us to view him both as unique and as potentially one among other bearers of God's saving grace in history. In fact, the very uniqueness of Jesus as the Christ can be seen to flow out of and terminate in simultaneous cancellation and preservation (Hegel's *Aufhebung*, Lonergan's "sublation") of "either-or dualism" into qualified "both-and non-dualism."

---

[1] David Tracy, *The Analogical Imagination* (New York: Crossroad, 1981), 408. All Tracy quotations are from this book. It should be noted that Tracy's definition of *dialectical* is Barthian rather than Hegelian. Several years ago I published a more extensive discussion of the two types of Christian imagination in "Non-Adversarial Criticism, Cross-Cultural Conversation and Popular Literature," *Proteus* 6,1 (Spring 1989), 6-15. See also my "The Catholic Imagination in Popular Film and Television," *Journal of Popular Film and Television* 19,2 (Summer 1991), 50-57.

[2] This is not Tracy's term, but I believe it is implied in his discussion.

These opposite, dissolving, and fusing "names" given to Jesus by disciples and theologians from Paul and the editor of John's gospel to Kierkegaard point toward Mystery: the ineffable and radically enigmatic at the heart of the Incarnation. They creatively and imaginatively juxtapose, join, and overcome opposites and transcend (not contradict!) common sense logic. Like Zen koans, they hint at the elusive, always just beyond the horizon Truth by breaking through the opaqueness of ordinary categories of reason, and rendering them translucent to the emergent meaning that illuminates its own genesis.

Jesus can best be "grasped" with analogical language. For us he reveals both the Ground of Being beyond time and space and the screaming, nursing, gurgling, peeing, sleeping baby boy born to the young Jewish woman Mary in the reign of Caesar Augustus; he manifests at once the Absolutely Other and the utterly us. He is the dynamic flow at the still center beyond either-or opposition. Like light, he is simultaneously quantum and wave, discrete packets and continuous flow, absence and presence, the Perfect Hologram—neither localized nor extended through space and yet *both* localized *and* extended through space.[3] He is the human manifestation of whatever comes "After the Absolute" (Leonard Swidler), the One Who Is Beyond Being and Becoming.

To recognize the pluralism of christologies is to admit two essential features of the christological task: that there can be no one way of talking about this Jesus, and that our efforts to talk about him embody an undertaking that is never accomplished (thesis 1).

Jesus continues to come to life in stories of faith that are told out of particular cultural contexts to preserve memories and weave meanings that are vital for (and at least in part unique to) the community out of which they grow. While these stories have neither a single, unchanging content nor an immutable form, they twirl and oscillate round a common axis: the axis of a God who loves us so much that he enters the finite world as a human baby and calls us to rebirth as well—to become healed, that is, holy, in the New Being in Christ.

Never mind that Easter outranks Christmas in terms of theological significance. For ordinary people, especially children, the birth story is the premier story of Christianity and their induction into the faith: a beaming new mother holding her baby the way all of us want to be held by our mothers—the same kind of biological triad reduced to a diad that establishes the primary family unit of mother and child—at once the

---

[3] See David Bohm, "The Implicate or Enfolded Order: A New Order for Physics" in *Mind in Nature: Essays on the Interface of Science and Philosophy*, ed. John B. Cobb, Jr., and David Ray Griffin (Washington, D.C.: University Press of America, 1977), 37-42.

uniquely universal Great Mother Madonna and Yahweh and the Primal Eagle hovering over its young. One can imagine burned-out cynics from practically any era or culture being touched by a ray of hope, an intimation of love, a hint of coherence and meaning when they see a mother and her child.[4] Even in such a patriarchal society as ancient China an abstract image of a mother holding her baby signifies love.

In this manner Jesus has taken on life for each new generation for almost two millennia in a shape distinctive to that generation, and yet a shape that can bear meaning, at least up to a point, in many different eras and cultures. Jesus comes for each person in a way unique to that individual, and yet, somehow, in that very diversity he also reveals himself as manifestation of the One who was, is, and shall be—the One who is "the dance and the dance goes on / I am the Lord of the dance, said He."

The more things change, the more they stay the same, and the primordial bond of mother and child is one that links Jesus not only to the universal givens of human procreation but back into our evolutionary foundations where

> Flesh and fleece, fur and feather,
> Grass and greenworld all together;
> Star-eyed strawberry breasted
> Throstle above her nested

> Cluster of bugle blue eggs thin
> Forms and warms the life within;
> And birds and blossoms swell
> in sod or sheath or shell.
> —Gerard Manley Hopkins
> *May Magnificat*

---

[4] Andrew Greeley is fond of telling about his "Madonna of O'Hare"—a woman holding a baby in the midst of a typical O'Hare holiday crush: "The weather is terrible, flights are delayed, the crowds are irritable and impatient. No one is smiling, I least of all." Suddenly he sees a young mother, "She is so proud of her child (blue means little boy, doesn't it I ask myself), so determined to protect him, so overwhelmed by his wonder, that she seems oblivious to the crowds, the noise, the electricity of tension and frustrations in the airport" (*Religion as Poetry* [New Brunswick: Transaction, 1995], 27-28).

As she merges into the crowd he walks toward the gate, a Christmas carol in his head, a smile on his lips, and a sense that the author of Ecclesiastes was only half right at best (or worst). He realizes—at least for the moment—that life is definitely more than chasing after the wind. For the harried priest in a cynical mood the young woman represents a sacrament of grace, and in her presence, in secular space, he experiences Jesus. Furthermore, in the retelling of the story she becomes a symbol of coherence, order, and meaning over and against chaos.

I clearly remember when Jesus became real for me. I was born in Austria in 1939 and spent the final years of the war in Schloß Freiling, a castle close to a military airstrip where my father worked as meteorologist. I remember howling sirens, magnesium flares we called Christmas trees in the night sky, the rumble of distant explosions, and evil black spiders ready to pounce from bright red flags. We didn't go to church, but one winter night my parents lit a candle on a spruce wreath and switched off the chandelier. The deer antlers on the wall cast eerie shadows and hollow-eyed skulls stared sightlessly at me in the gloom. I held my parents' hands and listened to my mother talk of the most special baby ever born, in a stable, many, many years ago, a child so good, so filled with compassion, that when it grew up its love brought peace to the world and turned enemies into friends. I looked at that bright flame and suddenly all my fears were gone. There, at age five, in the dark room with one steady flame, I knew that everything would be all right, for light was stronger than darkness.

Then the dreams started—nighttime dreams and daytime dreams of playing with a special friend who looked much like the fragile waxen figure in the crib on the floor under the tall spruce Christmas tree, but, unlike the pale, quiet Baby Jesus doll, my friend was exuberant and enjoyed joining me in everything I did from feeding chickens to building shrines in gnarled roots. Even today, I cannot write about this friend as boy or girl because in my imagination my friend was both or neither. But then, I really did not think of myself as "not-a-boy" either. In German, the word "Kind" (child) is grammatically neuter, and for me both my friend and I were "its"; my friend was simply a child like myself, different from me only in never even thinking of taking a secret bite out of a special pear or telling a fib. Years later, when I learned at school about the *Heilige Dreifaltigkeit*, the Holy Trinity, I began to merge my former playmate into young Jesus, unconsciously experiencing what I now think of as "reverse incarnation" or, maybe, "excarnation" from myself to my Friend to Jesus to the Father. I began to imagine Jesus as a caring, strong, and compassionate man, and finally as the personal face of the One who spoke the universe into existence and hovered over the primal waters and keeps drinking the bitter chalice and forever empties himself because he loves us and feels our creaturely agony and calls us to follow him by allowing ourselves to be conduits that pour love into the world, clear lenses that gather God's light and beam it into the night.

In grasping, describing, and proclaiming the **person** *and the* **work** *of Jesus, Christians can be open to new ways of talking, new images, deeper insights, yes, even re-visions of how God has acted and is acting through him (thesis 1).*

Stories of faith literally coalesce with tellers, listeners, and readers— and in that union their "truth" is revealed in as many manifestations as there are members of the participating community. Everything we know, our very categories of thought and imagination, is the result of our hermeneutic matrix; we interpret and give shape to what we call truth and experience as objective reality in terms of the categories we have absorbed unconsciously and consciously through our genes, environment, intellectual tradition, family, friends, books, church, and school. We tell our own stories, which harmonize with and play off the stories we have heard. For Christians, the very power of the stories of faith we imagine, tell, and absorb resides precisely in their adaptability to ever-new situations and surprising experiences of the living Christ. As Christians we tell *midrashim* on our central story and become agents and tools for the ongoing process of incarnation or christogenesis. A creative synthesizing of horizons in the christogenetic kaleidoscope results in a series of paradigm shifts of transformation. Whether we know it or not, we—global humanity—are ourselves the process toward the promised New Heaven and New Earth.

When this kind of reinterpretation introduces the engaged interpreter's authentic, insatiably curious, and attentive presence it constitutes not the abandonment of a tradition but rather its fulfillment, at least for a given temporal juncture. Serious subsequent interpreters come to the text out of their own personal historical context with new questions and the ability to uncover and generate aspects and levels of meaning that may not have even been possible for earlier efforts. Thus, subjects in process enter into intimate dialogue with subject matter in process, unpacking a fluid array of similarities, differences, and similarities in difference, daring to risk confusion as well as fusion.

As the text engages them they may not only discover themselves as finite beings, they may also come to understand their temporal finitude as the very horizon of eternity, and in that limit experience they may grasp the opportunity of self-transcendence and come to see both themselves and Christ in an utterly new light. They may even recognize that the formation of what Christians call the Cosmic Christ, like a symphony emerging from the supposedly silent music of the spheres, interweaves themes of countless religions in all their diversity and draws the entire human community toward the beatific—that is beautiful—vision of truth, justice, and love in practice.

But here many would voice a caveat: there are limits to such interpretations. Christology is not a free-for-all, an anything-goes venture. . . . Any new understanding of Jesus—his person, work, or uniqueness—must flow from and nurture a saving experience of and commitment to Jesus (devotion) and a resolute following of him in the world (discipleship). If it does not do this, it is heretical; if it does, it merits our serious attention if not acceptance (thesis 1).

What are the limits to these interpretations? While the christogenetic task is unending, it is not open to clear and distinct validation; we can never be absolutely certain whether the story we tell is a true story (we can, however, be sure that it is not *the* True story, for all finite, human positions are inherently limited, and stories, like other symbols, can wane and wax in power and even temporarily or permanently die). Yet we are not totally in the dark. We can assess our story like ordinary information by tracing its effects. A physician's diagnosis is considered accurate when the patient improves after treatment. I believe that we can analogously judge the origin and validity of a story of God by its fruits if we factor in the unnegotiable premises that God is Love and that we are free and responsible.

Surely no such story can be authentic, or more than partially authentic, if it inspires intolerance, bigotry, injustice, hatred, self-aggrandizement, ecological irresponsibility, and violence (beyond exerting the force necessary to keep people from oppressing their fellows and abusing our earth). An interpretation can be genuine if and only if it leaves tellers and their audience with deepened insight into the double commandment of love that links the two covenants, Old and New, the summary according to the rabbis of the entire Torah to love God and others as we love ourselves. This approach can discredit hate-mongering tellers of spurious tales from the outset.

I can think of no more powerful implementation of the ancient commandment to love God and others than the contemporary call to authentic dialogue not only among members of the various strands of Christianity but among followers of all the world's religions. This is no longer an option, it is a necessity. "If the always-already, not-yet reality of grace decisively disclosed in the Christ event is the focal meaning of Christian self-understanding," writes David Tracy, "then that actuality must impel Christian theologians to enter into conversation with all the other religions and their classics. Where that conversation will lead no one yet knows. But that it must occur—at the beginning, not the end of a Christian systematics faithful to our situation and its hopes and demands for a global humanity—seems clear" (Tracy 449). "We must love one another or die," writes W. H. Auden; "Death or dialogue," warns Leonard Swidler; "Dialogue is an ethical imperative," insists Paul Knitter.

If Christians think that they are in possession of the "fullness" of revelation and the norm for all truth, then no matter how much they might call for a dialogue "among equals," they retain the position of advantage. It is from **their** *vantage point that any conflict of truth claims must be decided. . . . Such a notion of an unsurpassable revelation would also seem to contradict, or rule out, the role of the Holy Spirit that Jesus, in John's gospel, affirmed: "I have many things to say to you, but you cannot bear them now. . . . The Spirit of Truth will guide you into all the* *truth" (Jn 16:12-13). If we believe in the Holy Spirit, we must believe that there is always "more to come" (theses 2-3).*

The present age is no different from other eras in providing us unique occasions for "more." It is unlike any earlier period, however, in that the rate of change is accelerating and the opportunities are intensifying. New dialogue partners are also entering the arena, most especially the voices of contemporary astronomy, quantum physics, molecular biology, and computer technology. Teilhard de Chardin[5] suspected something of the sort back in 1949 when he not only linked terms such as "ultra-hominisation" based on human effort to discover (109) with those fields, but anticipated an essential role for "those astonishing electronic ma-chines (the starting point and hope of the young science of cybernetics) by which our mental capacity to calculate and combine is reinforced and multiplied . . . [leading to] an auto-cerebralisation becoming the most highly concentrated expression of the reflective rebound of evolution" (111). Humanity emerged from the primeval mists and swamps when *Homo sapiens* began to use reason to forge cosmos out of chaos. Hence it makes less sense to imagine God erecting high-voltage electric fences around certain areas of knowledge than to imagine God watching with delight and parental pride as human beings use their divinely designed brains to refine the theory of evolution or go beyond relativity and quan-tum theory to what David Bohm calls "implicate order" or to decipher the genetic code of life. We try to lock Christ up in a book or building when we refuse to envision him bent over a Petri dish, eager to help us correct some copyists' errors that crept into the three billion "words" in the past six hundred million years. In this perspective there is no enmity between religion and science, the sacred and the secular, and the world is our scripture.

In other words, to know Jesus Christ is to feel that Buddhists and Hindus and Muslims need to know him too; this means they need to recognize and accept the truth he reveals, even though this does not necessarily mean that they will become members of the Christian community. . . . In a qualified but still real sense, persons of other religious paths are "unfulfilled" without Christ (thesis 3).

Clearly, this does not mean that non-Christians are unfulfilled unless they convert to Christianity, but that they are unfulfilled if they do not lead lives in the spirit of Christ, a spirit that can be followed without being a Christian—though, at least in theory, being a Christian should

---

[5] Pierre Teilhard de Chardin, *Man's Place in Nature: The Human Zoological Group*, trans. René Hague (New York: Harper & Row, 1956).

make it easier to do so. Conversely, it is not only probable but certain that many members of Christian churches lead equally—or even more— unfulfilled lives because they have never truly met Jesus and have no idea what it means to follow him. They may believe that the way to follow Christ is to attend church every Sunday and vote against political candidates who support passing out condoms to halt the spread of AIDS. They may justify lack of concern for the poor by quoting Jesus' words "the poor shall always be with us." They may oppose women's rights on scriptural grounds. It may never occur to them that at the very core of the Christian message there burns the live flame of love for God and neighbor, and that neighbor means not only friend but especially enemy.

In the spirituality of a pluralist Christian, therefore, Jesus certainly remains unique. But . . . his uniqueness is not a matter of superiority or arrogation of privilege; rather it is a matter of distinctness . . . that consists primarily and most importantly not in Jesus' ability to exclude or absorb others (although that can indeed happen) but rather in his ability to offer us a distinct, concrete, decisive way of knowing God and living God's life in this world. . . . In such an understanding of Jesus' uniqueness we are committed to Christ because of who he is and what we have found in him, not because we are certain that he is better than all others (thesis 5).

For us Christians, Yeshua is the one whom we must follow in order to keep from being restricted by self-centeredness (not to be confused with self-acceptance, which is essential for loving others) in the sense of being deaf to the call to be open to all other beings, to be living, germinating seeds that break through the shell that separates us from others. In Yeshua the Christ, God calls us to embrace and co-create the unfolding cosmos from family to friends to strangers to the natural world and ultimately the Source of All: Love, passionate, cosmic, absolute Love, which according to Dante "moves the sun in heaven and all the stars."[6] As Christians, it is by following Yeshua the Lover, who "walked his talk," that we can become ever clearer lenses to gather and transmit God's transforming light and in the process expand ourselves to become most fully ourselves. Ultimately, humanization and divinization are the same relational process viewed from the transcendent and immanent poles. We allow ourselves to be most fully transformed into those lenses and in a sense achieve ourselves as ongoing process by returning Yeshua's love with the kind of focused passion for which the beloved is absolutely unique. This is analogous to the way humans fall in love and have eyes only for

---

[6] Dante Alighieri, *The Vision; or Hell, Purgatory, and Paradise of Dante Alighieri*, trans. Henry F. Cary (New York: Hurst & Co., 1844), 600.

each other and want to fulfill each other's every wish. They consider their lover absolutely unique even though they rationally know that under different circumstances someone else might have taken the lover's privileged place. For Christians, Jesus is as unique a way as the Buddha is for Buddhists or Krishna for Hindus or the Tao for Taoists.

Philip Hefner tells the following story: When asked how she prayed, Parichart Suwanbubbha—one of his Theravada Buddhist students at the Lutheran School of Theology in Chicago—said, "I visit my grandfather and I go feed the fish."[7] Of course, attending church and other liturgical acts do not preclude performing acts of loving-kindness (the Confucian term *ren* comes to mind), and Christians are certainly encouraged to practice love in addition to fulfilling the "Sunday duty" (a Catholic notion but one not alien to some Protestants), but I strongly suspect that if the One Christians call God does indeed watch us, that God places loving action above ritual. This is apparently what Karl Rahner thought, and I am struck by his clear statement that people can meet and affirm Jesus without any knowledge that they are doing so, simply by unconditionally loving others and by unconditionally accepting their own humanity (*Menschsein*):

> Yes, there are those among us who have encountered Jesus Christ without knowing that they have seized hold of the one into whose life and death they have fallen as their blessedly joyous, redeeming destiny. The Grace of God and the Grace of Christ abide in everything as the secret essence of human options, and therefore it is not easy to reach for anything at all without somehow getting involved with God and Jesus Christ. No matter how distant they are from any specific revealed verbal formulation, those who accept their existence, their humanity, in tranquil serenity (or better: in faith, hope, and love—by any name) as the mystery that ensconces within itself the mystery of eternal love and bears life in the womb of death, say Yes to Jesus Christ, even if they do not know it, for as they surrender unconditionally and without limit to it they say Yes to something that is what it is because God actually filled it with the unconditional and limitless, that is, with Himself when the Word became Flesh. For those who let go and leap fall into the abyss that exists truly and not only as far as they have plumbed it. Those who fully accept their own humanness (and it remains obscure who really does so) accept the Son of Man because in him God has accepted and taken on humanity. When scripture says that those who love their fellows have fulfilled the law

---

[7] Parichart Suwanbubbha now teaches religious studies at Mahidol University in Bangkok; she received the Th.D. degree from LSTC in June 1995. Her dissertation is on grace (in Calvinism) and karma (in Theravada Buddhism).

then this is the ultimate truth because God himself has become this neighbor, and hence as we love and accept our fellow humans we always also love and accept this Unique One who is both the closest to us and the most distant from us.[8]

With an imprimatur of the Vicar General Dr. Schlund, dated 2 December 1975, Karl Rahner and Herbert Vorgrimler define Jesus Christ in such a way that it is possible to know Christ even if we follow the Buddha or Mohammed or no one, even if we are pagans or agnostics or atheists, as long as we lead lives directed toward others and accept our human condition "in tranquil serenity" and "faith, hope, and love—by any name." From the Christian perspective, the other's unwillingness or inability to accept and view Jesus the way Christians see him in no way detracts from Jesus as God's prime and eternally true Sacrament of Love. The insights of non-Christians, if they harmonize with the Christian view, can provide Christians with new and exciting horizons of understanding God. As Knitter puts it, the good news of Jesus *"defines* God, but does not *confine* God" (thesis 3).

If we can also learn to include nonhuman nature in the loving embrace of the Incarnation, then, I believe, we will reach an even deeper current of the universal law of love, one that allows a confluence of the religious stream of Abraham with the rivers of India and China as we share our stories of faith. In the words of David Tracy, "Then the autonomy of each will be respected because each will be expected to continue, indeed to intensify, a journey into her/his own particularity" (449). Tracy continues, "The actuality of variety and the demand for authentic particularity unite as the environment of all. An analogical imagination may yet free us to a communal conversation on behalf of the kairos of this our day—the communal and historical struggle for the emergence of a humanity both finally global and ultimately humane" (453). Then Yeshua, the man who was born in the reign of Caesar Augustus and lived and was executed and became the New and Timeless Ruler by whose appearance the calendar of Christendom would be synchronized, can indeed emerge as the standard of the Common Era as Yeshua gradually comes to unfold the eschaton in what Christians call Christself and symbolize the Cosmic Change Agent in ways that include, among countless others, the Christian *logos/hokmah*, the Taoist *yin/yang*, the Hindu *Atman/ Brahman-Ishvara/Shakti*, and the Buddhist *Kuan-Yin* as the *unique universal Ultimate*.

---

[8] Karl Rahner and Herbert Vorgrimler, *Kleines Theologisches Wörterbuch* (Freiburg i. Br.: Herderbücherei, 1976), 216-17; translation mine. I cite the Rahner-Vorgrimler paragraph in its entirety because it goes beyond the ordinary interpretation of Rahner's "anonymous Christian" and leads in the direction I see Paul Knitter going. It also underpins much of my own approach to christology.

Plurality of the Treasure in Earthen Vessels

SEIICHI YAGI

"But we have this treasure in earthen vessels, that the excellency of the power may be of God, and not of us" (2 Cor 4:7).

Paul had a subtle, correct insight into how the treasure is in our world. But what is the treasure? Apart from the exegesis of this verse, many answers are possible; tentatively, Christians, Christianity, right doctrines, the Bible, apostolic kerygma, Jesus Christ to whom the Bible bears witness, the universal Logos, the Ultimate, and so on. One thing is clear: we cannot separate the treasure from the earthen vessels in which the treasure is. The treasure is actual in vessels or, we can say, the reality of the treasure-in-vessels is the actuality of the otherwise transcendent treasure in the world. Indeed Paul could in this way identify Christ with the church as his body (1 Cor 12:12), or he was aware that his mission was the work Christ wrought through him (Rom 15:18).

On the other hand, it is also clear that we must make a strict distinction between the treasure and its earthen vessels because the nature of the treasure is such that it illuminates the earthen vessels as earthen vessels, forbidding one to confuse them with the treasure itself, as is shown in the latter part of the quotation.

Paul says, "For through the law I died to the law, to live for God. I have been crucified with Christ. It is no more I who lives, but Christ in me" (Gal 2:19-20). "Christ in me" is the Self of him, while "I," once dead and now living for God, is his ego, to and in which "the Son of God" was revealed (Gal 1:16), so that Paul as a human existence is now *the body* as a shrine of the Holy Spirit (1 Cor 6:19) and the structure of his subjectivity may be formulated as "Self-ego." In this sense "Christ in me" is the treasure-in-vessel par excellence.

This *"Christ* in me" is infinitely beyond my ego. But on the other hand, it is the Self of mine. I call this the "Self of mine," because I found that "the Formless Self," as Zen-Buddhists call it, or "the True Human of no Rank" who works in the body is the same reality that Paul called "Christ in me." I am not saying that I am the discoverer. By no means.

But this was to me one of the decisive discoveries that determined my thinking since then.[1]

But there are levels of the treasure (in vessels): divine Logos, Logos incarnate (*Christ* in me, the Self), Christian existence (Self-ego), Christian church (Bible, doctrines, and so on; see below), to which correspond on the side of, for example, Buddhism, *dharma-kaya, samboga-kaya, nirmana-kaya, samgha*, sutras, and so forth. Therefore, one must say also that they too are *vessels* of the treasure.

As the words "through the law I died to the law" suggest, this awareness of the treasure-in-vessel is conditioned by the freedom from the language (cf. "For the letter kills, but the Spirit gives life" [2 Cor 3:6]). Language is surely one of the most important vessels of the treasure. But it remains earthen, human. "Woe to me! for I am lost; for I am a man of unclean lips and I dwell among the people of unclean lips" (Is 6:5).

Religious language is an attempt to speak of what is beyond language. Seen from this point of view, Christian doctrines, Bible, and apostolic kerygma are the treasure-in-*vessels* and not the treasure itself, distinct from the vessels. But, one may argue, the language of the apostolic witness is constitutive of the gospel itself, because without it the salvation event of Jesus Christ cannot be made known (cf. Rom 10:14f.). The salvation event of Jesus is the event in history which must be told.

---

[1] Takizawa Katsumi (1909-84) made a distinction between "the primary contact of God with the human being and the secondary one." The former means the primordial fact given to every one unconditionally. He called it "Immanuel" (God with us) and identified it with "Christ." Not all persons are aware of the primary contact. But when a person awakens to it the person begins to live realizing the primary contact and Takizawa called this the secondary contact. Now, according to Takizawa, Jesus is the person who attained the secondary contact so completely that he could become the model of being human. That means that it is not the case that Jesus established the primary contact itself. But Christianity has ignored that and held Jesus for the primary contact itself so that Jesus has become the exclusive ground of human salvation. If one criticizes traditional Christianity at this point one sees that there are other real religions that have attained the secondary contact, and Buddhism is indeed one instance of this realization. Thus Takizawa held Buddhism to be a religion based on the same ground as Christianity and interpreted "the Formless Self" of Japanese philosopher Hisamatsu Shin-ichi (1889-1980), as well as the "True Human of No Rank" of Rinzai (a Chinese Zen Master of the ninth century, founder of the Rinzai-school of Zen) as the realization of the primary contact.

Yagi affirmed Takizawa's distinction *mutatis mutandis* and interpreted what Takizawa termed the secondary contact as the activation of the Self in individuals, so that the secondary contact means the event in which the ego awakens to the Self or the Self reveals itself to and in the ego (Seiichi Yagi, "Christ and Buddha," *Journal of Ecumenical Studies* 27, 2 [Spring 1990], pp. 306-26).

Of course the fact of the incarnation is the event in history. In other words, the reality of the treasure-in-vessel, Jesus of Nazareth, must be witnessed to. But, however "heretical" it may sound, the Logos became flesh—this is the salvation event—not in Jesus alone. Jesus is the model of the treasure-in-vessel, and, if one admits that, one will also admit that the language in itself is an *earthen* vessel for the treasure. It can become treasure-in-*vessel* but they cannot be confused with the *treasure*-in-vessel, which is beyond language. Christians are not always clear at this point, whereas Zen-Buddhists are—like mystics in Christian tradition— sharply aware.

"Ungan said, 'This summer I preached and preached for the sake of my brothers. Look, to see whether I have still eyebrows!'"[2] A dilemma: language is an inadequate vessel for the Ultimate, but without this vessel one cannot communicate it. The awareness of this dilemma can be found richly in Zen literature. Rinzai warned repeatedly against searching after the truth in verbal expressions. Bodhi-Dharma answered the Chinese Emperor Wu, who asked him what the ultimate formulation of the holy truth is—"Openness to all directions. Nothing holy"[3]—which in a way reminds us of John 3:8: "The wind blows where it wills, you hear the sound of it, but you do not know where it comes from, or where it is going." The Spirit-wind cannot be confined to any finite form.

In fact, the treasure is, as was said above, not actual in this world without the earthen vessels. This is the case primarily with human existence prior to its verbal expressions. When the Son of God was revealed to Paul he was qualified as the Apostle for the Gentiles and he received the formula of the Christ-kerygma most probably thereafter (cf. Gal 1:16; 1 Cor 15:3ff.). Thus we can make a distinction between the Logos incarnate itself and the Bible as the witness to it. The language is, as well as the ego, constitutive of, but not capable of containing the treasure fully. So is it in the Bible as the witness to it. The language is, as well as the ego, constitutive of but not capable of containing the treasure fully. So also is it in the case of Zen. Buddha-nature is actual only when one becomes aware of it, that is to say, when one's bodily existence as a whole actually becomes the vessel of it. Until that moment the Buddha-nature remains potential. In other words; its actuality is simultaneous with enlightenment. But the actuality of bodily enlightenment is distinguished from its verbal expression. Now precisely because of this correct "awareness" a certain propensity seems to develop at times. Buddhists occasionally seem to tend to lay emphasis on the actuality of

---

[2] *Pi-Yen-Lu*, Japanese, *Hekiganrou* (a classical Chinese Zen writing completed in the twelfth century), 8. It was said that the eyebrows fell off if one preached Zen in an improper way.

[3] Ibid., 1.

enlightenment rather than on its ground: Dharma. That then gives rise to a claim of the superiority, if not of the absoluteness, of certain enlightened individuals or the schools that hand down the enlightenment, though it is true that any enlightenment as a treasure-in-vessel is unique and individual.

We ask again what the treasure is, keeping in mind that the reality of the treasure-in-vessel is the actuality of the treasure in the world.

If one answers that God or the universal Logos or the Ultimate is the treasure in the primary sense, one assumes naturally that there are a number of vessels, for no finite vessel can confine the infinite exclusively to itself. Thus, if one lays all the stress on God, one tends to make light of the vessel with the result that religion becomes meaningless and God becomes an unfathomable X.

If, on the contrary, one holds the treasure-in-*vessel* not only for the indispensable moment of the actuality of the treasure but for the treasure itself—as is the case with traditional Christianity which preaches Jesus of Nazareth not as the most important treasure-in-vessel but as *the* treasure, that is, as *the* revelation of God as the *unique* salvation event for all humanity—that logically grounds not only the uniqueness and individuality, but at the same time also the claim of the absoluteness of Jesus and of the Bible as the witness to Jesus.

Today not a few Christian theologians want to avoid both extremes, absolutism and relativism. Then the solution is at hand: an absolutist-relativist view of Jesus—and therefore also of Christianity[4]—as the treasure-in-vessel, not as the treasure in the primary sense of the word. We do not assert this on grounds of the needs of our time, which seeks such a solution. The needs of the time are merely the occasion. The absolutist-relativist view must be based on the structure of human reality itself (Self-ego).

Now, if Jesus is a treasure-in-vessel—even if he is the most important one—there is nothing that prevents us from assuming a plurality of vessels, for the treasure is not confined to Jesus alone. Thus we come to the conclusion of this essay: If one admits that the reality of the treasure in vessels is the actuality of the treasure in the world, that is, that the human vessels are constitutive of the latter, we can name as "treasures" not only the treasure as distinct from the vessels (that is, the Ultimate itself), but also the treasure-in-vessels (though it may cause, indeed has caused, confusion), namely: 1) that which mediates between the Ultimate and humans (the Logos incarnate: "*Christ* in me"); 2) the humans as Self-ego; and 3) the expressions or the witnesses to the treasures.

---

[4] On the absoluteness of the relative religion see Langdon Gilkey, "Plurality and Its Theological Implication," in *The Myth of Christian Uniqueness*, ed. John Hick and Paul Knitter (Maryknoll, N.Y.: Orbis Books, 1987), pp. 37-50.

Then any religion that is a treasure-in-*vessel* is itself a treasure in the third sense: a real religion.

If one holds primarily the ultimate for the treasure, one's view as to the religion becomes relativist, whereas one becomes absolutist if one holds primarily a treasure in *vessels* (Jesus, Bible, Christianity) for *the* treasure. But we admit the levels of the treasure as well as the actuality of the treasure in plural vessels. We need indeed both views, which not only postulate but also relativize each other, relativist view as well as absolutist one. If one is absolutist, one should have an understanding for the *raison d'être* of the relativist view and vice versa, because without the ultimate the universe is *nihil* and without "vessels" the ultimate is not actual in the world. There are plural treasures: the Ultimate, the Logos incarnate, "Self-egos," and real religions.

Based on the discussion above, I agree with Paul Knitter's theses. If our view is right, it is evident that "previous understandings of the uniqueness of Jesus 1) not only can be," but also 2) "must be reinterpreted." Jesus is surely unique. But Logos became incarnate in such traditions as Buddhism. 3) "The uniqueness of Jesus' salvific role can be reinterpreted in terms of *truly* but not *only*," because such persons as Gautama also have salvific meaning. 4) Salvation means the reality of the treasure in vessel, which every religious person is. Namely, it is realized "in this world" in and through those who are awakened to the Self, which is actual in "their actions." 5) This view of Jesus does not prevent us from "a following of Jesus." By no means. If great religious traditions, which developed independently, witness together to the principally same reality of the treasure, this agreement is rather the guarantee of their truth than their diminution to "mere" relativeness.

The superiority complex has always caused discrimination. But that I learn much from Buddhism does not prevent me from following Jesus, just as my Buddhist friends who learn much from Jesus do not cease being Buddhists.

PART III

Paul F. Knitter Responds

Can Our "One and Only" also Be a "One among Many"?

A Response to Responses

PAUL F. KNITTER

It worked! The idea that Len Swidler and Paul Mojzes proposed to me when I submitted my Five Theses for publication in the *Journal of Ecumenical Studies* turned out to be a good one, I think. They thought that the way I formulated these theses on the uniqueness of Jesus could elicit a conversation among Christians that might serve both the academic and Christian communities. Over the past decade or two, the question of whether/how Jesus is unique among other religious figures has become somewhat of a theological stall, which to a great extent has blocked the flow of scholarly and pastoral traffic. The issue has been "driven" by so many people, with such "heavy feet," and in so many contrary directions that it seems to have broken down hopelessly. Indeed, there have been and continue to be voices, some of them in these pages, that urge Christians to leave the stall and move on to more productive concerns that will enlighten Christian theology and dialogue with other religions.

In fostering the conversation that this book contains, Swidler and Mojzes did not want to move this theological stall off the road but, rather, to put it back on track—a track that will enable it at least to move in new directions if not arrive at a common destination. After pondering—and being shaken, stimulated, and enlightened—by the commentaries on my Five Theses, I think the theological discussion on the uniqueness of Jesus has been moved forward. For me, and I hope for the churches and the academy, differences have been clarified, new common ground has been established, and new directions for shared efforts and possible consensus have been identified.

In this response and commentary I hope to lay out the ground Christians share, the issues that divide us, and the directions we can pursue in order to arrive at greater clarity and cohesion about who Jesus is for us and how we can speak about him in an ever more effective dialogue with persons walking other religious paths. As is evident, I'm talking with and to my Christian brothers and sisters. But I hope that any others who want to eavesdrop on the conversation will find it helpful and hopeful.

I've sifted through all the criticisms, caveats, applause, and suggestions that these conversation partners have offered, and I've formulated six areas or general issues in which I have found both promising agreement and promising differences: the Bible, the nature of dialogue, Jesus as savior and Son of God, the Reign of God, mission, and the Spirit. In a sense, I'm more encouraged by the differences than by the agreements, for the differences and criticisms have helped me better grasp the concerns of my critics as well as the limitations (or aberrations) of my own efforts to talk about who Jesus is for the Christian community.

I'm deeply grateful for and challenged by this conversation. And I remain optimistic that we Christians can get our christological and dialogical acts together. This conversation has helped me trust that the "one and only" whom we Christians experience in our communities can also be the "one among many" whom we proclaim in the broader community of religions.

I

To be orthodox, any reinterpretation of the uniqueness of Jesus must be faithful to the biblical witness.

But how is such fidelity determined and maintained?

This is an issue that will most assuredly elicit a nod of mutual assent from all the participants in this conversation; everyone would agree that the biblical witness, especially in what Christians call the New Testament, is *normative* for the way Christians seek to live and understand their lives. Thus, to engage in dialogue with other religious persons or to formulate "new" understandings of who Jesus is without listening and trying to be faithful to this scriptural norm might be acceptable for the philosopher of religion but not for the Christian theologian. Like any group of people who want to maintain a common identity and purpose, Christians have to be able to proclaim: "We hold these truths." Without the Bible, they don't know what truths they are talking about.

But this is where, according to many of the voices in this book, my proposal limps or collapses. In their view I am *not* faithful to the biblical witness about Jesus. I think I am. This shows that the nub of our discussion should be, not *whether* the Bible is normative, but *how* one determines and maintains that normativity. By reviewing and responding to their concerns about my biblical infidelity, I hope I can lay the groundwork for greater agreement on what fidelity means.

1. First, there is concern that I'm not listening to the Bible carefully enough to hear its normative voice. After all, as Karl-Josef Kuschel points out, I cite it only once in my essay. And because I'm not listening enough, according to Kajsa Ahlstrand, I'm not sufficiently armed against the temptations any Christian faces, namely, "the tyranny of current politically correct opinions" about Jesus or the temptation to want to "please believers outside the Christian community" rather than let them hear the sometimes harsh truth of the full gospel.

Whether I'm listening carefully enough or not, most of my biblically based critics are telling me that I haven't really heard or taken seriously what the Bible tells us about God and about Jesus. Regarding God, I've imposed on the biblical witness my own notion of Mystery (derived from the Greeks, according to John Sanders or from the post-modernists according to Kuschel). Kuschel reminds me that for the followers of Moses and of Jesus (and one might add, of Muhammad), God does not remain an "unsurpassable Mystery"; God does not play hide-and-seek with humanity. Rather, God has stepped from behind the veil of mystery and made the divine self known to humans. And although God may have revealed God's self in various ways, these ways are *not* equally significant or valid. According to Kuschel, Sanders, and Clark Pinnock, the New Testament, in its multiple traditions, is undeniably clear in announcing God's revelation in Jesus as "eschatologically final (definitive and unsurpassable)" (Kuschel). In Pinnock's view, Jesus understood himself to "occupy a position of unique mediation between God and humankind. . . . Jesus assumed unparalleled authority." Sanders reminds me that the early Christians made these definitive, unsurpassable claims about Jesus in a world teeming with religious pluralism; they knew exactly what they were doing when they proclaimed that Jesus was final and could not be surpassed by anyone else.

So Kuschel summarizes the good but astonishing news of the gospel in this way: "The infinite God reveals himself in a finite human being who is therefore God's Word, Image, the Messiah, the Son"—and then he immediately asks, "Is this idolatry?" Sanders takes Kuschel's question seriously and says that even if it were idolatry, it would be biblically approved idolatry, which he as a Christian would accept. "The making of idols may be illegitimate for us but may be quite legitimate for God."

2. Sanders' stunning statement helps me formulate my response and suggestions about how the Bible exercises its normativity in the Christian community. If Sanders were really convinced that the Bible was proposing idolatry, would he accept and practice such a proposal? I honestly don't think so. Archbishop Desmond Tutu once declared that if he found that the Bible actually propounded or justified apartheid (as many of his South African fellow Christians were arguing), he would abandon the Bible. I think Sanders would too. Certainly I would try to convince

him that he should! On what basis? On the basis of the way in which the Bible exercises its normativity in the first place; that is, the way it touches and illumines and shakes up our *experience*. The Bible does not function as the norm within Christian communities *all by itself*, simply by delivering decrees, as the popes have often done in the Roman Catholic community. Rather, the Bible "proves," as it were, or demonstrates its normativity by the way it addresses and elicits a response from the community. Thus, there are, I suggest, two central norms in Christianity—the Bible and the ongoing presence of the Holy Spirit within the experience of the community. One does not precede the other; one cannot function without the other.

To absolutize the authority of the Bible, to assert its authority independently of its ability to speak to and be received by the community, is to run the risk of idolizing the Bible (just as Catholics have idolized the pope by separating his authority from the sense of the faithful and the other bishops). If Christians do not also recognize the normativity of the Bible *together with* the normativity of the community, they all too easily end up identifying the Bible with God. Sanders rightly warns me against setting human norms over the authority of God; I fear that the Bible itself can sometimes be numbered among such human norms.

When I affirm God as unsurpassable Mystery or as ultimate Mystery incapable of being contained in human thought, I am doing so not because I have kowtowed to Greek philosophy or natural theology (Sanders), or to post-modern correctness (Ahlstrand), or because I am using a God-concept based on humanistic epistemology (Kuschel); rather, I believe my notion of God as unsurpassable Mystery is based on what I find in the contemporary conversation between the biblical witness and my experience within the Christian community. Without listing "proof-texts," I trust that while most Christians would agree that the Bible insists that in Christ Jesus God is indeed revealed "fully," we should never think that we have grasped the fullness of who God is. This is the paradox of incarnation that I tried to take seriously in my essay. Thus, while the gospels portray Jesus as assuming "unparalleled authority" (Pinnock), they also present him as reminding us that the Father is greater than he, that we should call no one (not even Jesus) Father, and that the Spirit will have more to say than Jesus did.

In insisting on Jesus' "unparalleled authority" and on Jesus' eschatological finality, my critics, I fear, are losing the essential ingredient of paradox in all Christian belief: in Jesus, God is revealed fully and yet there is more to come; in Jesus God's Reign is "already" but also "not yet." I would remind them that God is revealed totally and completely *nowhere*. To say that God is totally revealed anywhere is to open the door to idolatry. I think a glance at church history will show how that works.

3. But Kuschel, Sanders, and Pinnock will want to press their biblical concerns, saying I have not dealt with the explicit texts in the New Testament that hold up Jesus as "one and only" or as "once and for all." Kuschel has listed such biblical references and shown their multi-traditioned roots. My friends are right. I should have said more about taking such biblical texts seriously, for that is definitely what I want to do. Elsewhere, I have tried to do so—in *No Other Name?* and *Jesus and the Other Names*.[1] To carry this present conversation along, let me say briefly that although I try to share the *seriousness* with which my critical friends take such passages, I don't share their tight or literal *interpretation*. Such kerygmatic declarations about Jesus as the only one who "knows the Father" (Mt 11:27) or who "rests on the heart of the Father" (Jn 1:18), or who is "the image of the invisible God" in whom God's fullness dwells (Col 1:15, 19)—all such statements are religious confessions, using religious language, which is inherently symbolic or metaphoric. That, of course, does not deny that such statements are making real truth claims; yet these claims are delivered in language that is more poetic than propositional—or in pictures that are more impressionistic than photographic.

Therefore, I suggest that we can best interpret such "one and only" statements about Jesus by using what might be called a *hermeneutic of discipleship*. Just such a hermeneutic, I believe, is what John Mbiti inspiringly describes in his review of contemporary Asian and African efforts to reinterpret the meaning of Jesus in their contexts. Although the "one and only" biblical passages are certainly saying something about Jesus, their truth lies primarily in calling us to discipleship rather than in giving us a definitive, philosophical definition of who Jesus was and how he lines up with other religious figures. They are more calls to action than theological definitions; they are examples of performative language eliciting commitment to a way of life rather than philosophical language providing an ontological definition of Jesus' nature. In announcing Jesus as "no other name" (Acts 4:12), the Christian community was calling on itself and others to give full allegiance to Jesus and to turn away from any name or any thing that would impede that allegiance. In declaring Jesus to be the "one mediator" (1 Tm 2:5), the enthusiastic disciples of Jesus were extolling him as someone whose vision was entirely worthy of all one's trust and energies—not as a means of excluding others. I tried to describe such a hermeneutic of discipleship in thesis 4 of my essay; I should have applied it more explicitly to New Testament christology.

---

[1] Paul F. Knitter, *No Other Name?* (Maryknoll, N.Y.: Orbis Books, 1985), chap. 9; idem, *Jesus and the Other Names* (Maryknoll, N.Y.: Orbis Books, 1996).

By applying a hermeneutic of discipleship to the exclusivist New Testament statements about Jesus, we can also make sense of what John Macquarrie points out: that already in the New Testament there is a rich variety of viewpoints on the person and work of Jesus and that besides the exclusive statements about Jesus there are also New Testament perspectives that affirm the universal activity of God, outside of and distinct from Jesus. Such universal or pluralistic viewpoints, he urges, "need to be rescued from the obscurity cast over them by the dominant emphasis on the notion of 'only-begotten'" (Macquarrie). Once rescued, such universal perspectives, it seems to me, cannot be brought into balance with their exclusive New Testament counterparts if such exclusive language is taken literally.

Understanding the "one and only" New Testament texts from a hermeneutic of discipleship and trying to balance them with the more universal or pluralistic traditions of the Bible, we can better understand what the early Christian intended when they announced such exclusive-sounding claims about Jesus in a world of religious pluralism. In proclaiming Jesus as the "only begotten" or "one mediator," they certainly intended to, and did, *exclude* other religious options or figures. But they did so not because these other options were *other* (that is, different from Jesus) but because such options were *opposed* to Jesus' vision of the Reign of God. If other religions or religious prophets were not against the intent of God's Reign—if these other visions could either enhance or be enhanced by the Christian vision of how all may have life and have it more abundantly—then such other religious options are "with us" and not to be excluded or stopped (cf. Mk 9:40).

In general, especially amid the current recognition of the centrality of narrative in preaching and theology, I hope that all Christians can accept the advice of José Míguez Bonino, who points out that the New Testament presents us with stories (not with philosophical or theological treatises) that tell us how we can image God and how we can live God's life in this world. These stories, focused around Jesus, offer a clear enough and engaging enough picture of God and God's Reign to provide Christians with a solid place to stand and with a valuable, even necessary, contribution to make to the interreligious conversation. Thus Christians, both liberal and conservative, should have ample protection against the contemporary politically correct winds (whether those winds blow from the right or the left!). Proclaiming Jesus as his faithful disciples, Christians sometimes will have to announce and sometimes denounce, sometimes affirm and sometimes exclude, sometimes include and sometimes be included by other religious announcements of the good news. Jesus will be for Christians both their "one and only" and also "one among many."

II

Dialogue is a Christian imperative—necessary for Christians to live out the values and vision of the gospel in today's world.

But what does a conversation among religious communities really mean? What does it require? What are the prerequisites for genuine dialogue?

I trust I am not simply hearing what I want to hear when I transmit the following consensus, which I pick up from all the participants in this discussion, either in the foreground or the background of what they had to say: dialogue with pilgrims on other religious paths is for Christians not only something worthwhile but also something necessary. In this conviction, these theologians reflect what I think is a growing recognition among all the so-called mainline Christian churches, and even among some Evangelical communities.

1. But while everyone might recognize the need for dialogue, not everyone is agreed on just what it means—and especially, on what it demands of Christians. One of the staunchest criticisms that many of the commentators raised was triggered by what I proposed in thesis 2, when I asserted that the widespread inclusivist models for a Christian theology of religions become unintentional roadblocks to dialogue.

A variety of respondents, using a variety of arguments, all chimed in on a common insistence that such roadblocks are more imaginary than real. Both practically and theoretically, they argue, firm inclusivist convictions need not impede—indeed, they promote—interreligious conversation. Monika Hellwig looks at her long-time experience in interfaith dialogue and concludes, "It has not been my experience that such exchanges depended upon any particular interpretation of the uniqueness of Jesus." Indeed, she has witnessed vibrant dialogue among persons who take vibrant exclusivist positions.

Pinnock agrees: "Holding to the metaphysical singularity of Jesus as the unique Son of God does not threaten dialogue." He urges persons of different religions to imitate the way scientists pursue truth in their interscientific dialogue: each hypothesis is proposed to the community of scientists in a strong, often exclusive way, and from the ensuing discussion and experimentations the truth takes shape. Kuschel pushes forward Pinnock's suggestion. He argues that all religions, because of the nature of religious experience, naturally make strong, definitive truth claims. To require that all participants in the dialogue deposit their exclusive or definitive claims at the door of dialogue is to do violence to everyone involved. Kuschel also points out that Christian claims to an unsurpassable and definitive truth, though they may be "awkward and difficult to communicate," can still be expressed "in a non-absolutist and non-superior way as the faith witness of human beings who are willing to wager their very living and dying upon the reliability and trustworthiness of God."

Cobb, more simply and pragmatically, contends that it is a mistake to set up any prerequisites for dialogue before the process actually starts. If there are impediments to dialogue hiding in the attitudes of the participants, they will be revealed in the give-and-take of conversation.

I hope my efforts to take seriously and respond to what these friends are saying might introduce some helpful distinctions into our discussion. Hellwig and Pinnock are right that absolute, metaphysical claims need not interfere with interreligious dialogue, but only, I think, if the intent of such dialogue is limited to the promotion of greater information and mutual understanding. If, however, the participants want to do more, if they want not only to exchange information but to pursue truth together, then absolute, definitive truth claims are going to be problematic. The pursuit of truth means the readiness to change, the willingness to admit that there may be more to learn and that one's own view may not be the only or the best version of truth. But to take such a stand, it seems to me, is diametrically opposed to making assertions stamped *unsurpassable* and *definitive*. Here I would remind Pinnock that although scientists have advanced their cases with exclusionary vigor, they always propose such arguments as hypotheses. To claim that a hypothesis is unsurpassable or definitive is to argue for a square circle. One might say that it is the nature of scientific discourse to make absolute statements in a relative way.

And this is where Kuschel's comments helped me. At first I simply could not grasp his insistence that one can make "unsurpassable" claims in a "non-absolutist and non-superior way." But when he went on to explain that these claims are being made by religious believers expressing their trust in God, I realized that, yes, if we consider the *act of faith* (or the act of religious experience), then individuals or a community will speak in definitive, unsurpassable terms, for here they are expressing the total trust and commitment that a person feels when touched by the Divine. These are matters of the religious heart, and the heart trusts and gives itself fully into the fullness/emptiness of God or Dharma. But if we consider the *content of faith*, that is, if we try to express and talk about and put into words the Reality that has grasped us, then, as Kuschel admonishes, we cannot say that our religious views are necessarily "absolute" or "superior" to yours. These are matters of the head, of trying to understand and articulate the divine Mystery that has become so powerfully real for us.

The problem, however, is that Christians and religious persons in general often don't make such distinctions as they enter into dialogue. The vigor and fullness and unsurpassability that they feel in their religious commitments is translated into their language and into their religious doctrines and theologies. As Anthony Fernando points out, the absoluteness of the religious heart becomes the absoluteness of the religious mind—and eventually of the system. Or expressed differently: "Here is where I stand because God has called me here" becomes "Here is where I stand because this is the only place God has called me—or, the only place God calls everyone!" Jesus, whom I experience and proclaim as my "one and only," ends up excluding or subordinating other revelations experienced by others as their "one and only."

When I hold up my "one and only" as *necessarily* or *metaphysically* surpassing and providing the final word for your "one and only," then dialogue breaks down. To John Cobb I would venture to say that such has already been my experience of dialogue. Sufficient efforts already have been made in the arena of interreligious encounter for us to know what gets in the way and what doesn't. I would hope that all participants in the dialogue can come to mutual agreement on certain prerequisites or guidelines that will keep their discussions on track and avoid frustration.

This present conversation has helped me better understand that if one of the accepted guidelines requires participants to avoid making divinely approved "definitive" or "unsurpassable" declarations of truth, this does not mean that they have to check their "absolute" or "decisive" convictions and commitments at the door. What I'm trying to get at is expressed, I think, in Ahlstrand's distinction between a "subordinating inclusivism" and an "egalitarian inclusivism." Inclusive claims *subordinate* all others to themselves when they make absolute truth claims in an absolute manner; that is, when the absoluteness of the heart is translated into the absoluteness of the head. Inclusive claims are *egalitarian* and recognize the potential "inclusive" truth of others when they make absolute truth claims in a relative manner—i.e., when they recognize that their mind's grasp of the truth cannot be identified with their heart's commitment to truth. But in so stretching the word *inclusivism*, Ahlstrand indirectly asks whether such terms as *exclusivism*, *inclusivism*, and *pluralism* are appropriate for what we're talking about.

2. This question about terminology is pushed more explicitly and, for me, persuasively by Michael von Brück. He reminds me that every model for approaching the other will always be inclusive insofar as we unavoidably view the other, and so include the other, from our own given perspective, with our own norms for truth. But, echoing Kuschel, he immediately adds, "We have to say clearly that we do not regard our [inclusive] truth claims as superior." So, for von Brück, neither *inclusivism* nor *pluralism* describes what he thinks goes on in authentic

dialogue. He suggests, rather, a model of what he terms "partnership in identity" for religious pluralism. It is a model in which both the distinct identity and the inherent partnership or relatedness of each participant is affirmed and respected by all.

Thus, each participant in the conversation will assert his or her convictions in a clear, affirmative, yes, "normative" manner: "I hold these truths." This is part of maintaining one's identity. But at the same time, each will also allow and encourage the other to do likewise, recognizing that the other's truth claims might turn out to be normative also for oneself. This is part of respecting the other as partner. For me, such a model can best be described as *correlational.*

A *correlational model for interfaith dialogue* calls upon all to view and approach other religious believers in such a way that an authentic *co-relation* can exist among them. The goal is to maintain *real relationship*, to do all one can to keep from cutting off the relationship or maiming it by subordinating one participant to another. This means that while I will speak my convictions and my mind clearly and strongly, I will do so in such a way that allows you to do the same. This reflects what we said above about making absolute claims in a relative manner. In such a correlational model, all religions are viewed from the beginning of the conversation, *not* as necessarily being *equal* or the *same* in their truth claims (whether that is so can be known only in the dialogue[2]) but as having *equal rights*. Thus if I feel impelled to make normative or absolute truth claims in the conversation, I will do so in a way that still recognizes and allows for my partner to do likewise. This means that I am open to the possibility that my normative claim may be corrected or "normed" by what my partner has to say. So even though, as von Brück and Kuschel propose, we don't begin a correlational dialogue with pre-

---

[2] So I both agree and disagree with John Hick when he urges that to begin the multifaith conversation properly, we have to recognize not just the *possibility* but the *actuality* of genuine truth in our partners' religions. Methodologically and politically, I would disagree. All that is required of me to listen genuinely to the other is that I truly affirm the possibility, or probability, that what the other has to say is true and valuable; whether it is actually so can be known only from the dialogue. Hick seems to recognize this when he says earlier that whether a religion is "true and salvific . . . is not something to be determined by a priori dogma [I would add, either theological or philosophical] but by the observation of actual human behavior." Politically, we must be careful, as Pinnock warns, of universal, a priori declarations that all religions are true, for as history has shown and shows, there is much evil that marches under the banner of religion. And yet, practically and experientially, I do agree with Hick, for I believe that enough dialogue has taken place among various religious communities for all participants to know, from the ethical and spiritual "fruits" observed in their partners, that it is not only possible or probable but actual that there is much truth and goodness dwelling within the hearts and beliefs of their partners in dialogue.

established claims of "superiority," through the dialogue participants may come to the conclusion that a particular Christian truth claim is superior to a Hindu claim—or vice versa!

Thanks in part to this exchange, I have thus come to consider *correlational* a much better adjective than *pluralistic* to describe the kind of dialogue or theology of religions that many Christians are searching for.

III

Christians must continue to proclaim Jesus as savior and as divine.

But what do these announcements mean? And how can Christians continue to make these proclamations in such a way that they maintain the uniqueness of Jesus without closing themselves to the uniqueness of other religious figures and revelations?

Neither I nor anyone speaking in these pages would want to deny or diminish the biblical affirmations that Jesus is savior and Son of God (this includes, if I may be so bold as to speak for him, John Hick). On this there is widespread agreement in both the popular and theological contingents of the Christian community: Christians are people who experience and therefore must let others know that Jesus of Nazareth is truly *Soter* or health-bringer, and *Emmanuel* or God-with-us. Remove these central pieces from the Christian edifice, and the whole structure crumbles. But today, when the mix of other religions is not only near but dizzying, there is among Christians a growing awareness or desire that these two axial beliefs must be lived and announced in such a way that not only allows for, but stimulates, real respect for and cooperation with followers of other religious revealers and revelations. Just how this can be done—how commitment to Jesus as divine savior can be maintained alongside openness to others—is where differences, often impatient and harsh, divide the Christian ranks. Most of these differences and divisions surface clearly in the discussion contained in this book.

1. A number of my critic-friends fear that with my interpretation of "truly but not only," I am diluting the full and the healing content of what Christians have always meant, and must mean, when they announce that Jesus is savior. Michael Amaladoss sets the stage when he points out what was missing in my theses: " . . . [the] saving significance of the paschal mystery for all people. I do not see how one can set about solving the problem of the uniqueness of Jesus without even adverting to this central affirmation." For the Carmodys, to separate *only* from *truly* is to take a path never followed by the Christian community throughout its history. Integral to Christian self-identity is the knowledge that "no salvation occurs apart from Jesus." If many Christians are today ques-

tioning the aged adage *No salvation outside the church*, they still endorse, as they always have, *No salvation outside of Jesus*. Therefore, wherever salvation, or transforming knowledge and love of God, occurs beyond the Christian borders, it is, according to the Carmodys, within "an ontological Christian order of salvation." This sounds much like a restatement of Rahner's view of anonymous or nameless Christians who live far from, but still bear the same salvific genes as, their named Christian brothers and sisters.

Ahlstrand, Pinnock, and Amaladoss have a common soteriological problem with my understanding of Jesus as true but not only savior. They fear that by questioning "only," I am cutting away the ontological or operative muscle in the Christian experience of Jesus as savior. In their view Jesus, for me, is not the agent of salvation, who actually changes things and provides salvific power (in traditional terms, grace). Rather, I reduce ontological reality to ethical ideals. Jesus' saving power is dwindled down to the power of "an inspiring example" (Ahlstrand). Pinnock is more direct in what he hears me saying: "Jesus is a unique saint for the world rather than only the savior of it." A "unique saint," Pinnock warns, does not provide the ontological cement that all ethical programs need. For Amaladoss, all this represents a reduction of salvation to revelation: "Dr. Knitter seems to reduce the role of Jesus to mediating God's presence, communicating God-experience, or revealing the truth about God."

That last statement of Amaladoss stimulates a suggestion or clarification that I hope will carry forward this part of the Christian conversation on Jesus as savior: To experience and speak about salvation as revelation represents a valid, more ecumenical soteriology than the more prevalent salvation-as-historical-transaction perspective. Even in the New Testament there is a variety of models with which the early Christians tried to state how the death and resurrection of Jesus transformed and saved their lives. Besides the Paschal model found especially in Paul, which presents Jesus as *effecting* reconciliation between God and humanity, there is also the Wisdom model found particularly in John, which portrays Jesus as the embodiment of God's revelation or as "Sophia's prophet."[3] In more current terminology, Schubert Ogden has called this a "representational christology" to distinguish it from the widespread "constitutive" view of the way Jesus brings about salvation: Jesus' life-death-resurrection saves, not by constituting or causing God's saving love, but, rather, insofar as he *re-presents* for us the

---

[3] See Edward Schillebeeckx, *Jesus: An Experiment in Christology* (New York: Crossroad, 1979), pp. 429-32; James D. G. Dunn, *Christology in the Making* (Philadelphia: Westminster, 1980), pp. 209-12; Elisabeth Schüssler Fiorenza, *Jesus: Miriam's Child, Sophia's Prophet* (New York: Continuum, 1994).

re-creative love of God that is inherent in the divine nature and is poured out on all creation.[4]

Such a representational christology, I would point out for Amaladoss, has firm roots in the Catholic tradition, for *representational* is another word for *sacramental*. Jesus is the primordial sacrament who, in what he taught and wrought, embodies, incarnates, exemplifies, makes real (these are all synonyms!) for us the effective, transformative power of God's love and justice. When such an example or teaching is sacramental, it is more than just an example. As the old Roman theology would put it, *symbolizando causant*, "by symbolizing (teaching, showing), sacraments cause or effect what they symbolize." A representational or sacramental christology, therefore, *does* deliver the ontological reality necessary to steel the ethical vision. With such a christology, I can fully agree with Pinnock's declaration: "More than an ethical norm, more than God's love in action, Jesus is God's presence in history according to our canon and tradition."

But such a sacramental soteriology is also more ecumenical, for if the way Jesus saves is generally understood as embodying or *re*presenting the love of God already offered by God (but poorly understood or often scorned by humans) rather than as a one-time transaction that repairs what was totally broken down or constitutes what was nonexistent, then Christians can be open to the possibility of other representations or revelations of this same love. What Paul calls the Mystery of God's plan revealed so powerfully and savingly in Christ Jesus, can be revealed elsewhere and in sundry forms—without ever exhausting that Mystery. In Christ Jesus, Christians do know how that Mystery works, but at the same time they can be (should be) open and eager to learn more.[5]

2. The concern that a so-called pluralist christology jeopardizes the traditional Christian understanding of Jesus as savior expands into a similar concern about the understanding of Jesus's divinity. The Carmodys provide the headlines for this concern: first they express their fear that any inclination to rank others on the same level as Jesus will not do justice to the divinity of Jesus; then, toward the end of their comments, they give full expression to their fears that such a christology will become an "unnecessary forfeit of the full divinity of Christ, without which

---

[4] Schubert Ogden, *The Point of Christology* (New York: Harper & Row, 1982), pp. 148-49; idem, *Is There Only One Religion or Are There Many?* (Dallas: Southern Methodist Press, 1992), pp. 84-104.

[5] So, when Pinnock reminds us that "one cannot assume the universal salvific will of God, as Knitter does, without acknowledging the centrality of Jesus in which it is grounded," I would want to change his last word from "grounded" to "revealed." Then I can recognize that this love of God is broader than Jesus and can, perhaps, be revealed elsewhere in different but equally effective ways.

Christian salvation becomes only a shell of its traditional self, not the faith of Hebrews' great cloud of witnesses." Amaladoss gives this fear a Trinitarian underpinning: "If God is the Trinity, however this is understood, and if the Second Person of the Blessed Trinity became a human person, however this process is explained, then that person is not just unique as any other human person or spiritual leader is unique." Finally, Ahlstrand puts an eschatological twist on these admonitions: If Jesus, as it were, can have co-equals, then how are Christians to understand their belief in the second coming of Christ? Are there to be many "Returners?" If there can be "many" at the end of history, there can be "many" at the beginning; so Ahlstrand worries about a multiplication of Gods, fearing that "a consistent pluralist christology questions monotheism."

To carry on the conversation, I would invite these critics to look at what they already know: that all our words and images about Jesus as divine or Son of God or only begotten are but symbolic fingers pointing to a Moon we will never fully grasp. We must ask what these fingers are really pointing to, even while admitting we will never know fully. In my own efforts to do that, I believe I am following a common opinion among theologians trying to unpack the meaning of Christian belief in the divinity of Jesus; in footnote 20 of my essay, I tried to provide a thumbnail sketch of this kind of christology, which basically carries on the representational approach I outlined above. When Christians announce Jesus as divine they are attempting to articulate two realities, one functional and the other ontological: a) Functionally or personally, Jesus is for them the perfect sacrament of God—to meet Jesus is to meet the Divine; in the way he mediates God to them, he is God for them. b) Ontologically, in order to explain the way Jesus functions as such a sacrament, he must have been, and must be, "oned" with God in a manner beyond full human comprehension; his very being must participate in the being of God.

If such an understanding of Jesus' divinity (among many possible ways of understanding it) is valid, then I believe it allows for the possibility that what happened in Jesus in order to enable him to function the way he did (as God's sacrament) can happen, analogously, in other, very different instances or persons. Here I agree with Macquarrie: the reality that we are trying to express with our Christian symbol of incarnation need not be a one-time event. I still do not fully understand why, for the Carmodys, to question whether Jesus is the *only* sacramental incarnation of God must necessarily question his *truly* being such an incarnation. If the totality of Jesus' being was divine, that doesn't mean that he contained the totality of the Divine.

That's why I would want to talk further with Amaladoss about his trinitarian reservations. When he states that "if the Second Person of the Blessed Trinity became a human person, however this process is explained . . . ," I would urge that the "however this process is explained" is pivotal. If one *identifies* the Second Person with the human person of Jesus, then incarnation is limited, for there can be only one human being called Jesus of Nazareth. Even though the Council of Chalcedon spoke of one person in two natures, they did *not* identify the trinitarian Second Person with the person of Jesus. Such a replacement of the human person by the divine Person would have resulted in a dehumanized humanity of Jesus: a divine person walking around in a human costume. But if the Second Person is not identified with the person of Jesus, then that Person or Word of God is, as the early Fathers insisted, free to operate and take seminal form elsewhere. Even St. Thomas Aquinas, as Hick points out in his essay, recognized the possibility (but not the actuality) of other incarnations of the Word.

I hope all this might assuage the concerns that Ahlstrand has about a pluralist christology placing monotheism into question. Such a christology doesn't question the oneness of the Divine but the way Christians have tended to produce theological straitjackets limiting the movement and the expressions of the Divine to one event or one pattern. What this means, however, for belief in the second coming of Christ, I must honestly say, I don't know. Maybe we have to think more on the gospel text on the Last Judgment, when people realized that who Jesus really is came to them in forms very different from Jesus (Mt 25:31-46).

3. Another wave of criticisms concerning my pluralist efforts to reinterpret the uniqueness of Jesus comes from a very different direction: here the concern is not so much that such revisions of Jesus' uniqueness transgress traditional beliefs but that they will detract from, dilute, or derail the pressing need for Christians to meet their religious neighbors. Wesley Ariarajah, from his vast experience and bruises in promoting interfaith dialogue within the World Council of Churches, is the most vigorous voice for this concern. For him, to try to energize and direct Christians in their encounters with other believers by urging the kind of revisions of Jesus' uniqueness and decisiveness I have proposed is like pouring water into the churches' gas tanks. This is not going to move anyone, neither Christians nor their dialogue partners. The task at hand is for Christians to be *good disciples*—to follow Jesus faithfully, to witness to him boldly, and to listen just as boldly to the words and wisdoms of others—without any talk of who's unique or better. "These words [*unique, decisive, indispensable,* and so on], however carefully interpreted, have no place in our Christian witness" (Ariarajah).

Amaladoss, from his experience in trying to promote dialogue within the Roman Church, concurs. He encourages us to stop all this theorizing on Jesus' uniqueness and go forth to meet and respect and learn from other religious communities. It's fruitless to seek after "an overall theoretical framework of comparisons and contrasts, attempting to solve all problems of difference, a priori and in the abstract . . . " (Amaladoss). From an entirely different angle, Hick seems to agree. He warns that in trying to analyze and revise such traditional Christian notions as *unique* and *distinctive* and *necessary*, I may have to pay the price of theorizing and clarifying myself back to the imperialistic traditional position of inclusivism.

I hope I see the real dangers these friends are pointing out. Trying to get one's theological act together can indeed get in the way of acting altogether! Yet what brings me to the theological conversation contained in this book is not simply intellectual or speculative curiosity but personal and pastoral pain. Although the promotion of greater understanding and cooperation among cultures and religions is a top priority for me, I pursue that priority as a Christian, within the Christian community. Therefore, it is of vital concern for me that whatever model or theology of religions I am following be also *received* and, at least to some significant extent, affirmed by members of my Christian community. And both before and especially after the publication of *No Other Name?*, I have discovered, sometimes painfully, that issues of how we understand the role and uniqueness of Jesus *do* concern many (certainly not all) of my fellow Christians. Unless I am thoroughly misunderstanding him, I suspect that Ariarajah's assertion that words like *unique, decisive,* and *indispensable* "have no place in our Christian witness" would not play very well, not only in Rome and Geneva, but also in many local parishes and congregations. These words are part of our Christian witness. And most Christians, at least those in the West, feel they have to deal with them.

Actually, both Ariarajah and Amaladoss do deal, at least implicitly, with issues of how to understand basic Christian doctrines like that of Jesus as unique savior within the new context of interreligious dialogue. After chiding me about trying to construct "overall theoretical frameworks," Amaladoss ends his reflections with a challenge to Christian theologians: "In light of this experience [interreligious dialogue], we will have to revise our vision of God's plan for the world and our theology of history . . . revelation and redemption." That's part of what I'm trying to do with my suggested revisions of how to understand Jesus' uniqueness. And when one looks closely at Ariarajah's description of the kind of discipleship to which he is calling us, especially as exemplified among *minjung* Christians, it is a praxis that embodies and is grounded in an understanding of the uniqueness of Jesus similar to my theoretical proposals: Ariarajah challenges us to follow the example of *minjung* Christians, who take clear, uncompromising stands for the poor (such stands are decisive); all Christians are to "give an account of the hope that is in them" (that requires making universal claims); and they are to use "the values of the Kingdom" to discern whether the Spirit of God is active in other religious practices (such values are used as universal, decisive norms). So it seems to me that Ariarajah and Amaladoss are in agreement with me about the practice of dialogue; we differ on whether or how to name that practice.

4. Perhaps the suggestions of Cragg and Ahlstrand can help solve such theoretical differences. Maybe the word *unique* is off-putting for many non-Christians *and* Christians. Drawing on his exegetical expertise, Cragg reminds us that the word *unique* is not biblical language, especially when it is understood to imply exclusion or inclusion. Even the New Testament use of "one" or "only," Cragg points out, does not carry the sense of separating from others but rather connotes "entirely, completely, wholly." Thus, "only Son of God" affirms that Jesus is totally, entirely Son of God—not necessarily that there are no other Sons or Daughters of God. Therefore, for Cragg, a much more appropriate word for our christological vocabulary is *distinctive*. While *unique* signifies difference that excludes or dominates, *distinctive* affirms a difference that is connected with others: "'distinctive,' unlike 'unique,' does not totally exclude or need contrivance to include, since it relates multilaterally." If something is distinctive, it is always "within a unity." So Christ or Christianity "differ only to belong." What Cragg finds in the word *distinctive*, Ahlstrand seems to find in her suggested term, *special*. Christians should announce Jesus as *special* rather than *unique*.

All I can say is that the engaging content that Cragg and Ahlstrand lay bare in the terms *distinctive* and *special* is precisely what I hoped the distinctions I proposed in thesis 3 would reveal in (or instill into) *unique*. I wanted to stick with the traditional or familiar terminology in the hope that Christians could use old language in a new way; this can enable them to move forward with a sense of continuity with the past. In the final analysis, however, whether Christians talk about Jesus as "unique" or as "distinct/special" (none of these terms was coined in the Bible) makes little difference as long as their words encourage them to live out a full commitment to Jesus together with a full openness to others. Cragg's notion of distinctive as "differing only to belong" is an insightful and involving way of describing a correlational christology that would sustain the correlational dialogue that I proposed above: an understanding of Jesus the Christ that affirms his difference from others, but a difference that *requires* Christians to respect and enter into a genuine co-relation with others.

To affirm *that* Jesus is different leads to the issue of *how* he is different.

IV

Jesus' preaching of the Reign of God pertains to that which constitutes the identity and the distinctiveness of his person and his message.

But what did this symbol or ideal of the Reign of God mean for Jesus and what does it (should it) mean for Christians today? Does it require

an active engagement in promoting the well-being of this world? If so,
does this make Christianity unique among religious traditions?

I find it interesting, even ironic, that the criticism I drew when I questioned the uniqueness of Jesus in *No Other Name?* seems to be outweighed by the criticism stirred up by my recent attempts to affirm and especially to give content to Jesus' uniqueness. Thesis 4 has set off some of the most vigorous, but also the most challenging and helpful, interaction in this conversation. And yet, all these criticisms, despite their diversity, share (among themselves and with me) a large and relevant piece of common ground: although they qualify or reject my suggestion that the uniqueness of Jesus is found in his call to a this-worldly engagement, they do agree that an absolutely necessary requirement for understanding Jesus and his original mission is the symbol or ideal of the Reign of God. As New Testament scholars tell us (with a unanimity not generally found among their kind), to get at what Jesus was all about we have to take seriously the central place that the *Basileia tou Theou* occupied in his preaching, acting, and (as much as we can tell) his consciousness.

But from this common ground, opinions about what the Reign of God meant for Jesus and what it should mean for Christians today diverge like so many paths into a dark forest. Still, I believe that in discussing these differences, if we affirm and return to our common starting point, we *can* talk to each other from our different paths and so find the necessary light to come closer together. I hope something like that will result from this part of the conversation.

1. To start with the last of the controverted issues summarized above, even if my assertion in thesis 4 is correct—that an active involvement in this world is essential to the message of Jesus—would that make Christianity unique or distinctive among the religions of the world?

John Hick doesn't want to answer that question, because he doesn't want to pose it. Since such broad questions are based on sweeping generalizations, any answers are going to distort. Hick's fundamental problem is that the immense number of jig-saw pieces that make up any religion can never be assembled into one picture that would reveal the religion's distinct identity. Theologians, who love generalizations, should listen to historians, who love details: "Historians of religions are today generally too conscious of the immense internal variety of each tradition to indulge in such one-dimensional stereotyping." I think I was at least vaguely mindful of what Hick is talking about when in the first part of thesis 4 I pointed out that in trying to grasp the content of Jesus' uniqueness I am not searching for an *essence*—a one-time, immutable definition of Christ and Christianity's identity. Such an essence, I admitted, will always elude us because of Christianity's dynamism; Hick reminds me that it is also because of Christianity's diversity.

A historian of religion, committed to scholarship, would behold this dynamism and diversity of Christianity (or any religion) and refrain from any talk of unique identity. A theologian, committed to the promotion not only of scholarship but also of the living faith of his or her community, cannot so refrain. For faith to be not just professed and studied but to be lived and acted on in the world, the religious community must be able to say, to itself and to others, what it stands for at a given point in history; it must be able to read and respond to the "signs of the times." Religions, the theologian reminds the historian, are not just communities of belief and ritual; they are also *movements* (at least some, if not many, religions would so describe themselves). In order to move and call each other to joint action, members of a religious community must be able to say something about what is integral or distinctive or required for them to carry on the vision of their founder. If they can't do this, they can't be what they are. So even though the task of trying to formulate the uniqueness or distinctiveness of a religious community is difficult, and never done once-and-for-all, still, it remains, I think, a necessary part of the believer's and theologian's assignment.

This brings us back to the original criticism: granting that an active commitment to this-worldly well-being is something without which one wouldn't have authentic Christian faith, one must recognize that other religions are also so committed. Christians can't claim any uniqueness in this area. Raimon Panikkar attests that in his scholarly and personal pilgrimages throughout most of the religious landscapes of the world, he has found a broad display of "inner-worldly actions of love and justice." Michael von Brück, on the basis of similar experience, agrees: a "genuine life of unbounded love and justice is happening also outside the Christian tradition." Such a life, as Hick points out, has been embodied for all the world to see in Gandhi and the Dalai Lama, whose active historical work for peace and harmony is thoroughly Hindu and Buddhist. Finally, Cobb asks me, where did Jesus learn that to know God is to do justice? In announcing a God of history who calls us to historical engagement, Jesus was preserving a unique ingredient in Judaism. Islam, too, carries on this same unique concern for well-being in this world.

All of these reminders presume that if what characterizes me also characterizes others, it can't be unique to me. That is, indeed, the first definition Webster's dictionary gives for *unique*: "being the only one." But Webster tells us that *unique* can also signify "distinctively characteristic." And that's the meaning all of us, myself included, should feel and intend when speaking about the uniqueness of Jesus or Christianity—that which distinctively characterizes, or identifies, or constitutes identity. What makes one unique, in other words, is not what makes one different but what makes one oneself—that without which one would not be who one actually is. Uniqueness therefore need not depend on differences from others but on identity, or integrity, with oneself.

Therefore, the fact that other religions or spiritual leaders affirm the value of this world and the need to act for its betterment does not weaken the claim that the same quality is unique to, or distinctive of, Jesus. In *One Earth Many Religions*[6] I spent a whole chapter trying to show that all (or at least most) religions that have survived the centuries have traditions within them that call their followers to respond to the terrestrial needs of others. In some way, I would venture to say, all religions are actually or potentially "this-worldly." *But* when we look at the distinctive characteristics of each religion, when we study their identities, we find, I believe, that each of them is "this-worldly" in *different* ways. This is in conformity with what biology tell us—that the more we study carefully the particular identities of living beings, the more we marvel at the way each of them is different. No two living beings, no matter how similar they appear, are entirely identical. Thus, although we said that uniqueness does not depend on being different from others but on being oneself, we also have to admit that the more a being is itself the more it will be different. Nature loves patterns and similarities but also vast variety.

So even in attesting to the way all religions do or can promote this-worldly well-being, we have to be open to the differences in how they do it. Doing this, I think we will discover, first of all, that in the identities of many other religious communities the call to transform the world through concrete acts of love and justice does not occupy the same self-defining role that it does for the identity of Jesus. Historical involvement does not enter into the core of who they are as it does (or is supposed to) for disciples of Jesus. I think that this will be the case for many of the Asian or Indic religious traditions. For example, as Aloysius Pieris has pointed out, although *agape*, or active love of neighbor, is certainly alive in Buddhist spirituality, it does not occupy the focal place that *prajna* or contemplative wisdom does.

But even in those traditions or communities—such as the Abrahamic and perhaps also the primal—for whom the call of a historical or earthly Deity sounds from within the distinctive core of their beliefs and ethics, I think we will find significant and mutually enlightening differences in the way such historical involvement is grounded and practiced. Although Christians and Muslims follow the same God of justice and therefore have much in common in their "theologies of liberation," for instance, they are markedly and importantly different in how they understand the nature of justice and how it is to be realized in civil society. Below, I will be saying more about the distinctive characteristics of the way Jesus calls his followers to love and act for justice.

---

[6] Paul F. Knitter, *One Earth Many Religions* (Maryknoll, N.Y.: Orbis Books, 1995).

Yet, I don't want to end up with too great a stress on *differences* in proposing and describing the uniqueness of Jesus. What is essential and needed in the dialogue with others is that Christians work together in trying to grasp and live what is most important or pivotal for applying the gospel message to the world of today. It is the question that Jesus himself is said to have posed: "Who do you say I am?" (Mk 8:27)—in this very different world of the late twentieth century. In witnessing to this identity or uniqueness of Jesus, Christians will find that they have much in common with others but also much that is distinctive, different, and important for others to hear.

2. A number of my conversation partners wonder whether I'm more politically correct than biblically correct in the way I give the Reign of God such a heavy this-worldly content. I've identified three different reasons why they fear that the tight link that I (following the lead of liberation theology) find between the Reign of God and the transformation of this world runs the risk of skewing, even distorting, what Jesus and the early communities envisioned as the *Basileia tou Theou.*

a. Cobb and Hellwig are uncomfortable with my soteriocentric or this-worldly identification of Jesus' uniqueness mainly because many other Christians would not agree with me or would propose other elements as constituting the target of Jesus' mission. Am I being an exclusivist or inclusivist in the way I am defining who is or isn't a Christian?

I'm grateful for such questions or caveats. One can become carried away by the energies of one's convictions. I should have made clearer what I did try to recognize: that in attempting to describe the uniqueness of Jesus/Christianity (or of any religion) one is after not only a moving but a multiple target. There's no one way of stating, once and for all, what is for Christianity its "canon within the canon" or its "tradition within the tradition" or (in Luther's terms) the "belief by which the church stands or falls" (*articulus stantis aut cadentis ecclesiae*). I want to recognize more clearly that there are other ingredients that we may have to list in our attempts to describe what makes Christianity unique or distinct at the end of the twentieth century.

And yet—and here is the point of my response to Cobb and Hellwig—although there may be many colors on the Christian cloak, that doesn't mean that *any* color is appropriate. For instance, I would have to desist from, and resist, those Christians who claim that a male image of God (and a male image of the priesthood) is essential to Jesus' message. More important, there are some colors that, given the "signs of the times," I would argue have to be included on the unique Christian cloak. If they are missing, it's no longer Christian. A vision of and commitment to a new world order of greater justice and love is one of those essential colors. These are hard words. I want to apply them carefully and charitably. But I have no choice but to take them seriously.

b. Another theme of concern comes from various voices, all of whom would in no way deny that active, historical love of neighbor belongs to the core identity of Jesus and his followers; but they indirectly express their fear that in so stressing this historical love, we might lose touch with the deeper, animating part of the Christian heart. I might call this the mystical admonition. It is perhaps similar to the reminder that Jesus himself gently gave to Martha when he told her that because of her active love in the kitchen, she was missing the "better part" (Lk 10:42). These friends are asking whether I am concerned about so many this-worldly matters of justice and sustainability that I lose contact with the deeper part of Christianity's uniqueness: the personal, mystical experience of divine-human oneness that Jesus himself embodied and communicated. This universal, personal, mystical Mystery should be on the top of the list of any description of Christian uniqueness.

Seiichi Yagi draws his description of this mystical core of the Christ experience from the Buddhist thought of Takizawa Katsumi. There is a fundamental unity, a primary contact between the Divine and human, or between Buddhahood and all beings; yet this unity is not real unless it is realized in a secondary contact, that is, in the consciousness and experience of individuals. Jesus is an exemplary, sacramental realization of this secondary contact, and so he enables others to come to their own realization. Ingrid Shafer is urging the same concern, I think, with her preference for the "analogical" over the "dialectical"—or for the given unity between humanity and divinity that must be grasped, in analogously different ways in different religions, before any dialectical encounter with the world can take place. From a different, more Protestant perspective, von Brück is grasping for the same mystical pulse at the heart of the gospel when he suggests that the uniqueness of Christianity is better described, not as a "life of unbounded love and justice" (though that is certainly essential to Christian life) but as the experience and witness of the "unconditionality of the love of God," the existential realization that God's love "cannot be limited spatially or temporally, nor can it depend on the condition of knowing this fact."

But for me, it is Raimon Panikkar who most powerfully presses the priority of the mystical. For him, the uniqueness of Christ is to be found primarily in a personal, transforming grasp of a universal, ontological reality; Christ is the Christian way of speaking about the cosmotheandric Mystery—the given, dynamic, non-dualistic unity among matter-human-Divine. Panikkar writes, "Christ's uniqueness, for me, lies in the lived experience that I am at once finite, infinite, and on the way. This is a threefold but single experience, which by a thinking process I would apply to any human being." There is the one, universal, ineffable Mystery of connectedness or communication between Infinite and Finite; this mystery, according to Panikkar, not only manifests itself in but *is* or *has its being* in, the multiple expressions of the cosmos and religions.

"Now the Christian, but *only* the Christian, name for this link, for such a mediator [between the Infinite and the Finite] is Christ." Just as this Mystery of Christ-as-mediator has an ontological priority, so the experience of this Mystery should have an experiential priority in our efforts to grasp and speak about the uniqueness of Christianity. Without a sense of this Mystery, all our bustle to change and liberate the world will be just that—bustle.

Once again, I realize that these friends are telling me (and all liberationist-activist types) something I need to hear. On the one hand, they are offering the practical, necessary reminder that something is prior to, and therefore must come before, our zealous engagement to overcome injustice and to change the world. Unless our political-social efforts to transform structures are rooted in a mystical-interior transformation of the self, such efforts all too easily peter out or cause more problems then they solve. The centrifugal force of the prophet must be nourished and guided by the centripetal force of the mystic. On the other hand, these mystical critics are making a much broader and at the same time more christological point. Indirectly they are suggesting, I take it, that we are better off seeking to understand the particularity of Jesus within the *universality* of the divine-human relationship rather than vice versa. They find the power of Jesus' story and example within the larger, cosmic story of how the Divine is already present and communicating itself to all creation. The particularity of Jesus takes on meaning and transformative energy insofar as it becomes a name or a means by which humans can "plug in" and find themselves part of this Universal Love or Grace or Presence.

I resonate deeply with these perspectives. I have been a social activist long enough to know the practical, yes prior, need of mystical moorings for efforts to overcome death squads in El Salvador or myopic political agendas in Washington, D.C. But in taking this admonition to heart and practice, I would want to add that given my experience, especially with base communities in El Salvador, the priority of the mystical may be ontological, but it's not always or necessarily chronological. I have seen in others, and sometimes felt in myself, how persons can touch and be touched by the sustaining Spirit, by a power and source of hope they cannot explain, *in the midst of the prophetic struggle.* As Jon Sobrino, echoing his spiritual father Ignatius, teaches (and exemplifies) there is such a thing as *contemplatio in actione*—mystical experience *within action* itself. I would even want to suggest that unless one's *contemplative mystical experience* gained in liturgy and meditation is not balanced and clarified by this *prophetic mysticism* gained in the actual struggle, then one's mystical moorings will prove deceptive or wobbly.

A similar comment applies, I suggest, to the urging that the historical particularity of Jesus can best be understood within the mystical universality of God's relation to the world. Philosophically, as a scholar, I am a universalist; I need the big picture in order to understand the details; I need to integrate the Jesus story within the larger universe story. My intellect resists any picture of Jesus that ends up making him an anomaly or a scandalous contradiction to our knowledge of human nature or of the way the Divine seems to be at work universally. But practically, as a Christian activist, I'm a particularist. I find myself appealing or returning to the particularity of the Jesus story. As I marvel and rejoice at the way Jesus fits into the larger picture and at the way the larger picture casts unexpected light on the image of Jesus, I also realize that the particularity of Jesus enables me to understand the larger picture in ways I otherwise would never have seen it. In other words, in being subsumed into the big mystical picture, the particularity of Jesus enhances it. We're getting back to the meaning and necessity of Jesus' uniqueness.

This is where I want to offer a few admonitions to my mystical critics. If one tries to understand the particularity of Jesus or Buddha or Muhammad primarily or exclusively from the mystical universal of the cosmotheandric Mystery or the primary contact, or even God's universal affirmative love, one sets up a tent that too easily embraces everyone; it becomes very difficult, if not impossible, to discern who's in and who's out. Some mystics may rejoice at that, saying that such discernment can only lead to human hubris. But this is where the practical activist in me becomes very uneasy. There are many religious zealots in our world today, presenting their programs in the name of mystical enlightenment or as Jesus' or Allah's will, who are, I fear, not only wrong but dangerous; I realize that I not only disagree with them but that I must resist them. Our universal pictures need concrete, practical criteria to help us judge what is genuine mystical experience and what isn't.

Here I, as a Christian, turn to my particularities, to the Jesus story and what I think he adds or contributes to the big picture. More precisely, as I shall say more extensively in the next section, Jesus as the Christ tells me not only that there is a universal Mystery that holds earth-humanity-Divinity together, but that this Mystery beckons us to struggle for a different kind of world and to do so with a particular concern for the victims and outcasts. When I encounter people under the mystical tent who have no such concern whatsoever, I will have to raise words of concern and criticism.

c. At this point my understanding of Christian participation in the interfaith dialogue exposes either its solid basis or its Achilles' heel. On what grounds am I raising such criticisms in the dialogue? Just why am I claiming so adamantly that encounter with the Mystical must include a concern for worldly well-being? John Hick speaks for the many Christians who would argue that to place liberation and world transformation at the heart of the gospel is more politically than biblically correct. Hick pointedly but gently tells me that what I am holding up as part of the unique core of Christianity is "the very recent (dating from the 1960s), small, much contested, and officially condemned movement of liberation theology." Hick would align himself with E. P. Sanders and those New Testament scholars who hold that Jesus' eschatological orientation—his conviction that the end was near—precluded any real commitment to changing things in this world. Jesus announced God's Reign, but its coming was to take place soon, after the passing away of this world.[7]

Hick's words touch and weaken the bedrock of my suggestions for revisioning Jesus' uniqueness. In differing ways and degrees, many other participants in this conversation share his concerns about placing a this-worldly liberation at the heart of Christian life and belief. In the final part of this section I hope I can move the conversation forward by reflecting on these concerns and clarifying the reasons for designating love-with-justice as a unique and distinctive mark of Christian identity.

3. A subtitle for the third part of these reflections on the Reign of God might read: "Jesus' notion of the Reign of God does make Christianity unique, but relationally so."

Let me begin with the stickiest part of this conversation: what we can and cannot know about the historical Jesus. This is like stepping into a minefield where, with every assertion about what Jesus really said or did, one fears that the ground will blow up beneath one's feet. Still, I think it is relatively safe to claim that whatever else Jesus may have intended with his vision of the Reign of God, one of the essential pieces in his vision was the greater well-being of humans *right now*. This is so even though Jesus thought the "right now" was going to be very abbreviated. What Jesus was after with his efforts as a healer (historically reliable, according to most scholars) the Christian communities have reaffirmed through the centuries: "Thy Kingdom come, thy will be done *on earth* as it is in heaven." To use an eschatological scalpel to remove this central concern of Jesus for the suffering and need of persons in this world is, I fear, to deform what Jesus, especially as a Jewish prophet, was all about. And if we survey the shifting terrain of New Testament scholarship, it seems that the once unanimous picture of Jesus as a thoroughly eschatological prophet has blurred. Already in 1987 Marcus Borg ventured an assessment that has gained firmer foundations over recent years: "The consensus regarding Jesus' expectation of the end of the world has disappeared. The majority of scholars no longer thinks that Jesus expected the end of the world in his generation."[8]

---

[7] E. P. Sanders, *Jesus and Judaism* (Philadelphia: Fortress Press, 1985); John Hick, *The Metaphor of God Incarnate* (London: SCM Press, 1993), pp. 19-22.

[8] Marcus Borg, *Jesus: A New Vision: Spirit, Culture, and the Life of Discipleship* (HarperSanFrancisco, 1987), p. 14. In 1994 Borg reaffirmed: "Over the last ten years, the image of Jesus as an eschatological prophet, which dominated scholarship through the middle of this century, has become very much a minority position" (*Meeting Jesus Again for the First Time: The Historical Jesus and the Heart of Contemporary Faith* [HarperSanFrancisco, 1994], p. 29).

To venture a further, relatively safe, step onto the field of historical claims about Jesus, we can describe him in the general yet challenging terms of *a Spirit-filled prophet*. He was a person of evidently deep spiritual experience (a mystic) who as a wisdom-teacher spoke from what he deeply felt and was convinced of. But he was also a critic of the cultural-social status quo, proposing an alternate vision and founding a revitalization movement within his Jewish society that brought him into conflict with the dominant social-political paradigm. So I agree thoroughly and happily with the first of the "three additional dimensions of contemporary Christian spirituality" that Harvey Cox wants to add to our understanding of Jesus' uniqueness—namely, our increased knowledge of the historical Jesus, which reveals "the tough particularity of the Palestinian peasant, rebel rabbi, and freewheeling healer" and "the clearly political dimension of Jesus' mission in Roman-occupied Palestine."

Kenneth Cragg supports Cox by clarifying that what makes up the distinctiveness of a Jesus-based Christianity is not its announcement of a God of love but rather of a God of love who is rooted or incarnated in history and who wants this love to take on historical form. "Faith stands in and by evidentiality, and this, in part, means where and when and how. In this requirement the gospel will always be distinctive."

So when liberation theologians—and under that rubric I would place any Christian who understands salvation to include a healing of the sufferings of *this* world—hold up human and ecological well-being as distinctive of the identity of Jesus and his followers, they are not proposing only a recent, politically fashionable view of the gospel; no matter how controverted or even condemned such a view of Jesus may be, Christians who propose it would respond that they have good scriptural, theological reasons to do so. The Carmodys need not fear that such a stress on the this-worldly content of *soteria* will replace the mystical or transcendent strand of Jesus' message and example, for every Christian prophet or activist must, like Jesus, be Spirit-filled. Part of the control provided by the Spirit is contained in the reminder of Reinhold Niebuhr, passed on by Macquarrie (but not sufficiently recognized in my thesis 4), that as committed as Jesus' disciples must be to the building of God's Kingdom "on earth as in heaven," they should never think that they can finish the job. The Reign of God, though it is realized now, is always still to come. Any *final* plan or one-and-only picture of this Reign is idolatrous. Again, the need is to be as committed to what the Reign of God requires *now* as one is open to what it may be *tomorrow*.

Despite such reservations about making hard and fast declarations about God's Reign, I would like to go a step further in trying to articulate the distinctiveness of Jesus' vision. This step is prompted by the reminder that a number of the commentaries in this book made: that many, if not all, religions are in some way concerned about the well-being of this world. I think more can be said about what distinguishes the way Jesus calls us to historical engagement; it is something that I have frequently noticed in the interreligious conversations in which I have taken part. It can be summarized in the language of liberation theologians as the *preferential option for victims*. Affirming and embellishing a central note in the message of the Jewish prophets who preceded him, Jesus, as presented by the gospel writers (especially Luke), shows a special (not exclusive) concern for the little ones, those who are suffering most because, usually, they have been victimized most. Perhaps the clearest indication that the invitation to the table of the Kingdom was given especially to those who were excluded from the well-laden tables of the establishment was Jesus' scandalous "table fellowship" or "open commensality" with the riffraff of Jewish society— beggars, prostitutes, tax-collectors.[9]

Aloysius Pieris confesses that it was in the course of an interreligious exchange that a Buddhist reminded him that Jesus stands out from other religious messengers in revealing "God's defense pact between God and slaves."[10] Pieris's own experience confirms that such a claim is not made of any other founder of a religion, but also that such a claim has never been experienced by other religions as a threat to their integrity or value. So I would want to add to my thesis 4: Today, the uniqueness of Jesus can be found in his insistence that salvation or the Reign of God must be realized in this world through human actions of love and justice, *with a special concern for the victims of oppression or exploitation.*

I know that there are many fellow Christians and theological colleagues who continue to have reservations about the historical foundations for all these claims; we can't be certain, they insist, that Jesus was motivated by such a central concern for what today we call social justice and for changing the conditions of the oppressed and marginalized. There just isn't sufficient data. In an effort to carry on the conversation with those honestly burdened by the restrictions of historical method, let me offer a further, brief comment. Let's say that these critics are right, that because Jesus expected the imminent end of all things earthly he was not concerned about reforming social structures or achieving justice for the exploited. Even if this were true, another pivotal piece of Jesus' message would remain firmly in place: his call for radical love of neighbor. John's later reflection "They will know you are my disciples if you love one another" (Jn 13:35) reflects Jesus' original proclamation. I sug-

---

[9] Albert Nolan, *Jesus before Christianity* (Maryknoll, N.Y.: Orbis Books, 1978), pp. 39-40; John Dominick Crossan, *The Historical Jesus* (HarperSanFrancisco, 1991), pp. 261-64; Richard A. Horsley (with John S. Hanson), *Bandits, Prophets and Messiahs: Popular Movements at the Time of Jesus* (San Francisco: Harper, 1985), pp. 29-87.

[10] Aloysius Pieris, "Interreligious Dialogue and Theology of Religions," *Horizons* 20 (1993), 111-12; idem, "Whither New Evangelism?" *Pacifica* 6 (1993), 329. Both articles also published in Aloysius Pieris, *Fire and Water: Basic Issues in Asian Buddhism and Christianity* (Maryknoll, N.Y.: Orbis Books, 1996).

gest that today, when we are imbued by a historical rather than an eschatological consciousness, we cannot remain faithful to Jesus' challenge to radical love of neighbor without a commitment to social-ecological justice with a preferential option for victims. We can see more clearly, like the Samaritan, who our neighbor is. Perhaps more sharply and painfully than ever, we know and feel two realities: millions of our fellow human and other sentient beings are suffering the denial of their most basic needs, and that this denial is rooted in the way decisions are made and business is done. With such an awareness, for Christians to announce that they love all their neighbors without reaching out to those neighbors most in need and without working for justice is, I believe, to make a mockery of love.[11]

4. If for reasons of either historical evidence (as I believe) or applied logic we can locate the uniqueness of Jesus' message in his demands for an active historical love of neighbor, especially those neighbors suffering from various forms of slavery, we must also recognize that such a uniqueness is *thoroughly correlational:* a uniqueness that necessarily engages the message of Jesus and the Christian community in a life-giving relationship with others. By its very nature, such a commitment to what Christians call God's Reign will lead them to talk with and work with anyone else who, perhaps from vastly different perspectives, is concerned about the well-being of all sentient beings. Cox recognizes this when he notes that the "clearly political dimension of Jesus' mission . . . [suggests] a commonality that is not narrowly religious" and can be related to "shared structural elements with other cultures." Cox specifies and reclaims one of the more relatable elements in Jesus' liberative message, one which was obscured by later patriarchal developments: the female and sexual content of Jesus' good news and image of God now being *re*membered by women historians and theologians. So, as Pieris recognized, in proclaiming Jesus' unique vision of "God's defense pact with slaves" Christians are lifting up a difference that connects.

But we must be honest. Although these connections may be for the most part positive and mutually enhancing, as they have been for Pieris, this will not always be the case. Here I have to acknowledge Sanders when he asks whether I am using this notion of *soteria* or vision of social justice as a new absolute. In one sense I would say no, for although my commitment to the Reign of God is absolute, my knowledge of what it entails is not. Therefore I am open to the possibility that elements of my Christian vision of eco-human well-being may be surpassed by what

---

[11] This argument is made more adequately by Schubert Ogden, who hesitates to base the claims of liberation theology on the historical Jesus but who seeks an essential link in our contemporary awareness between Christian love and social justice. See his *Faith and Freedom: Toward a Theology of Liberation* (Nashville: Abingdon Press, 1979), pp. 43-55.

I discover from others. But in another sense, Sanders is right. There may be dialogical situations where my understanding of God's Reign places me in opposition to what I hear or see in other communities. As already stated, a correlational understanding of Jesus' uniqueness can sometimes be exclusive. My ideal is that such exclusion or opposition will always be carried out within the bonds of love, in which I will never view my opponents as enemies but oppose them in such a way that I continue to seek openings for reconnection.

5. A final comment in this section on the Reign of God is prompted by observations by Míguez Bonino and von Brück, who indirectly point out how in our contemporary new world order a this-worldly understanding of the uniqueness of Jesus bears a special appropriateness, maybe even necessity. When Christians bear witness to the need for an active involvement in confronting injustice, they are pointing to what Míguez Bonino contends should be the common context or common ground for interreligious discourse today. In other words, the vast human and ecological sufferings that so mark our world today can provide the "material" or the "hermeneutical starting point" with which the religious communities of the world seek to understand themselves *and* each other. Though each community may perceive and respond to this material differently, the material provides a common reference point for all of them.

In a sense, the much discussed common ground among religions is not to be found *within* each one of them, but *around* all of them. From the outside, it can seep inside and link them all. "A common context . . . is not an external reality but a commonality that—at least in part—is constitutive of encounter and consequently enters into any dialogue in which these people may engage" (Míguez Bonino). For Míguez Bonino, religious believers are better off starting their conversations with these common problematics of human and ecological suffering rather than with theological issues: "Do we not learn more about ourselves and our interlocutors, about our faith and theirs, by understanding how we and they live, interpret, and act out this common locus that we all inhabit than by merely comparing our 'religious views'?"

As all the religious communities examine and try to understand this common context of suffering, the distinctive Christian contribution to the exploration is extremely helpful, if not necessary: the perspective and experience of the victims, the marginalized, and the little people and creatures are needed in order to understand the nature of this context of suffering. Why? Von Brück responds simply but soberingly: "Interreligious understanding does not take place in a space free of power structures!" Míguez Bonino, from his Latin American experience of those power structures, expands on what this means: given the state of the world in which the Northern or so-called industrial-technological nations have power over the Southern, developing countries, those who speak as Northerners in the interreligious dialogue must know that their words will be heard differently than if they were speaking as Southerners. Language is always linked in some way to power; if we forget that, we slip, perhaps unconsciously, into a manipulative use of even the most dialogical of languages. As Míguez Bonino perceptively points out, it is not so much the uniqueness of our religious language that offends but the economic and military power that stands behind that language. As he writes, "Early Christians were able to make extraordinary claims about Christ because they made them 'from below' and supported them by their martyrdom and not by their legions."

It is precisely the Christian insistence on giving special or prior attention to the experience and voices of victims that can alert us to the reality of the unequal distribution of power and how this inequality plays out in our economic and religious relationships with others. It is only by humbly listening to and working *with* (not just *for*) the oppressed people and creatures of the world that those of us who consume and control most of this world's resources can begin the difficult, cooperative task of fashioning a more equal sharing of the earth's goods and of economic power among nations so that *all* beings, human and nonhuman, may have life and have it more abundantly.

V

Insofar as it is an inherently universal religion, Christianity must remain a "missionary" religion; it must share its vision of truth and well-being with others.

But can the missionary mandate (the Great Commission) be understood in such a way that both **mission** *and* **dialogue** *are fostered? How can the gospel be announced so that both the integrity of Christianity and the integrity of other religions are respected? Does conversion have a place in such an understanding of mission?*

Although the opening statement of this fifth issue would not stir applause from all the participants in this discussion, I think that all those seeking to speak from the evangelical and mainline churches would assent. If we understand a missionary as someone who has a message to share and is restless unless he or she does so, then every Christian is, or should be, a missionary. Like believers in so many other religions, Christians experience their "good news" to be good for everyone.

If, however, we take up the sub-paragraph of this opening statement, the inner-Christian conversation becomes more varied and complex but also more interesting and useful. A quick review of the various missionary concerns voiced by my conversation partners reveals the complexity and promise of these questions.

1. Macquarrie lays out the foundational question of whether with a pluralistic (I prefer correlational) christology, one can even speak of the missionary mandate of the Christian churches. Though he reluctantly recognizes some place for proclamation, he leans toward understanding mission as essentially dialogue, especially the kind of wordless, action-based dialogue that Mother Teresa carries on. Others, like Pinnock and Sanders, as well as Kuschel, fear that the way I have qualified the uniqueness of Jesus will lead to a rather lackluster Christian witness, one that even non-Christians will not take seriously because it does not make the kind of definitive, demanding claims that traditionally have been part of gospel proclamation. To my claim that if we Christians really love our neighbor we will respect and listen to them, Pinnock adds that if we really love them we will evangelize them. "Can we accept the sincerity of pluralist neighbor love if it does not lead to world evangelization?"

Another set of missionary criticisms comes from the opposite direction—not that I am being too lukewarm in the way I endorse mission but that I'm too fervent, to the point that I slip back to old proselytizing ways. Ariarajah comes right to the point. He fears that some of the adjectives with which I still want to describe Jesus' and Christianity's uniqueness end up making me a camouflaged inclusivist or exclusivist. He suggests that to hold that others "in a qualified but still in a real sense . . . are 'unfulfilled' without Christ" (quoting part of thesis 3) is "to remain inclusivist." No matter how gently or slowly, I'm still trying to sweep everyone under the Christian rug. Even more seriously, for Ariarajah, when I attest that what is true for me has to be true for others, I'm exposing "only the top side of the exclusivist position, softened up for the purposes of dialogue."

Hick raises similar concerns when he presses me on just what I mean by, or what are the implications of, my claim that Jesus' message remains "indispensable" for all. "Indispensable for what? What is it that cannot occur without this indispensable message having been heard and accepted?" Hick simplifies but sharpens his question: Do I think that Christ is indispensable for others as penicillin might be for a dying person, or indispensable as are vitamins, which may enhance our life, but which we can find in different sources or brands? If Christ is like penicillin, I'm an exclusivist missionary; if like vitamins, I'm a missionary presenting a product that can be found elsewhere.

Hick makes way for von Brück's missionary question: with my pluralist christology I have not made clear whether I want to "give up converting people of other religions." If I respond with something about wanting to convert others to the truth revealed by Christ but not to Christianity, von Brück pokes with a further question: is it possible to embrace a truth stripped of all its historical-cultural clothing? When one is converted to a particular truth, isn't one also converted to the context and community in which it lives? So, for von Brück, I still have to make clear what "conversion or *metanoesis*—individually and collectively—means in dialogue."

2. In trying to respond to these discomforting yet needed concerns and questions, I would like to make a suggestion that I hope will be acceptable to all and will therefore carry forward the conversation. I think that the integrity of both Christian identity and of other religions will be better fostered if Christians would understand mission, not as something they have to reconcile with dialogue, but *as* dialogue. In other words, dialogue is the broader, more inclusive reality. Dialogue is not to be included in mission, but mission in dialogue. The reason for this is basic, but not always evident, in the common understanding of dialogue. (I know we have to be careful of "common" understandings.) Even if we work with the cautious Vatican description of dialogue as a "witness given and received for mutual advancement" and as "interreligious relations . . . directed at mutual understanding and enrichment in obedience to truth and respect for freedom, [including] both witness and the exploration of respective religious convictions,"[12] then it becomes clear that what have always been considered the heart of mission—proclamation and witness—are an integral part of dialogue.

Active, functioning dialogue requires that everyone involved is both listening and speaking. Dialogue, as is sometimes suggested (perhaps by Macquarrie), is not just listening authentically; it also requires speaking honestly. In dialogue I not only want to understand the other and possibly be changed through that understanding; I also want the other to understand me and be changed by the truth that I feel has enriched my life. Therefore, Pinnock's concerns can be assuaged. What he understands by evangelization—announcing the good news broadly and vigorously—is still very much a part of what I understand as the dialogue required by a pluralistic or correlational christology. But at the same time, I trust that Ariarajah's fears can be calmed, for in calling upon Christians to evangelize in the dialogue, I am also calling upon them to *be evangelized*. If there is a hidden inclusivism in what I am proposing, it cuts both ways. What is true for one side of the conversation bounces back to be true for the other. As much as Christians, for instance, feel that Buddhists might be included or fulfilled in what Jesus has to offer, so must they be ready to be included and fulfilled in Buddha's message. This, I think, is a determining difference between a correlational and an inclusivist model for dialogue; the traditional inclusivist would find it difficult to allow for this effect.

---

[12] John Paul II, *Redemptoris Missio: An Encyclical Letter on the Permanent Validity of the Church's Missionary Mandate* (1990), #56; *Dialogue and Proclamation*, Vatican Council for Interreligious Dialogue and the Congregation for the Evangelization of Peoples (Rome, 1991), #9.

With an understanding of Christian mission *as* dialogue, the role of missionaries is not maimed or curtailed; rather, it is clarified and broadened, and, I suggest, made much more appealing for young people. If missionaries see their self-identity in terms of dialogue, they will continue to try to be good preachers of the Word incarnate in Jesus; but they will also seek to be good listeners to the Word that God may have cast like seeds among the nations (the *logoi spermatikoi*, Justin and Clement of Alexandria would say). In fact, by being good listeners, they will probably be better proclaimers. One big reason why the Christian church is still a Eurocentric religion and not, as Karl Rahner urged, a "world church" truly incarnated in multiple cultures is that missionaries have been better speakers than listeners.

3. At this point, John Hick will patiently press his question: In this view of mission as dialogue, am I still saying that the truth revealed in Jesus is indispensable for others? Yes, I am. But what does that mean? For the most part, I would not understand this indispensability to be like that of penicillin for the dying patient. But neither is it like vitamins available under different brand names but fulfilling the same function. Rather, what I intend by indispensability (and remember, Buddha may be as indispensable as Jesus) is better compared to a skill or insight that enriches our life profoundly and becomes integral to who we are, but which, we know, is not necessary to lead an adequate, contented human existence. I'm thinking of something like learning how to read and write; we know that we could live happily without these skills (and sometimes we envy the depth and vitality of oral cultures), but still we recognize that to read and to write are indispensable parts of who we now are and want to be.

Perhaps a better image of what I mean by indispensability can be found in friendship. After we have made a good friend and experienced how much that friend has changed and expanded our life, we can say that this friend is an indispensable part of our identity; yet we know that our lives would have been quite livable without that friend. Such a friendship can be indispensable and essential to one's life, and yet not make up one's primary relationship. This comparison touches my own experience, for, as a Christian, my primary relationship is with Jesus, and yet Buddha has become indispensable for who I now am and how I want to live—as a human being and as a Christian.

4. These clarifications for Hick help me respond to von Brück's questions about conversion. Because I feel the truth of Jesus to be indispensable in the sense just explained, I will indeed seek the conversion of others to this truth. I eagerly want them to grasp and take it into their life and culture. When they don't, I will naturally be disappointed—but not with the disappointment of the doctor when his or her dying patient refuses penicillin. In refusing the truth that has enhanced my life, I be-

lieve that my dialogue partners are depriving themselves of something that could make for profound differences in their lives, as writing or a new friend can transform someone's life. But I would not say that without these enhancing, even transforming differences my partners are "lost" or deprived to the point of not being able to live satisfying human and religious lives.

The kind of conversion I am seeking in this understanding of mission as dialogue *does* require a change, sometimes a radical change (*metanoia*), in how one sees and acts in the world; it does not necessarily require a change in one's religious community. Here von Brück warns that truth cannot be distilled from its cultural context. I want to appreciate what he's getting at. To grasp the truth of another culture or religion properly, I have to know and experience that truth within its own milieu. If I "comprehend" another culture's truth only from the perspective of my own culture, comprehension is really deformation. But *if* I carry out the process of what John Dunne calls "passing over" to another culture with as much openness and sensitivity as I can muster, I *can* learn something that I can then take with me when I "pass back" to my own culture. If something like this is not possible, if every truth is confined permanently in its own cultural trappings, then the extreme post-modernists are right and we are trapped in incommunicable cultural prisons. We can't really talk to and learn from each other.

In distinguishing conversion of the heart and conversion of community, I don't want to rule out the possibility that in the dialogue a person may decide to adopt not only truths from another community but the community itself. I have difficulties with those who would brand all such conversions as harmful to the individual or manipulative of the individual. Such changes can happen, and for good reasons. From a Christian perspective I would dub them the "work of the Holy Spirit," which means I cannot fully explain them, but I do trust that they are taking place as part of a life-giving process. One aspect of such a process has to do with how religious communities go about taking on new cultural identities. If Christianity is going to become more than a Eurocentric religion and if Buddhism is to move beyond its Asian identity, then some Japanese are going to have to become Christians and some Americans are going to have to become Buddhists.[13]

If I explore all the corners of von Brück's query, I have to add that there may be situations in which missioner-dialoguers do more than just sit back and allow conversions to Christianity to take place under the guidance of the Spirit. There can be occasions in which they actively seek to bring others into the Christian community—situations in which

---

[13] I am presupposing that some religions desire to expand culturally and that it is good for everyone if they do so. I'm not sure how all this would apply to "place-bound" religions such as the Native American traditions.

they judge the truth offered in Christian revelation to be as indispensable as penicillin is for the ailing patient. Admittedly, one has to exercise extreme caution and cultural sensitivity in making such evaluations. Still, it can happen that a Christian missionary will come to the conclusion that a person's cultural or religious community is an inherent obstacle to that person living or being treated according to the values of love and justice that the Reign of God demands. The social or religious milieu may be what some theologians term an instance of the "anti-Kingdom," and in this context the missioner judges that the well-being of the other can best be served by encouraging the person to join the Christian community. These are extremely difficult judgments, but I suspect they need to be made.

Examples of what I'm talking about are delicate and dangerous. Friends in India have suggested to me that something like this was the case when Christian missioners in India considered the state of certain Dalits or Untouchables to be such that they would be better off moving from a religious community that affirmed the caste system to one that at least was trying (in its better moments) to oppose caste. Something similar may be said of those Christians in the early years of Islamic expansion who became Muslims as a way of freeing themselves from their Christian imperial oppressors. Such "converts" may have made decisions that I would view as humanly and religiously defensible.

VI

Christology in general, and a theology of religions in particular, must be consistent with trinitarian theology; this means it must be more formed by a theology of the Holy Spirit.

But what is the relation between the "economy of the Spirit" and the "economy of the Word in Jesus"? How can christology be better balanced with pneumatology?

With this last issue we dip into some rather abstract levels of Christian theology. I suspect, however, that the abstractness of this issue is in direct proportion to the promise of its practical rewards. If Christian approaches to persons of other faiths were more grounded and guided by a sound understanding of why Christians affirm a trinitarian Deity in which Spirit plays an indispensable role, their ways of viewing and dialoguing with others would be both more effective and orthodox. I think that most of the contributors to this discussion would agree, especially insofar as Christian theologians generally affirm that all Christian life and practice should be informed by a trinitarian belief and experience. Such a general statement becomes more tuned to our issue when we add the observation, often heard among Protestants, Catholics, and especially Orthodox Christians, that the doctrine of the Holy Spirit has been neglected in our efforts to understand other religions and Christianity's relationship with them.

But as widespread as this assessment may be, it divides into diverse streams as soon as further questions arise about what difference a stress on the Spirit would make for understanding other religions and how the Spirit in the world relates to the Word incarnate in Jesus. Kuschel delineates the dividing lines on this question when he points out that I misunderstood the only New Testament text that I directly cite in my opening essay! I failed to realize that when Jesus in John's gospel speaks about "the Spirit of truth who is coming and who will lead you into all truth" (Jn 16:12-23), he is speaking about none other than "the Spirit and truth of Jesus Christ." I forgot, Kuschel reminds me, that John's understanding of the Spirit is the most "christocentric theology of the entire New Testament." Kuschel is raising precisely the issue that we can profitably explore in our further conversations about how a Christian theology of religions can be more pneumatological or Spirit-grounded. To begin this conversation, I suggest to Kuschel that Cox and Míguez Bonino offer some helpful caveats to his perhaps too certain or too quick assertions about the Spirit.

1. Both Míguez Bonino and Cox give voice to a growing uneasiness among Western, mainline theologians—an uneasiness stimulated by the Pentecostal Movement and, in a very different way, by Greek Orthodox theology: Western Trinitarian theology and christology run the risk of a form of "subordinationism," but this time not of the Word (or Son) to the Father (or Parent), but of the Spirit to the Word. Kuschel's formulation represents an example of such a danger: in almost identifying the Spirit of Truth with the Word in Jesus he runs the risk of removing the real differences between Spirit and Word and so of subordinating the Spirit to the Word. In Cox's recent masterful and challenging analysis of Pentecostalism,[14] he makes clear how the Pentecostals, with their experience and theology of the Spirit, are engaged in a "functional removal" of the "*filioque* clause"[15]; in Cox's estimation, so be it, for this clause has been "a long-standing obstacle to Christian unity and interreligious fellowship."

---

[14] Harvey Cox, *Fire from Heaven: Pentecostalism, Spirituality, and the Reshaping of Religion in the Twenty-first Century* (New York: Addison-Wesley Publishing Co., 1994).

[15] This represents the insistence of the Western churches, in opposition to the Orthodox churches of the East, that in the trinitarian relationships the Spirit proceeds from the Father *and from the Son*. This implies that the Spirit takes its role and identity from the Son and not just from the Father and so, as it were, can do nothing other than carry out or clarify what the Son has done.

Without placing culpability on the *"filioque,"* Míguez Bonino confirms Cox's concerns. He declares that Western theology of the Spirit has to a great extent "unilaterally 'restricted' the role of the Spirit to the work of the Son." Adding a typical liberationist political analysis, Míguez Bonino suggests that the motivation behind this limiting of the Spirit was an effort to preserve the "ecclesiastical monopoly of salvation." What is urgently needed in Western theology is a recognition that the economy or the mission of the Spirit has its own "dynamism and historicity," which is genuinely different from, though certainly related to, that of the Word.

I suspect that Greek Orthodox theologians would basically resonate with Cox's and Míguez Bonino's urgings. In fact, I have found the Orthodox theologian George Khodr to be especially helpful in working out a balance between pneumatology and christology, or between the universal activity of the Spirit and the particular incarnation of the Word in Jesus.

> The economy of Christ is not understandable without the economy of the Spirit. The Spirit fills everything *in an economy distinct from the Son*. The Word and the Spirit are called the "two hands of the Father." We must here affirm their *hypostatic independence* and visualize in the religions an all-comprehensive phenomenon of grace. Pentecost . . . is not a continuation of the Incarnation but its consequence. . . . Between these two economies there is *reciprocity* and *mutual service.*[16]

The balance here is finely tuned and admirable. Khodr affirms real difference and yet essential relatedness and reciprocity between Word and Spirit. This means that while the Spirit can never be understood and experienced without reference to the Word, neither can the Spirit, explicitly or implicitly, be reduced to the Word, subordinated to the Word, or understood as merely a different "mode" of the Word. There is "hypostatic independence," that is, real, effective difference. This is why Pentecost and the energy that it embodies and unleashes throughout history is to be understood not as a mere "continuation of the Incarnation"; that would make for subordination of the Spirit to the Word, or a form of "subordinationism." Rather, the economy of the Spirit is a consequence of the incarnation, originating from it (*filioque*) but living out its own identity (its own *hypostasis*). And yet, such independence is qualified, for both the economy of the Word and that of the Spirit are essentially bonded to each other in a relationship that is complete within the Deity (*ad intra*) but still in process of realizing itself and being discovered by humans in the history of creation (*ad extra*).

---

[16] George Khodr, "An Orthodox Perspective of Inter-Religious Dialogue," *Current Dialogue* 19 (1991), p. 27, emphasis added.

2. If such an understanding of the relationship and difference between Spirit and incarnate Word is taken seriously, Cox believes, it "will force us to redefine our regnant christologies." I'm not sure whether it would be a redefinition, but it would certainly be a clarification that would enable a more resolute openness to what the Spirit might be doing in other religious traditions. Recognizing this activity of the Spirit as genuinely different from but essentially related to what has been revealed in the incarnate Word, we would not be able to continue our insistence that Jesus brings us the "final" or the "definitive" or the "unsurpassable" truth about God and world, for such claims would subordinate the Spirit to the Word. But we could and would have to announce that whatever is found within the realm of the Spirit and other religions has to be brought into a sometimes confirmatory and sometimes critical relationship with the universality, decisiveness, and indispensability of what the Word of God has spoken in Jesus of Nazareth. Because of their real differences, the Spirit or the Word will sometimes reveal truths that are "greater" than what is contained in the other; but because of their relatedness, the truth of each will not contradict the other. What this means concretely, how to discern what is truly of the Word or of the Spirit of God, can be known only in the dialogue itself.

This response has turned out to be much longer than my initial statement. That's what happens in dialogue. Through the stimulation of differences and questions, more needs to be said. I hope that this "more" will foster further conversation by qualifying and clarifying what I think are some of the main issues in Christian efforts to understand the "no other name" of Jesus in the light of "other names." For this, I believe, is one of the most challenging and promising "Christian koans" facing the churches today: how our "one and only" can also be a "one among many," or how Christians can maintain a genuine commitment to Jesus the Christ and at the same time maintain a genuine openness to other religions and revealers. At the end of this theological conversation, the Zen masters would remind us that koans can be "solved" only through practice.

Epilogue

LEONARD SWIDLER

Most of the task of editing a book is thankless hard work. However, having read all these insightful essays in this book, I know that my effort was amply rewarded. It is clear that this has been an authentic dialogue: a sincere, sensitive listening with an attempt to cross over into the partners' minds and hearts so as to "cross back" enlightened and enriched.

The dialogue Paul Knitter entered into here with his many partners moved the contemporary understanding of the uniqueness of Jesus Christ into a stage of greater clarity. Through his careful, sensitive listening, Knitter either clarified or correspondingly modified his earlier thought so that all, I believe, would likely grant that his latter understanding and articulation is "better," clearer, more accurate, more helpful, than the former.

Perhaps the point of the greatest clarification Knitter made is his insistence that speaking along with listening are essential elements of dialogue, and that therefore it is best to see mission as a part of dialogue; or put otherwise, all mission is dialogue: evangelizing and being evangelized. Whether the term *correlational* rather than *pluralist* will become widespread remains to be seen. But the laying out of his understanding behind those terms would seem to bridge an important gap between "inclusivists" and "pluralists." I personally find myself in agreement with this, and the other positions, Paul articulated in his response—something that does not always happen in scholarly projects.

Let me point to where in his response I believe Knitter might have carried his argument a step further. Knitter referred to Macquarrie's insistence that in the New Testament there is not a single unified christology but numerous christologies. I believe he could add that these christologies are at times in tension with each other, and that Christians must choose which of them they will understand as dominant—in light of which the others will be interpreted. For example, will one follow the apparently "high christology" of John understood more or less at face value, and interpret the "low christology" of the Q Community as an incipient, not-yet-mature christology which finds its rightful completion in the Johannine

183

Logos christology? Or, will one follow the christology "closest to" Jesus, the low christology of the Q Community, and understand the high christology of John's gospel as a later "poetic/mystic" reflection on the Q Community's "teacher/Prophet" christology?

Human communities in general tend to follow the path of the former choice, and that is largely what happened in Christian history as well. However, in a historically conscious age, which ours is, the second appears to many to be more and more persuasive. The acceptance of historical consciousness without feeling that it undermines the heart of our previous understanding of the meaning of things—and in this case, the meaning of Jesus—entails a radical paradigm shift. This shift, although painful for many, in the end usually is experienced as liberating and deepening, and many are convinced it will happen eventually, despite all resistance.

Paul Knitter also referred to the Semitic thought world as one which used picture language rather than abstract language. He might well have also noted that nowhere does Jesus tell his listeners to believe in an "Uncaused Cause" or refer to the Father and the Spirit as "hypostases" or their relationship with each other as *circumincessio*. Jesus' listeners were not told they would gain salvation by accepting a list of abstract beliefs, as in creeds. Rather, they were informed that not everyone who cried "Lord, Lord" would enter into the kingdom of heaven, but "those who do the will of my heavenly Father." Thus, when responding to the accusation that he did not sufficiently cite scriptures in his initial five theses, Knitter could have cited the parable of Jesus about who enters into the reward of the Father—again, not those who make "orthodox" statements *about* Jesus, but those who *follow* him, and especially those who care for the least of this world by feeding, clothing, and sheltering them.

Knitter cites Clark Pinnock's claim that the Gospels portray Jesus as "assuming unparalleled authority," which then supposedly eventually leads to the claim of divinity. Knitter could have noted that in fact Jesus did not assume an unparalleled authority. A traditional Christian maneuver has been to point out that Jesus abrogated parts of the "Law," indeed even the written Torah—something a rabbi would never do. However, as Rabbi Phillip Sigal has pointed out: "The abrogation of specific precepts of the written Torah is not unusual for Jesus' milieu," and notes that the tannaitic (the period from about two hundred years before and after the birth of Yeshua) sage R. Nathan stated that when "one must act for the Lord, annulment of provisions is allowed. He maintains this in reference to either Torah, the written or the interpretative . . . no 'law' is absolute. What stands above all is the will of God,"[1] which is ap-

---

[1] Phillip Sigal, *The Halakhah of Jesus of Nazareth according to the Gospel of Matthew* (Lanham, Md.: University Press of America, 1987), p. 16. For a further discussion of this and related matters see Leonard Swidler, *Yeshua: A Model for Moderns* (Kansas City, Mo.: Sheed & Ward, 1988, 1993).

plied though the interpretative wisdom of the rabbi. One example of many of such rabbinic abrogations of parts of the written Torah is the rescinding of the trial by ordeal of the suspected adulterous wife (Nm 5:11-31) by no less than the contemporary of Jesus, Rabbi Yohanan ben Zakkai.[2]

Another area where Jesus was in fact very "distinctive," or "unique" as Knitter stretches the term, was his "feminism." Everything known about the Hebraic/Judaic culture of the time of Jesus points in the direction of a very patriarchal society[3]—as were practically all historical societies up to the present. The same is also clearly true of the Christian church, especially as reflected in the deutero-Pauline New Testament documents.[4] However, if one simply goes through the gospels, the image one finds of Jesus' attitude toward women is clearly egalitarian, that. is, feminist. Moreover, there is no way this extraordinary attitude can be attributed to Jesus' contemporary Jewish culture, or to the early church; everything in both those areas points in the opposite direction. Hence, the feminism projected by Jesus in the gospels must stem from him, in opposition to all that is around him. In his feminism Jesus was "unique," and that is a distinctiveness that both Jesus' fellow Jews and his subsequent followers, Christians, should be challenged by—and ultimately proud of.

Some of the essayists referred to Jesus as unsurpassable, and Knitter ably took the issue up. He might have added to his reflections that there is in fact something unseemly about Christians arguing for the unsurpassability of Jesus Christ. Most Christians would shrink from the idea of Jesus himself speaking like that "older adolescent" of a generation ago, Muhammad Ali: "I am the Greatest!" Still, many seem ready to follow the example of a child boasting that his father is stronger than someone else's dad. Already in New Testament times, some Christians seem to have forgotten that Jesus urged his followers to learn from him as "meek and humble of heart."

It is understandable and appropriate to stand in awe and to want to proclaim the praises of the true, the good, and the beautiful; these are authentic, valid human responses. But at times a kind of boastful hubris creeps into the Christian (and other religions' and ideologies') claims of superiority. Nevertheless, even though the claim that Jesus is the unsurpassable expression of the divine is contrary to the life and spirit of Jesus, the claim was made about him from very early on, and is still made today. Hence, it must be dealt with in a responsible manner.

---

[2] *Mishnah*, Sotah, 9,9.

[3] Cf. Leonard Swidler, *Women in Judaism: The Status of Women in Formative Judaism* (Metuchen, N.J.: Scarecrow Press, 1976).

[4] Cf. Leonard Swidler, *Biblical Affirmation of Women* (Philadelphia: Westminster Press, 1979; 4th printing, 1991).

It is one thing to claim that someone is the unsurpassed expression of the divine, but it is something quite other to claim that he is the unsurpassable expression of the divine. It is clear that the divine is manifested in many things and persons, but I personally find the transcendent most effulgently expressed, revealed in Jesus—and that is why I am a Christian. Hence, I can truly say that I find the divine revealed in Jesus in unsurpassed fashion. But this claim leaves at least three vital issues unresolved.

First, my claim to find Jesus the unsurpassed expression of the transcendent or the divine does not mean that I do not find transcendence and divinity manifested elsewhere, including in other religious figures and religious traditions. In fact, I do.

Second, even if I can with some confidence claim that I have investigated all known religious figures and find Jesus unsurpassed by any of them (which I do), I cannot know that I have investigated all possible cases, and certainly I cannot know possible cases of human expressions of the transcendent, the divine, in the future. Hence, it is not logically possible for me, or anyone else, to claim that Jesus is the unsurpassable expression of transcendence and divinity.

Third, we must be extremely cautious about claiming that our view of reality is *the* objective view, and all other views which deviate from ours are more or less mistaken distortions. This caution is most especially in order when we are dealing with statements not of "facts" (e.g., the door is open or closed), but of the *meaning* of something. In the last hundred years or so we have come to know that all knowledge is interpreted knowledge, all perceptions of reality are necessarily from the perspective of the perceiver; and when we are speaking of their *meaning* we speak from a perspective.

Or course, there must be fundamental commonalities in human knowledge and communication, otherwise there could be no such thing as language, communication, learning, and the like. But in trying to explain the ultimate meaning of life, and how to live in accordance with its character—which in brief is what all religion is—we must be extremely cautious in making absolute claims.

Now I am persuaded that these reflections are valid. And yet I am also deeply convinced that there is something extremely profound in the Christian claims of the unsurpassability or divinity of Christ. This conviction becomes all the stronger when I see stunningly similar developments in other religions, most particularly in Buddhism.

The parallels between Jesus the Christ and Gautama the Buddha, and their respective subsequent religious traditions, are extraordinary, much too striking not to point to something much deeper that is held in common by both Christians and Buddhists rather than any of their specific doctrines. To begin with, both figures are known not only by their personal names, Jesus (Yeshua) and Siddharta Gautama, but perhaps even more so by a particular title, "the Christ" (the Anointed One) and "the Buddha" (the Enlightened One). In fact, the religious traditions following each took their names from those titles: Christianity and Buddhism.

In both cases there is a shift from the teaching of the historical figure to the taught "entitled" figure; from the teachings and deeds *of* the historical Yeshua to the teachings *about* the Christ, from the teachings and deeds *of* the historical Gautama to the teachings *about* the Buddha; from the Yeshua of history to the *Christos* of faith, from the Gautama of history (Shakyamuni) to the Buddha of faith (*Maitreya Buddha* and *Amida Buddha*); indeed, in both cases, from the human to the divine.

Yet, the evidence indicates that there was very little historical influence exercised by these two religious cultures on each other in their great formative periods. Hence, it is clear that these prominent parallels point to a profound probing by the human spirit for a way to express something deeper than even the often profound specific doctrines, something at the very core of the human experience of life. Perhaps that deep insight into a sub-surface reality that both Christians and Buddhists were striving to express in their christologies and buddhologies could be at least inchoatively described as follows:

For Christians, Yeshua is the key figure through whom they get in touch with those dimensions of reality which go beyond, which transcend the empirical, the everyday. This is fundamentally what christologies are all about. All are attempts through the figure Yeshua to come into contact with the transcendent, the "divine," each christology being perceived, conceived, and expressed in its own cultural categories and images. Some do it better, even much better, than others.

Naturally they are all culture-bound. Otherwise they would not reflect and effectively speak to the people in that culture. But of course each christology is limited in effectiveness in regard to other cultures, whether the cultural differences result from variations in geography, time, class . . . or epistemology, as from an absolutized to a de-absolutized understanding of truth.

Thus, it should become clear to Christians, and others, that in moving from the human to the divine, from Yeshua to Christ, in talking about the unsurpassability of Jesus, we, like the Buddhists, attempt to express a reality that transcends everyday human experience and everyday human language. We assert that there is a deeper reality which goes beyond the empirical surface experiences of our lives, and for us Yeshua is the bond-bursting means to become aware of that deeper reality (as for Buddhists it is Gautama) which in fact is in each of us and in our encounters with each other.

For Christians, it is preeminently in Yeshua that we encounter the divine, and therefore our move to talk about the divine in Yeshua and thus to talk about the unsurpassable uniqueness of Yeshua. Hence, our attempt to speak of the divine in Yeshua the Christ is not a mistake but the result of the need to try to give expression to trans-empirical reality.

At the same time, however, we must be aware that when we attempt to speak of the transcendent we have to use trans-empirical language, that is, metaphor, symbol and the like. The mistake we must be cautious to avoid in this situation is to think that when we speak about the transcendent we are using empirical language. We are not. We cannot.

At the same time we must also be cautious to avoid being reductionist and erroneously thinking that all talk about the transcendent is merely fantasizing, thus assuming that, since Yeshua was merely a human being, all talk about the divine in him is simply romantic, superlative language with no referent in reality.

In fact, this superlative language is love language, and as such is a proper response to an experienced profound reality. It must not be dismissed but held onto for the vital insight into the meaning of human life it strives for—but it must be correctly understood for what it is, lest it become an idol, an image falsely adored, rather than the Reality toward which it points. When it is thus correctly understood and affirmed we will then have reached what Paul Ricoeur calls "second naïveté," that is, the state of awareness in which the affirmation of the symbol unlocks the portal to deeper, trans-empirical reality.

Paul Knitter spent a good deal of energy presenting, clarifying, and defending the need for all religious, and ethical, persons—and here, of course, particularly Christians—to collaborate in addressing the problems of the world. It seems to me that herein lies the primary common ground that we Christians share with each other, and with other religious and nonreligious ethical persons—the development of a global ethic. I am not talking about some abstract document, although documents have their indispensable contributions to make. Rather, I speak of the principles each of us employs in our dealings with ourselves, other persons and things, and the Source and Goal of all.

Of course, each of us has such principles, perhaps quite fuzzily perceived, but there appear to be significant asymmetries in their application to each other across religious and cultural lines. Christians often have such huge areas of ignorance and bias vis-à-vis non-Christians that our mutual ethical behavior is often confused and contentious. The problems of the world are so huge and are growing at exponential rates that we dare not drift and let a global ethic—understood as a minimal set of ethical principles arrived at by consensus through dialogue—develop haphazardly. Humankind desperately needs to get out in front of its global problems, such as environmental pollution; population explosion; mass poverty; widespread oppression of classes, races, women; ignorance; spiritual desiccation; deprivation of beauty.

Surely all Christians can agree that developing and practicing such an ethic on a global level is the essence of what Jesus was and is about—feeding, clothing, and sheltering the needy, teaching the ignorant, bringing spiritual drink to the thirsty, comforting the pained, opening to all the beauty of God's world. This is what it means to "love our neighbor as ourself," which in turn is the only true way we can "love God with our whole heart, mind and soul": "Those who say, 'I love God,' and hate their brothers and sisters, are liars; for those who do not love a sister or brother whom they have seen, cannot love God whom they have not" (1 Jn 4:20f.).

Other Titles in the Faith Meets Faith Series